Attitudes to Language

Just about everyone seems to have views about language. Language attitudes and language ideologies permeate our daily lives. Our competence, intelligence, friendliness, trustworthiness, social status, group memberships and so on are often judged from the way we communicate. Even the speed at which we speak can evoke reactions. And we often try to anticipate such judgements as we communicate. In this lively introduction, Peter Garrett draws upon research carried out over recent decades in order to discuss such attitudes and the implications they have for our use of language, for social advantage or discrimination and for social identity. Using a range of examples that includes punctuation, words, grammar, pronunciation, accents, dialects and languages, this book explores the intricate and fascinating ways in which language influences our everyday thoughts, feelings and behaviour.

PETER GARRETT is a Senior Lecturer at the Cardiff University Centre for Language and Communication Research. His recent publications include *Investigating Language Attitudes: Social Meanings of Dialect, Ethnicity and Performance* (with Coupland and Williams, 2003).

KEY TOPICS IN SOCIOLINGUISTICS

Series editor: Rajend Mesthrie

This new series focuses on the main topics of study in sociolinguistics today. It consists of accessible yet challenging accounts of the most important issues to consider when examining the relationship between language and society. Some topics have been the subject of sociolinguistic study for many years, and are here re-examined in the light of new developments in the field; others are issues of growing importance that have not so far been given a sustained treatment. Written by leading experts, the books in the series are designed to be used on courses and in seminars, and include useful suggestions for further reading and a helpful glossary.

Already published in the series:

Politeness by Richard J. Watts

Language Policy by Bernard Spolsky

Discourse by Jan Blommaert

Analyzing Sociolinguistic Variation by Sali A. Tagliamonte

Language and Ethnicity by Carmen Fought

Style by Nikolas Coupland

World Englishes by Rajend Mesthrie and Rakesh Bhatt

Language and Identity by John Edwards

Forthcoming titles:

Bilingual Talk by Peter Auer

Sociolinguistics and Social Theory by Nikolas Coupland

Language Attrition by Monika S. Schmid

Attitudes to Language

PETER GARRETT

CAMBRIDGE
UNIVERSITY PRESS

CAMBRIDGE UNIVERSITY PRESS
Cambridge, New York, Melbourne, Madrid, Cape Town, Singapore,
São Paulo, Delhi, Dubai, Tokyo

Cambridge University Press
The Edinburgh Building, Cambridge CB2 8RU, UK

Published in the United States of America by
Cambridge University Press, New York

www.cambridge.org
Information on this title: www.cambridge.org/9780521759175

First published 2010

Printed in the United Kingdom at the University Press, Cambridge

A catalogue record for this publication is available from the British Library

Library of Congress Cataloging-in-Publication Data

Garrett, Peter, 1950–
    Attitudes to language / Peter Garrett.
        p.   cm. – (Key topics in sociolinguistics)
    ISBN 978-0-521-76604-3 (hardback) – ISBN 978-0-521-75917-5 (pbk.)
    1. Language awareness.   2. Language and languages–Variation.   3. Sociolinguistics.
4. English language–Variation.   5. English language–Social aspects.   I. Title.   II. Series.

    P120.L34G37 2010
    306.44–dc22

                                                                2009047128

ISBN 978-0-521-76604-3 Hardback
ISBN 978-0-521-75917-5 Paperback

Dedicated to Mary and Ron Garrett

Contents

List of figures   *viii*
List of tables   *ix*
Acknowledgements   *x*

1 Introduction   *1*
2 Fundamentals of language attitudes   *19*
3 Main approaches to the study of language attitudes   *37*
4 Matched and verbal guise studies: focus on English   *53*
5 Matched and verbal guise research in more contexts   *70*
6 Attitudes to speech styles and other variables: communication features, speakers, hearers and contexts   *88*
7 Communication accommodation theory   *105*
8 Language attitudes in professional contexts   *121*
9 Societal treatment studies   *142*
10 Direct approach   *159*
11 Folklinguistics   *179*
12 An integrated programme of language attitudes research   *201*
13 Conclusion   *224*

Glossary   *228*
References   *230*
Index   *254*

Figures

2.1   Theory of Reasoned Action (adapted from Ajzen and Fishbein 1980)   *27*

9.1   Advertisement from *Y Drych*, August 1888   *148*

9.2   Advertisement from *Y Drych*, January 1908   *149*

9.3   Advertisement from *Y Drych*, March 1998   *149*

9.4   Advertisement from *Y Drych*, March 2001   *150*

9.5   Cowbois t-shirt: Merched Beca   *157*

11.1   Hand-drawn dialect map by Michigan respondent (from Niedzielski and Preston 2000: 58)   *181*

11.2   Hand-drawn dialect map by North Carolina respondent (from Niedzielski and Preston 2000: 60)   *181*

11.3   Hand-drawn dialect map by South Carolina respondent (from Niedzielski and Preston 2000: 62)   *182*

11.4   Hand-drawn map by South Carolina respondent (from Niedzielski and Preston 2000: 62)   *182*

11.5   Michigan 'correctness' ratings and map (from Niedzielski and Preston 2000: 64)   *184*

11.6   Southern 'correctness' ratings and map (from Niedzielski and Preston 2000: 65)   *184*

11.7   Michigan 'pleasantness' ratings and map (from Niedzielski and Preston 2000: 70)   *185*

11.8   Southern 'pleasantness' ratings and map (from Niedzielski and Preston 2000: 71)   *186*

12.1   Map of Wales, showing each of the six dialect regions   *202*

12.2   Teenagers: 'How Welsh do you think this speaker sounds?'   *213*

12.3   Teachers: 'How Welsh do you think this speaker sounds?'   *214*

12.4   Teenagers: 'Do you think this speaker is a good laugh?'   *215*

12.5   Teachers: 'Do you think this speaker is a good laugh?'   *215*

12.6   Teenagers: 'Do you think this speaker does well at school?'   *217*

12.7   Teachers: 'Do you think this speaker does well at school?'   *218*

Tables

4.1 Rank orders of accent evaluations with mean scores
on three dimensions (from Giles 1970) 54

4.2 Rank ordered evaluations (with mean scores) for Australian,
New Zealand, English and USA Englishes by Australian,
New Zealand and USA respondents (adapted from Bayard
et al. 2001: table 5, p. 39) 67

9.1 Languages and their stereotypical features in Haarmann's
study (based on Haarmann 1984) 144

9.2 Proportions of advertised products using English
(based on Cheshire and Moser 1994) 146

10.1 How the three regional groups (Wales, Patagonia
and North America) compared in their Welsh identities
and perceptions of the Welsh language 167

10.2 Comparison of prestige findings from Giles (1970)
and the BBC (2005) Voices study 173

10.3 Comparison of social attractiveness findings
from Giles (1970) and the BBC (2005) Voices study 174

11.1 Percentages of comments in each category
as a proportion of total comments made by each group
of respondents about each variety of English 189

12.1 Means and standard deviations of teachers' judgements
of the accent/dialect communities (1 = very, 7 = not at all) 204

12.2 Frequencies of categorised comments for the labelled areas 206

Acknowledgements

I am grateful to Wyn ap Gwilym and to Cowbois, Gweithdai Penllyn, Stryd Y Plase, Y Bala, Gwynedd, LL23 7SW, Wales, for allowing free permission to include the photographic image of the Cowbois t-shirt in chapter 9, and also to Arturo Roberts of Ninnau and Y Drych, 11 Post Terrace, Basking Ridge, NJ 07920, USA, for free permission to include advertisements from *Y Drych*, also in chapter 9. Permission has been purchased from Mouton to include Figures 11.1 to 11.8.

I have been delighted to collaborate with many excellent colleagues and friends during the time I have researched and taught language attitudes. I could not possibly list them all, of course, but Nik Coupland, Howard Giles, Tore Kristiansen, Dennis Preston, Angie Williams, as well as Colin Baker, Carl James, Phil Scholfield, and the late Harry Levin, simply have to be named before I end this paragraph. In a variety of ways, they have each played very significant parts over the years, and I am very thankful to all of them.

Not to be overlooked, though, is the part that very many students have had in this book. Its contents have evolved from lectures and seminars over a number of years, and seem to have stimulated a good many interesting student projects, and continue to do so. It is the students' curiosity and engagement with language attitudes that has made the task of compiling this book worthwhile. This book is for them.

1   Introduction

In October 2007, the *Sunday Telegraph* carried a report that Scottish actor Sean Connery had accused the British Prime Minister Gordon Brown of attempting to modify his Scottish accent in order to appeal to voters in England (Mandrake 2007). Connery was reported as saying that Brown's accent 'certainly isn't as pronounced as it was, but Gordon has to ride two horses down in Westminster. He knows it's difficult to appeal to people on both sides of the border, but he has to try, even if it means disappointing them both a bit.' Brown, the journalist suggested, was seeking to 'disguise his native tongue'.

Connery himself deployed his own Scottish variety of English when he played Richard the Lionheart in the film *Robin Hood: Prince of Thieves*. This portrayal of an English monarch with a Scottish accent was much commented on (as was US actor Kevin Costner's non-British accent in his role as Robin Hood in the same film). Audiences have expectations, it seems. These are clearly not based on any reality of how these characters might have spoken. Modern audiences would undoubtedly struggle with the English spoken at the time in which the tales of Robin Hood are set, for example, and Richard the Lionheart himself, though born in Oxford, was a French-speaking Plantagenet, who, according to Harvey (1977), may have spoken little English at all. But these expectations are doubtless based on a stereotypical notion in some that such famous figures in English history ought to sound, to modern ears, English. The breaking of these socially normative language expectations seems to generate salience. While some people might experience such a violation of expectations positively, and so be quite taken by the idea of Richard the Lionheart as a Scotsman, others clearly experience it negatively, leading to some discomfort and entrenchment. (Such ideas about meeting or breaking expectations are part of Burgoon's 1995 'language expectancy theory', to which we will also refer later.)

Language attitudes permeate our daily lives. They are not always publicly articulated and, indeed, we are not always conscious of them.

But many nevertheless are overt, and we probably notice them in particular when they are negative and articulated explicitly, and often argumentatively, in public arenas such as the media or in our day-to-day conversations. Although we may feel that there are many different ways of expressing our thoughts in our languages, language variation carries social meanings and so can bring very different attitudinal reactions, or even social disadvantage or advantage. As Coupland (2007: 88) says, 'dialect or accent variables may be alternative ways of achieving the same reference, but it certainly does not follow that they are alternative ways of saying, or meaning, "the same thing". Such sociolinguistic issues underpin this book.

People hold attitudes to language at all its levels: for example, spelling and punctuation, words, grammar, accent and pronunciation, dialects and languages. Even the speed at which we speak can evoke reactions. In this introduction, we will take examples from some levels of language. We begin at the level of words. In fact, this level of language has received less attention overall in sociolinguistic work on language attitudes (although chapter 6 reports some research into lexical diversity and provenance). Words nevertheless provide some good exemplification here of the scope and pervasiveness of language attitudes. The introduction also considers the levels of grammar and accent, and attitudes to 'whole' languages and to codeswitching, with an eye, too, on standard language ideology. It also gives some initial insights into some of the concepts and other issues around language attitudes. A closer look at the nature of attitudes will be a focus in chapter 2.

WORDS

Some words are expensive. They can get you into arguments and fights. They can cost you your job. On the other hand, some can help to bring you success and money. Goddard (2002) points to the huge sums of money that companies spend on choosing brand names in order to try to ensure that these trigger desired connotations and positive attitudes in potential customers. She gives the example of the formation of a new travel company created in the mid-1990s, which was given two main possibilities for a new brand name. One was 'Destinations' and the other was 'Going Places', and the company in the end plumped for the latter. Anticipating the social connotations of these two candidates, they felt that 'Going Places' would be more strongly associated in people's minds with the dynamism and mobility that their mass-market customers aspired to, and which the company itself wanted to project as its image.

Much strategic work on wording goes on in the political field too. In the USA, for example, Frank Luntz worked as a Republican political consultant, running focus group sessions (or 'Word Labs') with 'average Americans' to generate words and phrases to give to political candidates to use in their campaigns to help get the reactions they wanted from voters (Lemann 2000). Lemann writes 'Anybody who has to speak regularly to live audiences sees that some combinations of words do produce more and better reactions than others' (p. 110). Examples from Luntz's advice included using 'climate change' instead of 'global warming', 'tax relief' instead of 'tax cuts'. Luntz was also recommending the repeated use of the words 'listening' and 'children', because, he claimed, this would attract female voters. 'Why do you think Hillary Clinton went on a "Listening Tour" of New York?', he asked (p. 100). The idea of the Word Lab seems to be to discover how voters are already thinking and then to design language to convince them that politicians already agree with them. Whether we like this way of doing politics or not, through framing political debate in this way, this use of language is most certainly aimed at attitudes.

Personal names are also words that reflect and evoke attitudes, it seems. Crystal (1987 and 1997: 113) lists the top-ten given names for males and females in the USA and in England and Wales between 1925 and 1993. Cultural attitudes lead to a tendency for boys' names to be more enduring. For example, 'Michelle' was the top name for girls in 1970 in the USA, but does not appear in any of the other US top-ten lists between 1925 and 1993. In England and Wales, 'Trac(e)y' and 'Sharon' are in the top ten only in the 1965 list. In contrast, 'Robert' appears in the US top ten from 1925 through to 1982, and 'David' features in the England and Wales top ten from 1950 to 1981.

Attitudes to personal names can be looked at from other angles than simple preferences for one name or another, or even regarding levels of continuity. Barry and Harper (1995) studied the twenty-five most frequent given names of babies born in Pennsylvania in 1960 and 1990. By developing a 'phonetic gender score' based on features such as numbers of syllables, stress patterns and vowel qualities, they found that such features distinguished these popular names of males and females. Referring to previous findings by Duffy and Ridinger that female names were judged as more attractive and that male names were seen as more powerful, they suggested that 'phonetic attributes might contribute to the perception of a name as attractive or powerful' (p. 817). From this, then, we might surmise that a person's name can have implications at the level of impression formation, impacting on our (at least initial) disposition towards that person.

In a similar vein, Smith (1998) developed an analytical model called the 'Comfort Factor' to predict with reasonable accuracy the results of political elections. The model was constructed by assigning weights to a range of sound features in candidates' names in past elections. Acknowledging the role of political issues and party loyalty in elections, Smith thought that many voters (especially less decided ones) might nevertheless be influenced by the sounds of the candidates' names. Applying his Comfort Factor model, he claimed that it was able to predict 83 per cent of the winners of presidential elections. Apparently, then, the study was showing that phonetic qualities of candidates' names could have some effect on people's attitudes and on their behaviour towards the candidates in the electoral process.

A rather different study of names was carried out by Harari and McDavid (1973), this time in a school setting in the USA. They wanted to examine whether teachers' assessment of students' performance might vary according to what the students' names were: i.e. whether teachers' attitudes to their students' names might be reflected in the marks the students received for their work. Generating a set of essays and allocating a range of names to each one, Harari and McDavid found that the grades awarded (by experienced teachers) in their study were indeed significantly higher when the essays were apparently authored by students with names considered attractive.

An important difference between this study and those mentioned previously is the explanation that Harari and McDavid provide. In the previous studies, the main attention was on the sound features of the words – stress, rhythm, vowel qualities etc. – and how these seemed to affect attitudes. This was seemingly a phonoaesthetic approach (see Crystal 1995). Harari and McDavid do not focus on such qualities that might be viewed as inherent in the words themselves, but considered the social stereotypes associated with the names. Stereotypes are cognitive shortcuts. Here, then, when people hear about someone called 'Arnold', for example, they would tend to place them in a subjective category in which reside all Arnolds, and to then perceive and judge them in the same way, positively or negatively, as if they are all much the same. In interpreting their findings, Harari and McDavid employ the assumption that names that are more common and seen as more attractive connote favourable stereotypes, and those that are rarer and judged less attractive connote negative stereotypes. Social stereotypes will recur in this book, since they feature large in the language attitudes field. But it is also worth noting that we have touched on a controversy here: what is the basis of attitudes towards different language features, accents, etc.? Why do people tend to love some and hate others? Is it because of their inherent sound qualities (the 'inherent value hypothesis'), or is it due to their social connotations (the 'imposed norm hypothesis')? The latter is the generally held view (see, for example, Giles and Powesland 1975).

Names, whether personal names, brand-names or names of organisations, are of course certainly not the only words that people have attitudes towards or that can evoke attitudes. In the persuasion field, where there is often a focus on influencing people's attitudes, some research has been done on expletives, and whether their use is an aid or a hindrance in this attitudinal process. The general finding seems to be that the use of expletives is not advantageous in influencing other people's attitudes. One study, though, also found that, if they were used, they tended to work differently according to whether they were used by males or females. Bostrom, Baseheart and Rossiter (1973) grouped the expletives into three types: religious, excretory and sexual. In this US context, at least, females seemed to have more influence if they used sexual obscenities, whereas males seemed to have less influence with these than with excretory or religious ones. Interestingly, too, females achieved more attitude change overall through the use of more offensive language than males did, regardless of which of the three types they used.

While the study by Bostrom *et al.* included some important variables distinguishing different types of expletives and checking for differences in the reactions to speakers of each sex, subsequent theoretical approaches to communication have given more focus on how interactions engage with characteristics of the person at the hearing end. Communication accommodation theory (see, for example, Giles, Mulac, Bradac and Johnson 1987) argues that we have a tendency to adjust our style of communicating to those with whom we are communicating in order to gain their social approval and improve communication. So if we know that the person we are talking to usually uses a lot of obscenities, we might evoke more positive attitudes from them if we ourselves employ them. Communication accommodation theory is a significant theory in the language attitudes field and one we will look at more closely in chapter 7.

At the other end of the spectrum from the use of obscenities comes the careful choice of words to avoid causing offence. Political correctness concerns language referring to a variety of social groups: for example, non-racist and non-sexist speech. Its goal of projecting positive images is also intended to generate more positive attitudes and more constructive behaviour towards the social groups concerned and thereby lead to a more inclusive society. But what do we know about people's attitudes towards attempts at making speech more politically correct? Some research has demonstrated that using politically correct language can be a difficult even if worthwhile path. Seiter, Larsen and Skinner (1998), for example, looked at people's reactions to campaign materials designed to raise donations for people with disabilities. They were represented in four different ways: e.g. 'handicapable', 'confined to a wheelchair', 'uses a wheelchair' or 'abnormal'. Communicators using terms such as the first three were regarded as more trustworthy and competent than those using terms like the fourth. But the communicator who took the politically correct option and tried not to refer to people with disabilities as victims – i.e. the one who used terms such as 'uses a wheelchair' – was no more successful in raising donations than the one who used terms such as 'abnormal'. It seems that people have to present more urgency and need in their communication if they want to get people to give money.

There are two important points to take away from this study at this stage. One is that the relationship between attitudes and behaviour is problematic. In this study, respondents held a positive attitude to some communicators – seeing them as competent and trustworthy – but this did not translate into the positive action of donating money. The second is that a key feature in language attitudes research is the stereotypical view of speakers in terms of personality traits. Ways of speaking give rise to judgements of people's honesty, competence, intelligence, enthusiasm, etc. These are two more aspects of language attitudes that will be recurring in this book.

Other words evoke attitudes with a somewhat (though not entirely) different focus, relating to public controversies over language usage. In my school English lessons in England, attention was often rather tediously drawn to so-called 'vulgar influences' from across the North Atlantic. 'Hopefully' was a word that often surfaced. 'We continued hopefully on our way' was viewed as correct. But 'Hopefully, this film won't last long' was said to be poor English, because a film cannot last hopefully. 'I hope this film won't last long' or 'It is to be hoped that this film won't last long' were said to be the correct modes of expression. Crystal (1996: 177) also mentions the 'hopefully' phenomenon, and adds, 'It is unclear why this particular adverb should have attracted so much adverse criticism, when many other adverbs are used in a similar way: thankfully, regrettably, sadly, happily, etc.'

In any event, 'hopefully' has brought us into the arena of public arguments about English usage. Readers will doubtless be particularly aware of this area of attitudes about language and languages, in part because such complaints feature so commonly and explicitly in every-day discourse. Since these also relate to some concepts that are funda-mental to the language attitudes field, we will examine some of these in this chapter too.

STANDARDISATION IN LANGUAGE

Attitudes towards language, positive and negative, are often influenced by the process of standardisation in languages. Many languages are said to have a standard variety: Standard British English, for example. Milroy (2007: 133) writes that, in such instances, 'language attitudes are domi-nated by powerful ideological positions that are largely based on the supposed existence of this standard form, and these, taken together, can be said to constitute the standard language ideology or "ideology of the standard language"'. Generally, in day-to-day living, people are apparently not conscious of the influence of these ideological positions, but tend to work on the basis that such norms are simply a question of common sense.

Milroy (2007) stresses that standardisation of any kind is concerned with uniformity and invariance, and how, in standard language ideology, great emphasis is placed on correctness. Preston (1996) has observed in the USA the overwhelming degree to which appeals to correctness per-meate the way in which people talk about language. In standard lan-guage ideology, there are strong pervading common-sense views about which language forms are right and which are wrong. The notion of correctness is reinforced by authority. Standard languages are codified in dictionaries and grammar books, for example, and spread through educational systems. They are also reinforced by the awarding of prestige or stigma to language forms. The devaluing of some forms leads to a view of them as non-standard or substandard. Milroy (2007: 138) writes, 'all standard languages have to be given legitimacy, and all have to be maintained and protected through authority and doctrines of correct-ness. There is usually a tradition of popular complaint about language, bewailing the low quality of general usage and claiming that the lan-guage is degenerating' (p. 138).

In Crystal's (1981) list of the top-twenty objections about broadcast-ing language in the UK, one of the pronunciation gripes concerned the word 'controversy', and the claim that to pronounce it with the pri-mary stress on the second syllable – controversy – is wrong, and that the correct form has primary stress on the first syllable – controversy. To add a personal note, I recall this complaint, too, cropping up in school English lessons, with the first of these two pronunciations outlawed as a 'vulgar Americanism' (and therefore one we should never be caught using). Algeo (1998) also refers to this attribution of the controversy variant to American English (this time by 'a knowledgable British author'), and Algeo disputes this belief: 'this antepenult accent is unknown in the States, being a recent British innovation' (p. 177).

The example raises two issues. One is the difficulty in standardising and fixing a social phenomenon that is inherently characterised by change and variation, and the other is that many of the justifications for these attitudes are premised on misconceptions about language. Ideologies can promote strong common-sense notions that can be viewed as distortions or myths.

Trudgill (1998) writes about the myth that words should not be allowed to change or vary their meanings. He also points to how some people will look rather too much at the origins of words in order to argue their 'real' meaning. For example, he mentions how they might condemn English speakers who talk about there being 'several alternatives' on the grounds that 'alternative' comes from the Latin word 'alter' meaning 'second', and so there cannot be more than two choices (p. 1). Trudgill extends the argument to the word 'nice', the origins of which go back to Indo-European roots that would give it the meaning 'not cutting'. 'No-one in their right mind though', he adds, 'would argue that the "real" meaning of "nice" is "not cutting"' (p. 2).

GRAMMAR

At the level of grammar, Cheshire (1998) comments on the attitudes to the use of double negatives in English. 'You don't know nothing' exemplifies the type of double negative that arouses the strongest attitudes, and Cheshire notes that it featured in the top-ten complaints sent in to the BBC Radio Four series *English Now* in 1986, with some saying that it 'made their blood boil' (Cheshire 1998: 114). This is a way of expressing a negative that is condemned by standard language ideology in Britain. As Cheshire observes, it seems to be only in Standard English that such double negatives attract such negative attitudes. Complainers say that they are illogical and nonsensical, because the two negatives must cancel each other out to make a positive. Cheshire (1998: 120) points out that, in the real world, not only are such double negatives used unproblematically in the majority of the world's languages, but they are also found in all the rural and urban dialects of English in both hemispheres, as well as in African-American English and in all English creoles. Within Standard English, though, they are stigmatised and tend to be associated with low-status groups in society. Such associations between language and social groups are a pervading feature in language attitudes.

The disapproval of this kind of double negative in Standard English is almost certainly identifiable with the eighteenth-century hope that language could be fixed, a time when grammarians were trying to construct a set of norms in order to establish and then preserve good usage. Such attempts have been referred to as 'an illusion based on misunderstandings about the nature of language, values and human nature' (Algeo 1998: 178). Nevertheless, the process has left a strong mark on modern-day attitudes, amongst some at least.

The apostrophe has also attracted considerable comment at times. It has an interesting history in English, and is something of a latecomer in its present usage, in that it was not until the nineteenth century that grammarians tried to impose the current grammatical rules (see Austin 1989; Garrett and Austin 1993; Truss 2003). Modern attitudes are varied, and exist alongside a great deal of lingering uncertainty about standard usage. Garrett and Austin (1993) asked groups of university undergraduates in Britain and Germany, and a group of trainee English language teachers, to say how serious they judged various apostrophe errors to be in English. Errors where apostrophes were included in plurals (e.g. we sell car radio's) were seen as more of a concern than others, but overall, none of the errors were judged to be particularly serious (no higher than about the mid-point on a five-point scale from 'unimportant' to 'very serious'). The respondents attributed least importance to cases where apostrophes were simply omitted. It is clear, too, that apostrophe omissions, unlike the double negatives above, are not associated solely with low-status social groups. Reputable British institutions such as Harrods, Selfridges, Boots and Lloyds Banking Group seem at some stage to have made policy decisions not to use apostrophes in their names (see Crystal 1996).

There are many other usages that some people are vexed by. Ending sentences with prepositions (as I have just done), splitting infinitives, saying 'It is me' rather than 'It is I' are other favourites, again attempts by grammarians to impose standard norms, and sometimes by referring to the grammatical rules of a language that works very differently from English: Latin. Infinitives are single words in Latin. Although there are some instances of single words sometimes being split in colloquial English speech – 'absobloodylutely' – Latin infinitives were not, it would seem reasonable to assume, split. English infinitive forms have two components – to speak, to walk, etc. – offering scope for splitting.

The English rule itself – that nothing should come between 'to' and 'speak' etc. – was also formulated rather late, in the nineteenth century. So these negative attitudes to splitting infinitives are comparatively recent. Crystal (1984) notes that there were no complaints about them before the nineteenth century.

Preston (1996) points to how, when there is persistent use of non-standard language forms, people often refer to the 'internal recognition system' that users of these forms have, which allows them to infer not only the 'error of their ways' but also what the features of the 'real' system are. So there appears to be a folk-view that 'Non-standard speakers are not simply those whose environment, class, and lack of opportunity have failed to equip with the standard variety; they are also persons who have somehow rejected the deeper internal knowledge which they surely have about the correct way to behave (at least linguistically)' (p. 58).

Indeed, debates about the importance of standard language also extend to arguments about maintaining other kinds of standards. Alongside the enduring notion that the language is going to the dogs is the notion that people who do not adhere to the rules of standard language are themselves going to the dogs. To illustrate, Graddol and Swann (1988: 102) cite Norman Tebbit, former Conservative Cabinet Minister in Margaret Thatcher's Conservative government:

> If you allow standards to slip to the stage where good English is no better than bad English, where people turn up filthy . . . at school . . . all those things tend to cause people to have no standards at all, and once you lose standards then there's no imperative to stay out of crime.

This close association between judgements of language and judgements of the people who use the language is what underlies the stereotypical evaluations of language considered throughout this book.

LANGUAGES

There are also strong negative attitudes about 'whole languages' rather than aspects of usage within a language. Bauer (1998) points to claims sometimes made that some languages have no grammar, for example. She notes that, if something is a language, then it must by definition have a grammar. Similarly, there is a common belief that some languages are incapable of fulfilling a wide range of functions. They are often claimed not to be suitable for writing literature, for example, or for conducting affairs of state. These sorts of attitudes are often *articles about m?*

expressed about minority languages. Harlow (1998) refers to a newspaper article about Maori, for example, which claimed that Maori was no good because it needed to borrow words from English to express new ideas. Evans (1998), writing about Aboriginal languages, also mentions this stereotype, illustrating the flawed basis of such claims by referring to the adaptation of Walpiri, and the fact that Walpiri can now be used to discuss nuclear physics.

These are important matters. In the case of indigenous minority languages, for example (Welsh in Wales, Maori in New Zealand, etc.), such attitudes can play a key role in whether they survive, revive, reflourish, or whether they die out, as parents stop using them with their children. It is no co-incidence that much language attitude research is carried out in settings where languages are in competition and where some speakers feel under threat. As will be seen later in this book, a great deal of research has been carried out in settings such as Canada and Wales.

The labelling of language behaviour and languages is also a window into people's attitudes. Jørgensen and Quist (2001: 42), for example, write about how in-migrant minority languages in Denmark are viewed as a 'nuisance'. In-migrant minority languages tend to attract the most negative attitudes from majority language communities. In addition, pidgins, which are language systems that develop when people do not share a common language but need to communicate (for example, for trading), and which are the 'main means of communication for millions of people' (Crystal 1997: 334), have sometimes been characterised as 'baby talk', reflecting primitive thought processes, and labelled 'mongrel jargons' or 'macaroni lingos' (Holmes 2001: 84). Creoles (pidgins that have expanded in functions and structure and have gained native speakers) are often viewed equally negatively by outsiders.

CODESWITCHING

Amongst bilinguals and multilinguals, codeswitching is a powerful feature of informal communication. Speakers may switch between languages, without necessarily being aware of it, to signal solidarity with a particular social or ethnic group, for example, or to express their attitude towards the listener (friendly, distant, etc.). But codeswitching is often frowned upon, especially by monolinguals, and dismissed as 'gibberish' (Edwards 1994: 78), and given labels such as 'Tex-Mex', 'Franglais', 'Japlish', usually meant derogatorily.

Often the evaluative discourse around codeswitching is set in terms of 'laziness' and 'impurity', qualities extended to speakers as much as referring to language. But there are also powerful issues of social identity present for the speakers themselves. Tok Pisin, the most widespread creole lingua franca in Papua New Guinea, now with the status of official language, is 'a language of solidarity between Papua New Guineans with different vernaculars' (Holmes 2001: 90). Codeswitching, too, may be used to emphasise one's social identity and membership of a community.

A classic demonstration of a form of codeswitching as a marker, and indeed assertion, of social identity occurred in a study by Bourhis and Giles (1977) exploring communication accommodation theory, to which we referred earlier when considering expletives. In this study, the researchers were investigating people shifting their speech in various ways towards (convergence) and away from (divergence) their interlocutors (whether making shifts within a language or switching across languages). Welsh language learners in a language laboratory listened to a set of questions recorded by a British English speaker with Received Pronunciation (RP), and had to speak their answers into a microphone, and these were recorded. Some of the learners were taking the Welsh-language course for career purposes, with their employers paying for the course and allowing them to pursue it in their work hours, whereas others were taking the course in their own time and at their own expense because they valued their Welshness. After hearing some general questions and recording their answers in English, the learners heard the recorded speaker challenging them as to why they were learning a 'dying language with a dismal future', talking in terms of 'us' and 'them' and mentioning that he was from an English university. In this final phase, the second group of learners began to strengthen their Welsh-accented English, with some of them introducing Welsh words and phrases into their responses. One of them simply fell silent for some time, and then calmly conjugated an obscene Welsh verb into the microphone: an unambiguous assertion of social identity in the face of threatening and demeaning opposition.

ACCENTS

Apart from the complaint tradition in the media around grammatical usage, pronunciation of particular words etc. that were considered above, there are also frequent stories in the media concerning the attitudes to various accents and their effects on people's life opportunities.

Hernandez (1993), for example, in an article in the *New York Times*, described how many immigrants into the US, although fluent in English, often seek speech therapists and tutors in order to 'reduce' their accents. Morrish (1999) reports the same phenomenon in Britain. While many worry whether by taking such courses they are sacrificing their cultural identity, Hernandez notes that 'remarks, gibes and ridicule about accents' caused anger, insecurity and shame and a feeling that they were being cheated of the opportunity to assimilate. Hernandez reported one Colombian student as saying 'this class is my last hope. If it doesn't work out, I'm going back to my country. I was practically raised in this country . . . But I have this accent. Does this mean that I am not an American? I don't know.' References to 'accent reduction classes' often crop up in the media, as some people find that they sound 'too different' and feel that they face social or career barriers, whatever the legal protection. (See, for example, Swift 2007.)

Stories about British regional accents range from positive to negative attitudes. A survey reported on the BBC News website (BBC 2005) claimed that some regional accents were bad for trade, particularly Liverpool, Birmingham, Cockney, Geordie and the West Country accents. In contrast, Home Counties, along with Scots, American, European, Indian and Asian accents were viewed as a sign of success. Morrish (1999) reported how, in the 1970s, one boy at his school was not allowed to be a member of the TV 'Top of the Form' school team because the school regarded his Bristolian English as 'unsuitable for broadcasting'.

Attitudes to regional accents seem to get a variable press. Writing in the *Guardian*, Ward (2000) reported that the Liverpool (Scouse) accent had turned Liverpool into a favourite location for call centres in Britain, and quoted an investment manager as saying 'It is not seen as a barrier to business.' Khan (2003) reported 'The dominance of soft regional accents in call centres may be put down to the establishment of operations in areas where land is cheaper and jobs harder to come by than in the South East, but telecoms bosses admit that accents played a part in determining where they settled.' In the media itself, Khan noted that in the previous decade, the BBC made a conscious move to diversify accents on its Radio Three and Radio Four, feeling that it was lagging behind 'the sound of the nation' and 'beginning to sound a bit antique'.

One of the most famous stories of a pioneering BBC move towards the use of regional accents dates back to the Second World War, when Wilfred Pickles was the first national newsreader to speak with a northern English (Yorkshire) accent, along with one or two dialect features. The Ministry of Information was already concerned that Nazi propagandists had become adept at speaking with 'BBC Oxford' accents, and was keen to minimise the risk that, if Britain were invaded, the public might be misled by orders issued by the enemy over the radio. One strategy, then, was to use accents that were much harder for them to imitate. But, in addition to this, and in a clear display of language attitudes of the time, the Deputy Prime Minister (Clement Atlee) argued that the monopoly of upper-class readers on the BBC news was offending working people. The Ministry of Information therefore suggested that 'something might be done to diminish the present predominance of the cultured voice upon the wireless' (Curran and Seaton 2003: 142). But, Wilfred Pickles' newsreading attracted an avalanche of complaint from listeners. Pickles (1949) himself wrote that he was the 'central feature in a heated national controversy'. He was 'caricatured mercilessly' (Hargreaves 2004) by London cartoonists, drawn with cloth cap and rolled-up shirtsleeves. If stereotypes are 'pictures in the head' (Lippmann 1922), simplified images of what groups look like and what they do, then this is a good visual instance of how language features can trigger a whole set of associated attributes that go far beyond the language itself.

Media reports of dismissals from jobs on accent grounds are even more striking. O'Mara (2007) reported that an Indian-born customer advisor from the UK, who was employed to train staff at a communications firm's office in New Delhi, was dismissed because he spoke with an Indian accent and so his accent was 'not English enough' to be working with these people in New Delhi. He successfully brought a charge of racial discrimination against the employer.

However, RP is not immune from such controversies, a sign perhaps of how the balance of attitudes towards RP has changed within the UK (e.g. see Mugglestone, 2003, on 'the rise of the regional' in and since the 1960s). Nowadays, according to Morrish (1999), 'RP is much more popular with the 1.5 billion speakers of English abroad.' And indeed British actor Stephen Fry is reported in the *Daily Telegraph* (21 March 2007) as saying 'I sometimes wonder if Americans aren't fooled by our accent into detecting a brilliance that may not really be there.' In Britain itself, Zenab Ahmed, who was suddenly dismissed from her job as a BBC news presenter, wrote the following letter to the *Daily Telegraph* (30 October 2003):

> The BBC has sacked me for sounding too posh. At the moment, the World Service is on a mission to sound classless – hence the proliferation of Scottish, Welsh, Irish and Australasian voices. My accent – received pronunciation – is associated with a white, middle class demographic. Which is ironic, because I am a mixed-race South Londoner: half-Pakistani, half-English and from a very ordinary background.

India Knight (2001) maintains that RP speakers in Britain are nowadays 'immediately viewed with hostile suspicion, the implication being that you are probably some ghastly plummy nob, your very existence confirming the fact that there are still people who sneer down their long, well-bred noses at the plebs'. We shall be coming across RP a great deal in this book, since it has been the focus of much research in the language attitudes field over the years, both within the UK and internationally.

Such evidence of changing language attitudes suggests some qualifying or reappraisal of Milroy's (2007) ideas about standard language ideology set out earlier in the chapter, and indeed other views on standard language ideology have recently been emerging. Coupland (2009), for example, emphasises the social change of recent decades, and the social conditions of the present day (late-modernity). He points to features of late-modern life, such as mediatisation (with far more diverse media formats than previously) and the growth of service-based employment, which often place greater demands on individuals to present themselves attractively and competently. He argues that these require, generate and reflect a sociolinguistic diversity that works against the singular value system contained within the notion of standard language ideology suggested by Milroy. Coupland (2009) proposes that 'linguistic varieties referred to as "standards" and "dialects" are coming to hold different, generally less determinate and more complex values in a late-modern social order' (p. 43).

CONCLUSION

In this chapter, then, we have looked at language attitudes at a variety of levels, and in a variety of contexts. The field of language attitudes indeed encompasses a broad range of foci, and there can also therefore be a range of reasons for studying them. For sociolinguists, one important goal has been to construct a 'record of overt attitudes towards language, linguistic features and linguistic stereotypes' (Labov 1984: 33). From this perspective, language attitudes research provides a backdrop for explaining linguistic variation and change.

But language attitudes issues extend to all manner of sociolinguistic and social psychological phenomena, such as how we position ourselves socially, and how we relate to other individuals and groups. They may affect behaviours and experiences. For example, do some language attitudes lead to certain groups (e.g. speakers of certain dialects or minority languages) faring better or worse in labour markets, or in the educational, health and legal systems? Will such experiences affect people's language behaviour (e.g. avoiding the use of certain words or grammatical structures, taking accent reduction programmes, or ceasing to use a minority language, or even promoting it more). Another goal is to try to establish what gives rise to these attitudes. Many sociolinguists have tended to focus on particular linguistic forms: for example, Labov's early sociolinguistic work on the social meanings of postvocalic |r| on the eastern seaboard of the USA. Social psychologists of language have tended to work at a less specific level regarding linguistic features: e.g. 'Scottish English'.

Language attitudes studies can also tell us about differences within and across communities. If attitudes are learned, then some sources of learning are related to social group membership. So attitudes may vary according to ethnic, regional and social and professional groups, for example. It is generally difficult to distinguish attitudes to language varieties from attitudes to the perceived groups and community members who use them. Language varieties and their forms are often not simply characteristic of a community, but even enshrine what is distinctive in the community and in a sense 'constitute' that community. In addition, language attitudes researchers are interested in how attitudinal judgements are affected by the social contexts in which the language occurs. A particular language variety or way of speaking can, for example, meet with advantageous attitudes in some specific contexts, but detrimental ones in others, and perhaps more so in this late-modern epoch.

Some of the points and stories touched on in this chapter will undoubtedly not be entirely unfamiliar ground to some readers. But treading a path through these has drawn together attitudinal material from some very diverse contexts to demonstrate the extensive significance of language attitudes in our everyday lives. It has also allowed a first foray into some of the issues that are central to this field of work: for example, language ideologies, notions of correctness and purity, some language myths that underpin attitudinal stances, language features and communication behaviours aimed at changing or forming specific attitudes in other people, social and cultural stereotypes leading whole clusters of attributes to be associated with language, from personality traits, moral standing, even dress styles.

LATER CHAPTERS

Following on from this general orientation to language attitudes, chapter 2 looks more systematically at some core theoretical issues regarding what attitudes are, to provide a foundation for understanding this field of research. Chapter 3 outlines and exemplifies the main ways in which researchers have approached the study of language attitudes. This lays the ground for the general arrangement of the subsequent chapters in terms of research carried out under each of these approaches: studies in the tradition of matched guise and its variants, societal treatment studies, studies using various direct methods, and finally a more integrated approach. The book reaches back to the early development of language attitudes research, particularly from the 1970s and 1980s, working through to contemporary work, particularly in the later chapters, showing the historical growth of the field. It thus aims to show how our knowledge of language attitudes has grown over the years, and indeed how some of the earlier studies have since been extended or undergone some replication. It will also be more evident how many methodological debates have persisted and developed over time.

To some extent, the geographical and cultural contexts covered in the book tend to reflect, on the one hand, those on which there has been much research published, and, on the other, those in which the author has had most involvement. Wales, which has always enjoyed a great deal of research activity in language attitudes, features frequently therefore, but many other contexts are also included.

FURTHER READING ON CHAPTER 1

For more on misconceptions about language:

Bauer, L. and Trudgill, P. (eds.), 1998, *Language myths*. London: Penguin.

For further reading on language ideology:

Coupland, N., 2009, Dialects, standards and social change, in M. Maegaard, F. Gregersen, P. Quist and J. Normann Jørgensen (eds.), *Language attitudes, standardisation and language change*. Oslo: Novus.
Lippi-Green, R., 1997, *English with an accent: language, ideology, and discrimination in the United States*. London and New York: Routledge.
Milroy, J. and Milroy, L., 1998, *Authority in language: investigating standard English*. London: Routledge.

QUESTIONS FOR CHAPTER 1

1. In this chapter, we looked at how some language features can evoke strong reactions in people, make their blood boil etc. Can you add to this list – in any language with which you are familiar?

What sorts of explanations do people give for their reactions? What is your own view?

2. How do people talk about the various languages spoken in your country, and the people who speak them?

3. What is your view on 'accent reduction classes'?

2 Fundamentals of language attitudes

This chapter covers some of the fundamental issues around attitudes, such as their constitution, origins, functions, qualities of stability and change, and their relation to stereotypes and ideology. Inevitably, these basic aspects tend to concern attitudes generally, rather than language attitudes specifically.

DEFINING ATTITUDE

In early work on attitudes, Allport (1935: 801) claimed that attitude was the most indispensable concept in social psychology, and it has been a core concept in sociolinguistics since Labov's (1966) seminal work on the social stratification of speech communities, and how language change is influenced by the prestige and stigma afforded by speech communities to specific linguistic features. The concept of attitude, however, is not easily defined. Definitions vary in their degree of elaboration and in the weighting given to different features of attitudes.

To take one or two examples, Thurstone (1931) defined an attitude as 'affect for or against a psychological object', emphasising the positive and negative emotional responses that attitudes embody. A well-cited definition was given by Allport (1954): 'a learned disposition to think, feel and behave toward a person (or object) in a particular way'. This one, then, highlights that attitudes concern more than affect alone, and extend to thought and behaviour too. Oppenheim (1982) also incorporates cognitive and behavioural aspects, but includes in his definition more elaboration of the ways in which attitudes are manifested:

> a construct, an abstraction which cannot be directly apprehended. It is an inner component of mental life which expresses itself, directly or indirectly, through much more obvious processes as stereotypes, beliefs, verbal statements or reactions, ideas and opinions, selective recall, anger or satisfaction or some other emotion and in various other aspects of behaviour (p. 39).

These three definitions set out a range of issues that get talked about in relation to attitudes, and these are taken up in the following sections.

Oppenheim's definition opens with the explicit statement that attitude is a psychological construct. Constructs cannot be observed directly, and so we have to rely on our abilities to infer them from the sorts of things that Oppenheim lists: emotional reactions, statements etc. The fact that we cannot observe attitudes directly does not mean that they are bogus, that we are just 'imagining things'. Perloff (2008: 58) argues that mental and emotional phenomena are no less real than physical behaviours. In another often-cited statement, Allport (1935) maintains that

> Attitudes are never directly observed, but, unless they are admitted, through inference, as real and substantial ingredients in human nature, it becomes impossible to account satisfactorily either for the consistency of any individual's behaviour, or for the stability in any society (p. 839).

The status of attitudes as psychological constructs brings difficulties in accessing them. This is the reason why there is always a great deal of debate about how we can study them, throughout attitudes research, and throughout this book.

Beyond this basic characteristic of being a construct, it is useful to take a general and simple 'core' definition and then to elaborate on it by looking at various aspects of attitudes about which there is reasonable consensus. Sarnoff (1970: 279) provides such a core in his definition of an attitude as 'a disposition to react favourably or unfavourably to a class of objects'. Using this as a starting point, it is taken as a given that an attitude is an evaluative orientation to a social object of some sort, whether it is a language, or a new government policy, etc. And, as a 'disposition', an attitude can be seen as having a degree of stability that allows it to be identified.

FACETS AND MANIFESTATIONS OF ATTITUDES

Attitudes are seen as complex through their possessing various facets and manifestations. To take an example from an educational context, if we wanted to study students' attitudes towards their Swahili language lessons, we would need to establish the relevant facets of these attitudes: what do we (and the students) mean by and include under 'Swahili language lessons'? The facets involved could include the Swahili language itself, classmates, teachers, teaching methods, materials and activities, types of assessment, perhaps even the physical environment of the classroom. When we consider manifestations, we are concerned with how these attitudes will reveal themselves to us (as in Oppenheim's definition above): what will we search for in our research in order to identify and try to interpret, measure or assess attitudes? We might simply see what the students have to say about their feelings and experiences by interviewing them individually or in groups, or by asking them to write a few paragraphs for us, or even to keep diaries as the course progresses. There is also an option of asking them to complete attitude rating scales, or we could try to infer their attitudes from how attentive and productive they are in these lessons. If resources allow, we might think it useful to look at a range of different manifestations and see if they seem to tell us the same story or, together, give us a fuller story. Decisions on facets and manifestations are central to designing the research.

ATTITUDES AS INPUT AND OUTPUT

It is also generally accepted that attitudes can function as both input into and output from social action. In areas such as educational research and language planning, this potential duality is particularly important. To take the case of Welsh-language education in Wales, Baker (1992: 12) sees attitudes towards the Welsh language as an important input factor to the learning and general revival of the Welsh language. Favourable attitudes may provide the impetus towards high levels of achievement in Welsh language programmes. From the other (i.e. output) direction, success in a Welsh-language course for beginners may create more positive attitudes to the language. Language planners and educationists often pursue their projects with the hope that attitudes will serve this kind of two-way function.

Beyond the educational context, attitudes also play a role in both the reception and the production of language. Language attitudes and the socio-cultural norms that they relate to are an integral part of our communicative competence (Hymes 1971), so in terms of our everyday use of language, language attitudes would be expected not only to influence our reactions to other language users around us, but also to help us anticipate others' responses to our own language use and so influence the language choices that we make as we communicate. In an effort to gain the specific responses that we seek from other people, we might 'fashion' our speech in various styles. Thus, we might try to be seen as friendly, as intelligent, as being a member of a particular community, as dynamic and as the best person for the job etc. (See Coupland 2007.)

In the reception and production of language too, then, attitudes can be understood in terms of input and output, as a cycle of influence between social cognition and language variation. Considering this dynamic relationship between 'language' and 'language attitudes', Giles and Coupland (1991: 59), in fact, argue that the two need not even be separated conceptually. One point to bear in mind here, though, is that when attitudes are considered in these terms of input and output, they are essentially being strongly linked (as input to or output from) with behaviour. The relationship between behaviour and attitudes is considered when we look at ideas about the structural composition of attitudes.

ATTITUDES ARE LEARNED

Allport's definition of attitude points to attitudes as being things that we learn, rather than as innate. In fact, there is some recent research that hereditary factors may also influence attitudes (Tesser 1993). A study of twins in the USA and Australia concludes that both genetic heritability and social environment contribute (Alford, Funk and Hibbing 2005). There is as yet, though, no clear evidence that such influences impact on language attitudes specifically, and so this is not pursued here. Suffice it to say for our present purposes that we learn attitudes, and that we do this through a variety of means (for a brief overview, see Erwin 2001: 21ff.). Two important sources of attitudes are our personal experiences and our social environment, including the media.

Various processes may be involved in our learning of attitudes. One of these is observational learning, which involves noticing the behaviour of other people and the consequences of that behaviour. Another is instrumental learning, where we attend to the consequences of attitudes and whether these bring rewards or detriments. For example, some fundamental language attitudes (evaluatively distinguishing a familiar non-standard language variety from a standard one) have been found to become established as we enter the school system as children (e.g. Day 1982). This suggests that parents and teachers can have some role in the development of such attitudes at the person-to-person level, consciously or not. Parents might indicate approval or agreement at times when their children express attitudes with which they themselves concur. Our experiences of the media may also influence attitudes in some areas. (We may also of course oppose the specific attitudes that the media – and indeed individuals – project.) Media portrayals of the elderly, for example, have been found generally to stereotype them as frail, unattractive, useless (Williams and Giles 1998), though with some more positive stereotypes emerging in some recent studies (e.g. Williams, Ylänne and Wadleigh 2007). And television advertisements have been found to reinforce rather than bring into question conventional attitudes to gender roles (Manstead and McCulloch 1981). Language controversies, as shown in chapter 1, also frequently surface in the media, and in so doing keep these issues on the public agenda, as a focal point for the shaping, reinforcement or change of attitudes.

ATTITUDE STRUCTURE

Attitudes have often been talked about in terms of three components: cognition, affect and behaviour. All three are evident in the definitions by Allport and by Oppenheim mentioned at the start of this chapter. Attitudes are cognitive insofar as they contain or comprise beliefs about the world, and the relationships between objects of social significance: e.g. judgements of standard language varieties tending to be associated with high-status jobs. Attitudes are affective in that they involve feelings about the attitude object. This affective aspect of attitudes is a barometer of favourability and unfavourability, or the extent to which we approve or disapprove of the attitude object. This positive-to-negative directionality of attitudes is usually augmented by an assessment of intensity: for example, whether we mildly disapprove of something or we well and truly detest it. Thirdly, the behavioural component of attitudes concerns the predisposition to act in certain ways, and perhaps in ways that are consistent with our cognitive and affective judgements. In terms of language, then, if we were considering a student's attitude towards Spanish as a foreign language, we could talk about a cognitive component (she believes that learning Spanish will give her a deeper understanding of Spanish culture), an affective component (she is enthusiastic about being able to read literature written in Spanish), and a behavioural component (she is saving money to enrol on a Spanish course).

There is some questioning over the status of these three components in relation to attitudes. Recent views warn against equating them with attitudes themselves. Cognition, affect and behaviour can instead be seen more in terms of causes and triggers of attitudes. Hence, for example, an emotional reaction (affect) might bring to mind an attitude object and its associations. Or the activation of an attitude might trigger a set of emotions. (See, for example, Clore and Schnall 2005; Preston, in press.)

STRUCTURAL RELATIONS OF ATTITUDES

Although attitude is often viewed in terms of cognition, affect and behaviour, there is some difficulty in determining the interconnectedness of these, and the extent to which we should anyway expect them to be in agreement all the time. This is an important issue in the attitudes field. Gass and Seiter (1999: 41), for example, go as far as to claim that 'there wouldn't be much point in studying attitudes if they were not, by and large, predictive of behaviour'. A common-sense view about the relationship between attitudes and behaviour can lead people to assume that if they are able to change someone's attitude towards something, then the person's behaviour will also change accordingly. Common-sense views can also lead people to assume that, if we look at how people behave, we can safely infer what their attitudes are. A further common assumption is that if we can get someone to start behaving in a certain way, their attitudes will simply follow along afterwards to support the new behaviour. It may well be that this is indeed the way that things often work. One would expect, for example, that it is usually safe to conclude that someone walking down a Cardiff street wearing a Cardiff City football shirt has a favourable attitude towards Cardiff City Football Club, or at least that they do not hold an unfavourable attitude.

Congruity among cognition, affect and behaviour is indeed also foregrounded if attitudes are seen in terms of input and output in the way described above. Much advertising and marketing, in fact, bases itself on such assumptions. For example, marketing managers are often keen to get us to try out free samples, or to try a product for a free trial period (or your money back if not fully satisfied) on the rationale that, once we have tried out the product, we will develop favourable attitudes to it. Festinger's (1957) theory of cognitive dissonance proposes that we prefer to keep our beliefs, attitudes and behaviour in tune with each other.

There are occasions, however, when attitudes and behaviours appear far removed from such alignment. Hewstone, Manstead and Stroebe (1997) posit the example of going for a dental check-up. Cognitively, most people would view this as a sensible routine for health reasons. Affectively, though, our feeling about making a particular visit may lack the same level of positivity as this cognitive orientation. Our behavioural inclinations, too, may be out of step with our belief that it would be a sensible thing to do, and we may rather readily find some reason to cancel our appointment.

One often-cited study of how far cognition, affect and behaviour operate independently is one by Breckler (1984), in which he studied people's attitudes to snakes. Breckler used and compared two research approaches. In one of these, a snake was physically present when people's attitudes were studied, and in the other, the respondents were asked simply to imagine that a snake was present. In the first of these conditions, Breckler found only moderate correlations between behaviour, cognition and affect, whereas in the second, he found much higher correlations. It would seem from Breckler's study that the degree of alignment found among cognition, affect and behaviour can vary according to how the studies are designed and conducted, and that there is value in assessing each of the three separately rather than assuming alignment.

Ostrom (1969: 27) pointed to a heavy bias in attitudes research towards affect, and, indeed, Thurstone's definition at the start of this chapter prioritises this. Occasionally, though, as Cargile, Giles, Ryan and Bradac (1994) point out, attitudes do appear largely or entirely affective. Hence, a person may hear a language that they are unable to identify but which they nevertheless judge to be pleasant or ugly, and this may even affect their responses during the encounter (van Bezooijen 1994). Nevertheless, research suggests that there is generally a close link between the cognition and affect (Erwin 2001: 14).

It is in the third component of this triadic model of attitudes – behaviour – where much of the controversy lies. It is perhaps telling that we tend frequently to talk in terms of 'the relationship between attitudes and behaviour' as if taking it for granted that attitudes are primarily related to cognition and affect combined, with a tendency to work together independently of behaviour much of the time. Yet the relation between attitudes and behaviour is a hugely important issue in attitudes research. For many professional persuaders, most notably in fields such as policy making, campaign and programme organising and design, and advertising, this is the relationship by which much of the rationale for researching attitudes stands or falls (Perloff 1993: 79). Hence, we devote some space to this aspect of the nature of attitudes in this chapter.

The most famous study into this question of behaviour was conducted by La Piere (1934). For two years in the 1930s, at a time when there was considerable prejudice in the USA against people from the Far East, La Piere travelled around the USA with a young Chinese student and his wife. On their tour, they stayed at sixty-six hotels and other types of accommodation, and visited 184 restaurants and cafes. Only once were they refused service. Six months after their return, La Piere sent questionnaires to the establishments they had been to. The questionnaires included the question 'Will you accept members of the Chinese race as guests in your establishment?' After some persistence by La Piere, completed replies were received from eighty-one restaurants and forty seven of the accommodation locations. 92 per cent of the restaurants and 91 per cent of the accommodation locations answered 'no' to the question. All but one of the others said that it would depend on circumstances. This study is frequently cited as showing a weak link between the attitudes that people say they have and their behaviour (although La Piere himself drew the conclusion that questionnaires were not good indicators of social attitudes).

Though extensive, this was only one study, however, and more evidence for the problematicity of any link between attitudes and behaviour comes from Hanson's (1980) review of forty-six attitude studies. Twenty six of these were laboratory studies, in which there is a great deal of control over the conditions, and the other twenty were field studies, where there is inevitably less control. The results were quite different for these two types of studies. Hanson found eighteen of the laboratory studies showed a positive relationship between attitudes and behaviour, while sixteen of the field studies failed to show any relationship. This suggests that outside the laboratory, there are probably a great deal more situational constraints on attitudes following through into behaviour. Some attitudes may come into conflict with other attitudes, for example (Erwin 2001).

The work of Ajzen and Fishbein (1980) has been of importance in the attitudes field with regard to establishing the structure and internal relationships of attitudes. They have proposed the Theory of Reasoned Action to accommodate some of the difficulties referred to above into an explanatory model.

Rather than focusing directly on behaviour, the Theory of Reasoned Action considers behavioural *intentions* as an intermediate step. Looking at Figure 2.1, we see that the basic determinants of behavioural intention are twofold. Firstly, there is the person's attitude to the behaviour itself, influenced by their beliefs about the consequences of carrying out the behaviour and their evaluation of the consequences. Secondly, there are the person's normative beliefs about how other people would judge such behaviour (with hostility or with approval, for example), along with the degree to which the person wants to take their views into account.

An example:

> *Beliefs about consequences*: 'My speaking RP on the phone to Mrs Smith, who is inviting me to go to an interview for a job, will increase my chances of getting the job.'
> *Evaluation*: 'I want this job, so this would be a good thing to do.'

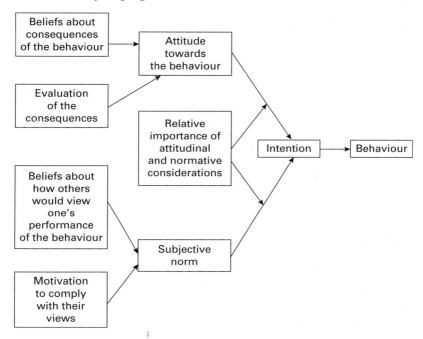

Figure 2.1 Theory of Reasoned Action (adapted from Ajzen and Fishbein 1980).

Normative beliefs: 'My sister who is sitting here in the same room with me will mock my behaviour and call me a slimy posh prat for talking RP.'
Motivation to comply with their expectations: 'I don't want to end up like my sister. I need this job, and I'm not going to stick around here much longer anyway, especially if I get it.'

Considering behavioural intentions in this theory, rather than going straight to behaviour, allows situational variables an explanatory role in attitudes that do not lead to action. For example, somewhat reminiscent of the story in chapter 1 about the BBC and Clement Atlee, Mrs Smith might conceivably open the telephone conversation referred to above by rashly saying that she is keen for this person to be interviewed because there are rather a lot of candidates whom she feels talk too posh and will simply irritate potential clients.

A number of factors, in fact, can intervene between intended and actual behaviour. To begin with, Ajzen and Fishbein (1980) propose that attitudes and behaviour are likely to be more strongly linked when they are both investigated at similar levels of specificity. If we simply measure the attitude of some non-German speakers to the German language and find that it is highly positive, this will not help us predict whether they will learn it. We might get closer if we instead assess their attitudes to learning German.

Secondly, the behaviour itself needs to be within our actual or perceived control. Internal and external factors can impact on this control. External factors include such things as time available, opportunities, facilities and the degree to which we are dependent on other people. Internal factors include such things as whether (in actuality or in our perceptions) we have access to the skills, knowledge and abilities needed to perform the action, and whether we are able to plan adequately. (For a useful summary of these points, see Hewstone *et al.* 1997: 249ff.) The importance of control factors in moving from attitude to behaviour led Ajzen (1985) to develop the Theory of Planned Behaviour, in which these kinds of volitional control factors were added to the framework of the Theory of Reasoned Action.

One phenomenon that could be added to such internal factors is whether the behaviour follows a 'script'. A script is 'a knowledge structure governing perceptual and cognitive processes (or) an organised bundle of expectations about an event sequence' (Abelson 1982: 134). Scripts can make attitudes less likely to translate into behaviour. Hence, Abelson writes of La Piere's study:

> In script terms, we would say that when the Chinese arrived, the management representatives played standard script scenes from their role perspectives. In the restaurant, the crucial scene is 'seating the customer'; in the hotel, 'registering the guest'. Given very well-practised scripts, the action rules – the policies for whether to enter the scripts – are presumably very well learned. What a hotel manager is likely to check before registering a guest is whether a room is available and the guest looks able to pay. Hotel managers (and clerks) are very well practised at going ahead if the answers are yes, but refusing the guest politely if either answer is no. On the other hand, it seems quite unlikely that managers would ask themselves, 'Do I feel favourable towards these potential guests?' (p. 135).

So having pointed earlier to the argument that the value of the study of attitudes lies in their ability to predict behaviour (Gass and Seiter 1999; Perloff 1993), it is clear that the opposite viewpoint is also valid; the variables that stand between behavioural intentions and behaviour itself, and perhaps in particular in the field of language attitudes, are often very much of interest. Links between people's attitudes towards language varieties and their own behaviours are likely to differ according to the complexity of domains in which language is used.

At another level, we may have a very positive attitude to learning a minority language, but be very aware that (like forming some kinds of friendships, for example) language learning involves a sustained long-term commitment, compared to, say, buying a new toaster. Perhaps on the basis of our personal experience, we may not feel confident of maintaining that level of commitment into the future. Or it may be that the only opportunities for learning the language involve paying expensive fees (again, over a long period of time) to a private language school. At times, too, our attitudes may be in competition: a candidate at an interview for a job may strategically adjust their speech style in a way that diverges from (or conceals) the dialect they in fact have a very strong loyalty to, if they feel this enhances their chances of satisfying other important attitudes, such as getting the job, thus helping them to fulfil their career ambitions, and/or pleasing significant others, such as a partner or parent.

STABILITY AND DURABILITY IN ATTITUDES

> When we talk about attitudes, we are talking about what a person has *learned* in the process of becoming a member of a family, a member of a group, and of society that makes him [sic] react to his social world in a *consistent* and *characteristic* way, instead of a transitory and haphazard way. (Sherif 1967: 2)

This view by Sherif not only considers the formation of attitudes as an essential part of human socialisation, but also stresses the durable qualities of attitudes as socially structured and socially structuring phenomena. Alongside this, though, are some important considerations in the persuasion literature. Fink, Kaplowitz and McGreevy Hubbard (2002), for example, review research into the fluctuation ('oscillation') that can occur as we establish or revise attitudes and beliefs or arrive at decisions, and they argue that 'it is reasonable to expect oscillatory dynamics for cognition' (p. 17). And Sears and Kosterman (1994: 264) argue that attitudes can differ in their levels of commitment. Some attitudes are more superficial and unstable, even to the point where they can even be labelled 'non-attitudes' (Ostrom, Bond, Krosnik and Sedikides 1994). 'Non-attitudes' include instances where people make up evaluations on the spot, perhaps responding for the first time to a new topic, or one that is too complex to engage with fully before feeling required to express a view. Sears (1983), though, suggests that those attitudes acquired early in the lifespan tend to be more enduring. Given that many of our attitudes to language, like language itself, are acquired early in the lifespan, this view from Sears suggests that at least some of our language attitudes are likely to be more enduring than some other attitudes.

In addition to the above, strong questioning of claims about stability and durability in attitudes comes from Potter and Wetherell (1987). Arguing from a discourse analytic perspective, they demonstrate their view by providing discourse from New Zealanders about Maoris. In the example, individuals are expressing their attitudinal positions during the course of their social interaction. They change from moment to moment and show substantial variability and volatility in their attitudes. This dynamic and constructive process of social categorisation and social evaluation, Potter and Wetherell say, is not captured by traditional approaches to studying attitudes.

Their view is well argued and demonstrated, but the implication that research into social evaluation should confine itself to the qualitative analysis of individuals' talk in interaction nevertheless seems overly restrictive (cf. arguments by Liebscher and Dailey-O'Cain 2009: 218 for the pursuit and integration of discourse and indirect approaches). There is much to be gained from taking an open view of research methods and interpretation and to allow approaches that aim at reaching generalisations about community-level phenomena. Most of the work conducted into language attitudes over the years has been situated in group-focused empirical work in the fields of sociolinguistics and the social psychology of language, and so this is inevitably reflected in this book. In chapter 10, though, we look at a study in the discourse tradition by Hyrkestedt and Kalaja (1998), investigating attitudes to English in Finland.

Theoretical questions such as how stable or ephemeral attitudes are, and of context-dependent and context-independent attitudes, are important. Social evaluations may indeed vary across or within social situations, and, as mentioned above, some attitudes may indeed also be less stable. But this does not mean that the variation is not normally bounded in some way or that there can be no stable subjective trends at higher levels. A degree of 'systematic variation' (Potter and Wetherell 1987: 45) need not be seen as entirely contradictory to the idea of durability.

OTHER TERMS RELATED TO ATTITUDES

There are a number of other terms that seem so closely connected to attitudes that they are often used almost interchangeably. It is useful to gather some of these together and try to define them and, as far as is feasible, to differentiate amongst them. Those pursued here are: habits, values, beliefs, opinions, and two concepts touched on in chapter 1: social stereotypes and ideologies.

Habits

Habits share some of the qualities of attitudes insofar as they are learned and, as with some attitudes, they are normally stable and enduring. They differ from attitudes in that they tend to be viewed primarily as behavioural routines, whereas attitudes are not seen as essentially behavioural phenomena, even if they may link with behaviour. For Perloff (1993: 29), a further difference between attitudes and habits is that people generally have more awareness of their attitudes and are able talk about them more than is the case with their habits. It is important to keep this claim in proportion, though, since one of the main difficulties in attitudes research is estimating how much reflexive awareness people actually have of their various attitudes. (See the comparison of attitudes and opinions, below.) Awareness may vary with different attitudes and in different contexts. Reflexivity is an important window in the empirical study of people's attitudes, but it can also lead to systematic error in our measurement of attitudes.

Values

Oskamp (1977) sees values as more global and general than attitudes, and as 'the most important and central elements in a person's system of attitudes and beliefs'. Rokeach (1973) differentiates 'terminal values', such as freedom and equality, from 'instrumental values', such as the importance attributed to being honest. For Rokeach, terminal values are the more global and general, and they may generate a range of highly differentiated attitudes. For example, the value of equality may drive attitudes towards a particular political party, anti-discrimination legislation, language policies in multilingual settings. Values, then, can generally be seen in terms of superordinate ideals that we aspire to.

Beliefs

Beliefs are usually talked about in terms of the cognitive component of attitudes. How uniquely cognitive they are is arguable, though. They might not have any affective content themselves, but they may trigger and be triggered by strong affective reactions. In terms of the structural components of attitudes, it is rare for the cognitive component to evoke judgements that are devoid of affective content (Cargile *et al.* 1994).

Opinions

Opinion and attitude are two terms that tend to be synonymous in everyday usage (Baker 1992: 14) and even in the discourse of many researchers (Perloff 1993: 29). Like beliefs, opinions are often said to be cognitive and lacking any affective component (e.g. Baker 1992: 14; Perloff 1993: 30), although, again, one could argue that they may trigger or be triggered by affective reactions. Baker (1992: 14) also suggests that 'opinions are verbalisable, while attitudes may be latent, conveyed by non-verbal and verbal processes' (contrasting, then, with Perloff's comparison of habits and attitudes above). Baker's distinction is useful, suggesting that opinions are discursive, while (at least some) attitudes may be harder to formulate. It allows for instances where a person's articulated opinion does not necessarily reflect their underlying attitude. This is a methodological and interpretive matter that underlies a great deal of attitudes research, as we shall see.

Social stereotypes

Cognitive processes in language attitudes are likely to be shaped by the individual and collective functions arising from stereotyping in relations between social groups. The basis for such stereotyping is social categorisation, which means dividing the world into social groups, classifying individuals as members of social groups on the basis that they share certain features of a particular group (Smith and Mackie 2000: 160). Such groups can be diverse in nature: people from a particular country, region or city, people who drive a particular type of car, people who ride bicycles, used-car dealers, academics, people of a particular ethnicity, males and females, and even, in Harari and McDavid's (1973) study in chapter 1, people with a particular name. Social categorisation tends to exaggerate similarities among members within a social group and differences between groups, and thus provides a basis for stereotyping. Stereotypes can include many types of features, such as how trustworthy, skilful or lazy group members are, their typical interests and occupations, their emotional dispositions, even physical appearance, such as height (see Cheyne 1970). One social group may be viewed with disdain, and another with admiration. Labels used to refer to the groups often imply or reveal these standpoints (e.g. the term 'wrinklies' for the elderly). In this way, stereotypes may be negative or positive. So although viewed as a cognitive process, stereotyping is not entirely divorced from affect. Stereotyping is seen as incorporating the affective response evoked by the other groups (Smith and Mackie 2000: 163).

Stereotypes are generally difficult to change. Some studies have found that attempting to suppress them can even lead to our being more influenced by them at a later stage (Wegener 1989; Macrae, Bodenhausen, Milne and Jetten 1994). Social mixing and exchange with members of opposing groups (outgroups) as a way of changing negative stereotypes – the Contact Hypothesis – do not necessarily have significant effects. For example, males and females are two social groups with a great deal of contact. Also, newly gained friends from an outgroup might be seen as exceptions, and so leave the negative group stereotype intact. For contact to alter group stereotypes, it seems that certain conditions have to be met. Instances that are inconsistent with the stereotype have to be experienced on repeated occasions across a large number of members, who, despite the inconsistency, must still be regarded as typical of their group rather than exceptions (Smith and Mackie 2000).

In the language attitudes field, then, language varieties and styles can trigger beliefs about a speaker and their social group membership, often influenced by language ideologies, leading to stereotypic assumptions about shared characteristics of those group members. A number of functions are attributed to this social categorisation (Tajfel 1981). At the individual level, one function is to bring some order to a complex social world, making it easier to predict and negotiate. At the intergroup level, stereotypes serve a social differentiation function, enabling us to preserve and enhance favourable distinctions between our own group (ingroup) and relevant outgroups. And linking to the concept of ideology, they also serve a social explanatory function, meaning that they create and maintain group ideologies that justify and defend relations between the groups, and how members of outgroups should be evaluated and treated. Hence, as we saw in chapter 1, there can be implications for how people behave towards each other. Recall, for example, Morrish's (1999) story of the student whose Bristolian English led the school to feel justified in excluding him from the school team on a television quiz show.

Stereotypes, then, play a role in maintaining inequalities which advantage some and disadvantage others (Smith and Mackie 2000). According to Milroy (2001), social class background (which people may deduce – correctly or incorrectly – from language use) is still a powerful factor as regards income and opportunity in the UK, whereas the corresponding factor in the USA is still race. The system of beliefs that maintains, triggers and directs such discrimination is often referred to as ideology. Social stereotypes tend to perpetuate themselves and be self-fulfilling, acting, like ideology, as a store of 'common-sense' beliefs or filters through which information and social life generally is conducted and made sense of.

Ideology

Although social stereotypes and ideology have just been mentioned in the same sentence, the concepts come from different traditions. While social stereotypes originate from the field of social psychology, the notion of language ideology mainly emanates from linguistic anthropology. One might argue that language ideologies can influence social stereotypes through the process of social learning, although social stereotypes have multiple sources within social interaction and specific contexts too.

The concept of ideology has attracted a great deal of attention in social science in recent years, with the revived interest in the political landscapes and climates in which social life is conducted. As we saw in chapter 1, ideology comprises a patterned but naturalised set of assumptions and values about how the world works, a set which is associated with a particular social or cultural group. A right-wing political ideology might represent the privileges associated with wealthy and powerful social groups as 'freedom of the individual', while representing left-wing political policies as features of 'the nanny state'. Ideology is a pivotal concept in critical discourse analysis (see Fairclough 1995), in which often hidden, taken-for-granted values that structure linguistic representation are scrutinised and exposed (see Jaworski and Coupland 1999).

Within sociolinguistics and language attitudes, language ideology has come to the fore as a politically more sensitive backdrop to investigations of language variation and language change and the values placed on linguistic alternatives (see, for example, Irvine and Gal 2000). It has become an important concept for understanding the politics of language in multilingual situations, in such areas as social inclusion and exclusion (e.g. Blommaert and Verschueren 1998), and also in monolingual contexts. In chapter 1, we saw a view of standard language ideology as built on the overlapping principles of correctness, authority, prestige and legitimacy. Milroy (2007) writes, 'The maintenance of standard language depends on obedience to authority' (p. 136) where 'some groups have more authority than others' (p. 137). Standard languages are given legitimacy and prestige over non-standard alternatives. Speakers tend to confer prestige on language varieties that are seen as those of higher social classes. Some legitimacy is also achieved through the writing of histories of languages, which can be seen largely as codifications of the standard language, legitimising it, in part, through supplying it with 'continuous unbroken history' (Milroy 2007: 138). Against such a backdrop, then, language attitudes can be viewed as being influenced by powerful ideological positions.

Research into language ideologies is not linked to any specific methodological tradition, although critical discourse analytic procedures constitute one approach within sociolinguistics. Language attitudes research can arguably be seen, though, as one set of methodological options for studying language ideologies. The programmatic language attitudes research reviewed towards the end of this book in chapter 12, for example, can be seen as providing some access to differentiated ideological accounts of language within a community.

CONCLUSION

In this chapter, then, we have engaged with matters concerning what attitudes are and what their composition is, and we have looked at some of the debates around their durability, their relationship to behaviour, and their links with concepts that are strongly grounded in 'common-sense' ideas that we are not necessarily conscious of in our interactions. These underlying factors continually come to the fore as new research is conducted and data interpreted. They contribute to making language attitudes difficult to research, especially when set alongside some of the methodological issues raised in chapter 3, but they also undoubtedly add to the interest and challenge of this field.

FURTHER READING ON CHAPTER 2

An extremely important text on attitudes generally (rather than language attitudes specifically), which questions the focus on consistency in much attitudes work, and emphasises variability in attitudes, is:

Potter, J. and Wetherell, M., 1987, *Discourse and social psychology: beyond attitudes and behaviour*. London: Sage.

Two sources on how contextual factors can impact on evaluative reactions to language are:

Coupland, N., 2007, *Style: language variation and identity*. Cambridge: Cambridge University Press.

Preston, D., in press, Variation in language regard, in E. Ziegler, J. Scharloth and P. Gilles (eds.), *Empirische Evidenzen und theoretische Passungen sprachlicher Variation*. Frankfurt: Peter Lang.

The following is a valuable and varied collection of research papers that give attention to the nature of attitudes and the concomitant difficulties in researching them.

Acta linguistica hafniensia, Volume 37. This is a yearbook on the topic 'Subjective processes in language variation and change', edited by Tore Kristiansen, Peter Garrett and Nikolas Coupland, 2005.

QUESTIONS FOR CHAPTER 2

1. In the study questions at the end of chapter 1, you were asked about people's attitudes towards particular features of a language with which you are familiar, and to other languages and their speakers in your own country. Do you think these attitudes have existed for a long time, or have just developed recently? Do you see these attitudes as durable, or do you feel they might be changing, or change in the near future?

2. Make a list of any attitudes that you hold that you do not translate into action? (Perhaps a language you would very much like to learn but never have, for example.) What are the reasons why you have not followed them through? What sorts of barriers can you find between your attitudes and behaviour?

3 Main approaches to the study of language attitudes

Many authors identify three broad approaches to studying people's attitudes towards language (e.g. Ryan, Giles and Hewstone 1988), and so these are used as a framework for grouping studies in this book. These approaches are called the analysis of the *societal treatment* of language varieties (also referred to as 'content analysis' by Knops and van Hout 1988: 6), *direct measures* and *indirect measures* (indirect measures are sometimes referred to as the 'speaker evaluation paradigm', or 'the matched guise technique' in the language attitudes literature). As with any research methods, the methods within each of these approaches have their own strengths and weaknesses. In this chapter, these three approaches are exemplified, outlined and considered.

As mentioned at the end of chapter 1, there is stronger reference in these early chapters to some of the early work in language attitudes, showing how the field was 'laid down'. A greater proportion of more contemporary research comes to fore as the book moves forward.

DIRECT APPROACH

MacKinnon's study of attitudes to Scottish Gaelic

MacKinnon (1981) reported a large-scale survey of attitudes to Gaelic in Scotland. In total, attitude data was collected from a sample of 1,117 respondents, aged fifteen and over, living in the Scottish Lowland and Highland regions, Skye and the Western Isles. The survey employed a questionnaire which contained sixteen questions, and respondents chose one of six possible responses: 'strongly disagree', 'disagree on the whole', 'no feelings either way', 'agree on the whole', 'strongly agree' and 'no response'. The respondents were asked the questions orally by interviewers (rather than filling in the questionnaire themselves), and the interviewers wrote the responses on the questionnaires.

The questions included the following:

1. Do you think that the Gaelic language is important for the Scottish people as a whole?
2. Do you think that Gaelic should be officially recognized in Scotland?
3. Should Gaelic speakers be allowed to use Gaelic when dealing with public authorities?
4. Should children in any part of Scotland be able to learn Gaelic at school if they or their parents want it?
5. Would you yourself welcome more opportunities for adult education in Gaelic?
6. If Gaelic became more noticeable in everyday life, in what way would this affect you?

For this last question, which was the last of the sixteen questions on the questionnaire, the interviewers wrote down the various comments made by the respondents, and these were later analysed by identifying the main themes that emerged. For example, comments such as 'It would be rather attractive', 'It would suit me', 'It would boost my morale' were grouped into a theme called 'personal satisfaction'.

The results, overall, for the survey seemed encouraging. At the time, Census figures showed only 1.6 per cent of the population of Scotland as a whole reporting themselves as Gaelic speakers, and only about half of these reported themselves as literate in the language. (Percentages were not even across Scotland, of course, but were much higher in the more 'Gaelic' regions, such as the Western Isles.) Baker (1988: 126), with some caveats, summarises the findings on most of the major issues as showing between 40 per cent and 50 per cent of the sample positive towards Gaelic, and the remainder either neutral or negative. We will return to one or two specific findings from this study later.

Sharp *et al.*'s study of attitudes to Welsh

Sharp, Thomas, Price, Francis and Davies' (1973) large-scale study in Wales involved 12,000 children aged 10–11, 12–13 and 14–15, with the 'post-junior' students drawn from grammar schools (selective state secondary schools) and technical schools, as well as secondary modern schools. To collect their attitudinal data, they employed a combination of scales. That this is a direct approach study is evident from the instructions given to the students. These made it very clear what the researchers' objectives were: 'The following exercise is designed to find out what kind of idea you have of *the Welsh language*' (p. 167).

They found that, while at the age of 10–11 the great majority of children were mildly positive towards Welsh, there was an overall trend to a relatively neutral attitude by the fourth year of secondary education. This was paralleled by an increasingly favourable attitude towards English, creating a 'see-saw' effect. Attitudes towards Welsh in bilingual schools followed a different pattern, however. Despite a decline in positivity, they nevertheless remained on the positive side. It was not clear whether these findings supported bilingual education policies. This is because the creation of bilingual schools resulted from parental pressure, so the positive attitudes in these students might have been fostered as much by their parents, family and community as by the policies themselves. This is suggested by the fact that these latter students also *started* with a comparatively more favourable attitude.

These two studies exemplify the *direct approach* to studying language attitudes. Typically, as in these studies, people are simply asked questions directly about language evaluation, preference, etc. They are invited to articulate explicitly what their attitudes are to various language phenomena. So it is an approach that relies upon overt elicitation of attitudes. At one level, it may seem the most obvious way to get at people's attitudes: i.e. to ask them what their attitudes are. But, as we shall see, things are not always that simple.

INDIRECT APPROACH

It is against this backdrop that the *indirect approach* emerges. Compare the two studies below to the ones above.

Lambert *et al.*'s study of attitudes towards Arabic and Hebrew

In this study by Lambert, Anisfeld and Yeni-Komshian (1965), a text was recorded in Arabic, in Yemenite Hebrew (spoken by emigrants from Yemen), and in Ashkenazic Hebrew (spoken by Jews of European descent). The recording was made by two speakers who were both bilinguals. One had Hebrew as his native language, while the other's first language was Arabic, and both were judged to speak both languages well enough to be taken as native speakers of either of them. These three audio-recorded versions of the text were heard by Arab and Jewish teenaged school students in Israel, who then had to rate the speakers on a number of scales. For example, they had to make personality ratings of each speaker. For this, they were given a number of personality traits (e.g. friendliness, reliability, good-heartedness) and had to indicate their judgements for each of these on a scale calibrated from one to six (i.e. a six-point scale) with one end labelled 'very little' and the other 'very much'. The two voices of each speaker were maximally separated on the audio-tapes, so as to decrease the likelihood of the respondents recognising that they were listening to the same speaker twice. To help achieve this, an additional voice was also included, and this one was not used in the analysis. The instructions given to the respondents were that they were to listen attentively to a series of speakers reading a passage and to imagine, much as you do when you hear a voice on the air or over a telephone, what type of person each person was. They were informed that some would be speaking Arabic and some Hebrew, but they were to disregard the language differences, which, it was said, had only been used to make the task more interesting, and they were to focus on the speaker instead.

Amongst the many results, statistical analysis showed that the Jewish respondents, when judging the recorded voices, rated the Arabic speakers significantly less humorous, less friendly, less honest and less desirable as friends or potential marriage partners. The Arab respondents, in turn, judged the Hebrew speakers as less intelligent and confident, less good-hearted, friendly and honest, and less desirable for marriage.

Remember that the 'Hebrew speakers' they heard were in fact two different bilingual people, each from different communities, while the two Arabic voices they heard were also two bilingual people, each from different communities. But the statistical divide in the ratings suggested that the respondents identified the two voices speaking the same language as two people from the same community.

Giles' study of attitudes towards regional and foreign accents in British English

A study by Giles (1970) used the same sort of technique, though it differed in a number of ways. He studied the evaluations of secondary school students in the UK to a range of UK accents, along with some foreign accents of English frequently heard by people in the UK. The teenagers listened to tape recorded voices produced by one male speaker, who read the same passage in thirteen different accents. Giles notes that 'The speaker attempted to assume the same speech-rate, vocal intensity, pitch and personality throughout the recordings' (p. 214), so that, as far as possible, the only difference in the recordings was the accent that was used in each case. The students, however, were told that they should listen to a series of different speakers reading the same factual passage in their own particular regional or foreign accent. The students then had to note their evaluations of each voice on three seven-point scales (e.g. how much status they associated with the accent). It is worth noting here that, to increase the likelihood that the students would not realise that the voices were all produced by the same person, they were told before the task began that the researcher had gone to considerable lengths to obtain the services of all these thirteen speakers (Giles 1970: 216). And, at the end of the task, when the students were 'debriefed' (informed of the true nature of the experiment, in order to meet ethical requirements), some of the respondents expressed surprise that the voices had been produced by the same person (Giles and Powesland 1975: 28).

The results showed that the respondents evaluated these voices in ways that differentiated them. Since the researchers had attempted to ensure that the only difference between the voices was their accents, the different evaluations of the voices are regarded as different evaluations of the accents themselves. For example, they judged RP more positively on all three evaluative scales than the other varieties. We will not comment further on these results here, since we will revisit this study and comment more on the results in chapter 4.

As is evident in these examples, the *indirect approach* to studying language attitudes means using more subtle, even deceptive, techniques than simply asking straight questions about what people's attitudes are to something. In attitudes research generally, the indirect approach comprises several techniques (Dawes and Smith 1985), but in research into language attitudes, the indirect approach is generally seen in terms of the *matched guise technique*. Typically, respondents in matched guise studies hear an audio-tape recording of a single speaker reading out the same text a number of times, with each reading differing from the others in one respect only, as far as possible. For example, if the focus of the study is on regional or social accent variation, then the text will be read in a number of relevant accents, but with other features remaining as constant as possible (e.g. speech rate, pauses and hesitations, etc.), as in the Giles (1970) study above. Respondents are told that they will be listening to a number of different speakers. They are not told that the speaker is in fact the same person speaking in different 'guises', and it is assumed that this deception lasts for the duration of the evaluation task. They are asked to listen to each speaker, pausing after each one in order to fill in attitude rating scales. Attitude rating questionnaires are therefore used in such studies. Listeners are aware that this is an attitude rating task, but it is an indirect approach because the respondents are not aware of exactly what they are rating (e.g. accents). A variant of this technique, which we look at more in the next chapter, and which features in many studies in this book, is the *verbal guise technique*, in which the language varieties are recorded by different speakers.

Why are there these two approaches – direct and indirect? Does it make any difference which one you choose? Firstly, we take a look at another part of each of the matched guise studies we set out as examples above.

In the same study by Giles (1970), he also gave out a simple written list of accents, similar in range to those in the matched guise task. The respondents had to rate these accents on scales of the same kind as before. Because, this time, the respondents were responding to accent labels (rather than vocal guises), they were well aware that they were evaluating accents, and so this part of the study was using a direct method rather than an indirect one. So were the results any different? Giles found that, apart from a trend for accents to be regarded slightly more favourably when presented in a list, the results from the two parts of the study correlated very highly (+0.79 for pleasantness, +0.87 for communicative content and +0.88 for status). In this study, then, it did not seem to matter which method was used, and going to all the time and trouble of finding someone who could produce the accents and then preparing the audio-tapes seemed not to be necessary.

In the other study (Lambert *et al.* 1965), there was also a second task: the Jewish students had to complete a number of additional scales. This time, they completed them, not in response to the audio-recorded voices, but to questions referring to 'Ashkenaic Jews', 'Arabs' and 'Yemenite Jews' (i.e. using group-labels rather than voices), so, again, making this a direct method. For example, they had to indicate on a scale whether they thought that 'Arabs in general' were boring. In addition, though, there were some particularly striking differences between the findings for the audio-recordings and the findings for the labels. Specifically, in the labels procedure, the Arabs were judged relatively less good-looking, intelligent, self-confident, reliable and leader-like, whereas in the voice procedure, Arabs were seen as less honest and less friendly, but not significantly different as regards appearance, intelligence, self-confidence, reliability or leadership.

Why should the use of direct and indirect approaches make a difference in one study and not another? Lambert *et al.* (1965) concluded that the matched guise technique, in contrast to the other measure in their study, probably evoked more private emotional and conceptual reactions. So it may be that in some contexts there is a difference between people's private attitudes and the ones they are normally prepared to tell people about. Indeed, Lambert and his colleagues originally developed this technique in Montreal in the 1950s because they were sceptical as to whether local people's overt responses to direct questions truly reflected their privately held inter-ethnic views. The context in which Giles was studying attitudes was perhaps a much less highly charged environment linguistically and ethnically than bilingual Montreal, and that could account for the close similarity of attitudes from the indirect and direct parts of his study.

In some contexts, too, people may operate with two value systems (or two sets of attitudes) alongside each other, while only being conscious of one of them. Kristiansen (2009) concludes from his research into language change in Denmark that such change is governed by subconsciously held values (more likely, then, to be accessed through indirect research methods) rather than by consciously offered ones (accessed through direct methods). The latter tend to reproduce the ideology of elite discourse. Such 'ideologised values' are something we return to in later in this book.

There are all sorts of ways in which we can compare indirect and direct approaches, and more will emerge as we report more studies in this book. At this point, though, we will look at some of the factors that tend to be discussed in relation to direct approach studies (though indirect studies are not necessarily immune from all of these). Firstly, there are some problems that regularly occur with the formulation of the questions that the respondents are asked.

Asking hypothetical questions

Hypothetical questions ask about how people *would* react to a particular object, event or action. And in terms of the relationship between attitudes and behaviour (see chapter 2), the responses to these sorts of questions are often poor predictors of people's future behaviour in a situation where they actually encounter such objects, events or actions. Remember, too, that in chapter 2, we referred to Breckler's (1984) study looking at attitudes towards snakes. When there was no snake present, and respondents had to say how they would feel and behave if there were one there (i.e. approach the issue hypothetically), the results were quite different from when a snake was actually present. So if you are investigating attitudes in the hope of gaining insights into likely behaviour arising from them, the use of hypothetical questions may be less likely to give such insights.

Asking strongly slanted questions

Some questions contain relatively 'loaded' words that tend to push people into answering one way. Oppenheim (1992: 130 and 137) lists a number terms that are often seen as best to avoid: e.g., *Nazi, Reds, bosses, strike-breakers, healthy, natural* (though these presumably have to be judged in context). Questions may also be slanted less by individual loaded words, but more by their overall leading content: e.g. 'Do you disagree with our well-considered view that Welsh children should be perfectly entitled to learn Welsh?' Care needs to be taken to avoid this. Baker (1988: 128) suggests that some of McKinnon's questions in his study of attitudes to Gaelic were slanted in their wording. He gives the example of question 1 in our list of interview questions provided earlier being slanted through its use of the word 'important': 'Do you think that the Gaelic language is important for the Scottish people as a whole?'

Asking multiple questions

Multiple questions are questions where a positive answer can refer to more than one component of the question, or they can be types of double negative questions to which a negative answer would be ambiguous. Baker also points to an instance in MacKinnon's Gaelic survey. One of the questions (number 4 in the list earlier) was: 'Should children in any part of Scotland be able to learn Gaelic at school if they or their parents want it?' By including children 'or their parents', in effect, the question ends up as two questions. In fact, the responses to this question differed considerably from those to other questions. 70 per cent were positive, compared to the general norm of 40 to 50 per cent. It may be that there were combined responses relating to both children and parents.

In addition to the wording of questions (whether written on a questionnaire or spoken in an interview), there are certain inclinations (or 'biases') that can occur in people's responses.

Social desirability bias

This bias is the tendency for people to give answers to questions in ways that they believe to be 'socially appropriate'. In other words, the respondents tell you about the attitudes that they think they ought to have, rather than the ones they actually do have. According to Cook and Sellitz (1964: 39), for example, people in the USA are often inclined to give replies that make them appear 'well-adjusted, unprejudiced, rational, open-minded, and democratic'. Questions aimed at tapping attitudes towards racial, ethnic and religious minorities often are hampered by a social desirability bias. Respondents who hold negative views towards a particular group may not wish to admit this to the researcher, or even to themselves, and so 'they may avoid giving answers that would make them look like bigots' (Perloff 1993: 44). Also, one of the reasons for guaranteeing anonymity, or at least confidentiality, to respondents is to reduce the risk that they will just give socially desirable responses. One cannot be sure, of course, that even this will be effective. Oppenheim (1992: 126) argues that the social desirability bias is of more significance in interviews than in questionnaires. Logically, then, one might expect the greatest risk of social desirability bias in interviews with whole groups of respondents (e.g. focus group interviews), too 'public' to afford individual anonymity.

Acquiescence bias

Acquiescence bias (Ostrom *et al.* 1994; Fabrigar, Krosnik and MacDougall 2005) can be a further difficulty. Some respondents prefer to agree with an item, regardless of its content. The preference may only be marginal, but it may still be significant (Baker 1988: 128). They may see this as a way of gaining the researcher's approval, giving them the answer that they think they want. This, too, then means that the responses do not reflect the respondent's actual personal evaluation of the attitude state-ment, and therefore raises issues of validity. Acquiescence bias can occur in response to questionnaire or interview items, although some claim that it is especially pronounced in face-to-face interviews (Gass and Seiter 2003: 47).

Social desirability and acquiescence biases doubtless affect some attitudes more than others, and some people more than others. For example, it may well be that they have a greater effect where the issues are of some personal sensitivity, or where the issues are less likely to have been well thought through. As far as respondents are concerned, there is some evidence that people who are more 'ego-involved' (i.e. when an issue is of great personal significance to them and/or their sense of self) are less likely to present or tolerate a view that is at odds with their own (see, for example, Bettinghaus and Cody 1994: 168ff.). Nevertheless, these biases are pervasive phenomena in language attitudes research that can prevent researchers tapping into the 'private attitudes' of respondents, and it was these sorts of difficulties, and the importance of accessing such private attitudes, that led Lambert and his colleagues in Canada to develop the matched guise technique, trying to distract respondents from the real nature of their research questions.

Characteristics of the researchers

Qualities of the researchers may also affect the quality of attitude data, reflecting what might be termed an 'Interviewer's Paradox' (*cf.* Labov's 1972 'Observer's Paradox'). Responses to questions posed by the researcher may be affected by ethnicity and sex on both sides, for example. Webster (1996) investigated these issues in relation to Anglo and Hispanic males and females in the USA. She found that better response rates were achieved when interviewers and respondents shared the same ethnicity (especially in the case of Anglos, and especially when questions related to cultural issues). A language attitudes study in Wales conducted by a Japanese researcher produced results that differed from comparable data collected by Welsh or English researchers (Bellin, Matsuyama and Schott 1999). In addition, the language employed by researchers in data collection may also have an impact on language attitudes results, particularly where language is a very salient dimension of intergroup comparison. In their matched guise study of attitudes of Welsh children (ten to twelve years old) towards RP and the English and Welsh accents of West Wales, Price, Fluck and Giles (1983) found that some results differed depending on whether the children did the evaluation task in Welsh or in English. Specifically, the West Wales accented English speaker was judged to be less intelligent than the other two when the test was in Welsh, and more selfish than the other two when it was in English. In both instances, no such differences emerged when the testing was conducted in the other language.

SOCIETAL TREATMENT STUDIES

Schmied's study of attitudes towards English in Africa

Schmied (1991) sought to uncover the various attitudes in favour of and against English across many African contexts. In one part of his study, he looked at letters to the editor in African newspapers. By examining these, with their focus on specific language issues, he identified the types of arguments put forward for and against English, which, he said, then reveal the writers' attitudes (p. 168). So his study sought to achieve a kind of map of attitudes from material occurring in the media.

One might argue that this is not much different from a direct approach study, with the letter writers consciously expressing their attitudes to language, and indeed, there are certainly some similarities with the social constructionist study by Hyrkestedt and Kajala (1998) reviewed in chapter 10. Categorisation is seldom clear cut. But Schmied's study is included here since his letters were taken from the media, in this case newspapers, rather than being elicited from respondents by researchers for the purposes of a particular study.

Examining these letters from these African media sources, Schmied found that, although the arguments covered a spectrum of negativity and positivity, the kinds of issues they addressed nevertheless fell into five principal categories: communicative, national, personal, educational and cognitive. The typical arguments found were as follows.

Communicative arguments

A1: An African language is more effective for communication than English.

A2: Complex concepts can be expressed more easily in English than in an African language.

National arguments

A3: Favouring English means neglecting an important aspect of the national identity.

A4: Favouring English may create class differences in the nation.

A5: A decline in the use of English would strengthen national unity.

A6: English medium education means equal chances for all children because English is the basis for all further education.

A7: Only sufficient knowledge of English can keep science and learning in the country in touch with world-wide developments.

A8a: The discouragement of English language teaching is harmful to our national interests.

A8b: The discouragement of English use is harmful to our national interests.

Personal arguments

A9: English is useful for getting a better job.

A10: For a career in the civil service, it may be better not to use English but African languages.

A11: Speaking good English shows that someone belongs to the modern educated society.

A12: English is an elitist language, thus separating educated Africans from the common people.

Educational arguments

A13: Switching to African languages as a medium of instruction would bring down the educational standards.

A14: If a student is good at English, he is good at other subjects too.

A15: Favouring the students' use of English too much undermines principles of national education.

A16: It is easier to understand concepts when they are explained in African languages.

Cognitive arguments

A17: Knowing African languages only means being less educated.

A18: People who do not know English or European languages in general lack certain basic cognitive concepts.

A19: Being a foreign language, English is not suitable for the African mind.

A20: English makes Africans too European-minded.

To some extent, it is possible, simply from the gathering of data from various sources and from familiarity with the context, to contextualise these arguments. So, for example, A3 is seen as a cultural argument relating to the nation-building process, whereas A4 is seen as an argument occurring more in the context of discussion about the democratic participation of all social groups in this process. Similar factors make it possible to proportionalise them. For example, Schmied feels that A8a is more likely to meet with more support than A8b, because A8a is connected with the use of English as an International Language whereas A8b is more an argument associated with English as a Second (i.e. internal) Language.

Schmied points to the methodologically restrictive factors that can often feature when researching in parts of Africa. These include a lack of reliable statistical data, unreliable postal services and, perhaps even more importantly, some populations that are unused to questionnaires and interviewers from foreign countries.

Kramarae's study of attitudes towards gender differences in speech behaviour

Kramarae (1982) studied beliefs about gender-related differences by analysing publicly available literature and documentation of various kinds. We will look at aspects of her work that illustrate what is here being referred to as the societal treatment approach. One strand was her survey of more than 100 advice books that had appeared over the past 150 years. By 'advice books', she meant books that are 'intended to provide self-training for women and men who want to do and say what is proper and or effective' (p. 88). Across the 150 years, she found some clear similarities. It was clear too that most of the books were directed at women rather than men. Essentially, the story coming out of these books was that women are innately more modest and proper than men, and that, innate though these qualities might be, women evidently need to take a lot of care to make sure they surface. Here are some representative attitudes found by Kramarae in these books, and some of her citations of their authors (see Kramarae 1982 for details of these sources).

Referring to advice in Loeb (1954): 'Women should not make derogatory remarks or questionable jokes about others.'

From Hertz (1950: 30), Kramarae summarises: 'The problem of conversation between the sexes is made difficult because when girls are together, they "chatter" endlessly about clothes and dates, while boys together "discuss" sports.'

Illustrating the general tone in much advice, that women should inform themselves about topics liked by men, while at the same time understanding that women can never expect to discuss them authoritatively with men, Kramarae quotes from Witan (1940: 25): 'A safe subject is always the boy himself.'

'The perfect secretary should forget that she is a human being, and be the most completely efficient aid at all times and on all subjects . . . She should respond to [her boss's] requirements exactly as a machine responds to the touch of a lever or accelerator. If he says "Good morning," she answers "Good morning" with a smile and cheerfully. She does not volunteer a remark – unless she has messages of importance to give him. If he says nothing, she says nothing, and she does not even mentally notice that he has said nothing' (Emily Post 1945: 548).

'Once during an evening is enough for women to state a definite and unqualified opinion – and even then it should be some-thing constructive or a defence of someone or something' (Wilson 1947: 206).

Quoting from Wright (1936: 99ff.), she adds that if 'by some freak of nature' a woman should shine at activities which take a logical mind, 'it will be found that she has a man's mind'.

In another strand of her data on social attitudes related to gender and speech, Kramarae (1982) reviewed documentation in the form of historical records. These were concerned with the struggle over a period of 150 years by women to gain public speaking rights.

Some of the findings from her examination of treatment by the media are reminiscent of the stories we looked at in chapter 1. In 1926, the British press reported a considered decision by the BBC not to employ women radio announcers, because they would be 'hopeless', especially for reading the news (Kramarae 1982: 89). A few years later, though, the BBC had a change of heart, and decided to experiment by employing a woman announcer. The decision aroused a great deal of discussion in the media, including mention of the salary she would receive for her job (information that was not mentioned in the case of male equivalents). Encouragingly, comment after the first broadcast was positive, with much admiration expressed for her 'cool, business-like, commanding . . . authoritative tone' (*News Chronicle*, 29 July 1933). Nevertheless, she was sacked a few months afterwards on the grounds of technical problems, according to the BBC. Subsequently, however, the BBC acknowledged that they had been inundated with letters complaining that her salary was too large, since she was the wife of a pensioned naval officer (*Daily Express*, 7 March 1934).

In contrast to men, then, women are advised to modify or restrict their speech in mixed-sex contexts. Kramarae's data revealed that the attributions in such advice to women include, with some consistency, references to such things as voice qualities, reticence and intelligence, and familial and social duties. Her research was also a good demonstration of the value of the societal treatment approach in gaining historical insights into attitudes. This is something that this research approach can deliver that lies generally beyond the reach of direct and indirect approaches. This kind of historical material 'helps explain the support for and extent of the contemporary expressions of attitudes toward women's speech' (Kramarae 1982: 90).

Kramer's study of speech gendered behaviour in cartoons

Kramer (1974) also examined stereotypes of women's speech, this time by looking at contemporary, rather than historical, data in the form of how males and females were portrayed through their speech in cartoons in large circulation magazines. This type of research material was viewed as fruitful because 'in few places are the stereotyped differences presented in so concentrated a form' (p. 625).

Her research extended beyond the societal treatment analysis of texts, since she asked respondents to examine a sample of captions from cartoons (without the cartoons themselves). They were told that these were statements taken from magazines, and were asked whether they thought they would originally have been presented as coming from male or female speakers in the magazines, and then to explain why they thought that. The students tended in their responses to describe the communication gender stereotypes. From an analysis of the students' responses and the original cartoons themselves, Kramer found the stereotype for female speech to be

> stupid, naïve, gossipy, emotional, passive, confused, concerned, wordy and insipid, ineffective, and also restricted, in the sense of not being spoken in as many different places as men's speech, and dealing less forthrightly with topics that hold importance in our culture, such as finance and politics (1974: 626).

Male speech, on the other hand, was seen as logical, concise and dealing with more important topics, as well as more likely to be putting down the other person.

Kramer concludes: 'One male commenting on the captions wrote: "The roles portrayed through these statements were created by our society, and have been learned by me. I will probably teach them to my children, consciously or unconsciously." Unless the situation changes, he will have help from the cartoons in mass-circulation journals' (p. 630).

The value of societal treatment studies

Societal treatment studies tend to be relatively overlooked, in fact, in most contemporary reviews of language attitudes research. As can be seen even from these few examples, though, it is a useful way of obtaining insights into the social meanings and stereotypical associations of language varieties and languages, and the 'treatment' meted out to languages and language varieties 'out there' in society. Typically, then, it involves analysing the content of various sources in the public domain, such as prescriptive (or proscriptive) texts, language policy documents, media texts and various kinds of advertisements (some also include ethnographic research under this rubric: e.g. Ryan, Giles and Hewstone 1988). The approach is sometimes viewed, especially by those working in the social psychological tradition of language attitudes research, as somewhat informal, and not lending itself to the rigour of statistical analysis and generalisation to broader or specific populations. Hence some tend to view such studies more as a preliminary to more rigorously designed surveys. Knops and van Hout (1988) suggest that the approach is more appropriate in contexts where time and space limitations do not allow access to respondents directly, or where respondents can only be accessed under somewhat unnatural conditions. But far from all would agree with this. There is a large body of work in discourse analysis and text analysis (looking at attitudinal and ideological positions in the media, for example) which is firmly based on the premiss that this work is of immense importance in its own right.

CONCLUDING POINTS

Before ending this chapter, there are one or two additional comparisons of the approaches to be made in order to bring some of the threads together. To begin with, we can say that both the societal treatment and direct approaches employ a wide variety of techniques and methods, and we shall see much more of this variety later in this book. The indirect approach, in contrast, has tended, in language attitudes research, mainly to be characterised by the use of guise techniques.

In addition, in the societal treatment approach, the researcher has to infer attitudes from various kinds of observed behaviours and sources. In the direct approach, the respondents themselves infer and report directly their own attitudes. Arguably, ticking boxes on a questionnaire in a direct survey of attitudes (or indeed in an indirect study) is also a kind of behaviour from which researchers have to infer attitudes, but this kind of inference, on the basis of specifically targeted questions, is at one remove from that which characterises the societal treatment approach. A further difference between the approaches is that the societal treatment approach is the least obtrusive overall, in that it generally works from texts or observations of various kinds rather than through eliciting responses. As this book progresses, these three approaches will be covered in more depth as we examine some of the work on language attitudes that has employed them.

FURTHER READING ON CHAPTER 3

For more on designing questions, questionnaires and interviews:

Oppenheim, A., 1992, *Questionnaire design, interviewing, and attitude measurement.* London: Pinter.

For more on language attitudes research in Africa, see:

Adegbija, E., 1994, *Language attitudes in sub-Saharan Africa.* Clevedon: Multilingual Matters.

QUESTIONS FOR CHAPTER 3

1. In your own words, summarise the three main approaches to language attitudes research introduced in this chapter.
2. Think of a language issue that has appeared in the media in your country recently (perhaps one concerned with language in schools, for example). What sorts of arguments have been made? Do any of them fall into any of the categories that Schmied identified in his study in this chapter? Can you find other categories?
3. Take the issue that you talked about in question 2. Could you find out more about such attitudes by using direct and indirect approaches? In your context and on this issue, do you think that using an indirect approach might reveal more about people's attitudes than a direct approach study would?

4 Matched and verbal guise studies: focus on English

The main focus in chapters 4 and 5 is on studies employing the matched guise (and verbal guise) approaches. In this chapter we shall start by revisiting the study by Giles (1970), briefly introduced in chapter 3, to draw out some of its features and findings regarding UK attitudes to different accents of English. We shall then discuss advantages and disadvantages of this approach to studying language attitudes. We shall then review a number of studies that have investigated attitudes to native varieties of English in other English-speaking countries. This gives the chapter something of a native speaker English tone, with attention largely focused on 'inner circle' Englishes ('inner circle' Englishes is a term from Kachru 1985, 1988 referring to the Englishes of Australia, Canada, New Zealand, the UK, the USA, and other countries where English is said to have a traditional basis). In chapter 5, though, we will extend to more contexts. Research methods issues will continue to be picked out in context as we go along.

UK: MORE DETAILS AND FINDINGS FROM GILES 1970

Giles' (1970) study presented accents of English to 177 secondary school students in South Wales and South-west England. The students were told they would be listening to different people, each reading in their own accent, although in reality the readings were all by the same person. The students answered three questions about each speaker: how pleasant they thought the accent sounded, how comfortable they would feel if interacting with the speaker and how much prestige or status they associated with each speaker. They did this by completing seven-point semantic differential scales (e.g. bounded with labels 'extremely pleasant' = 1, and 'extremely unpleasant' = 7).

The results of this matched guise part of the study are set out in Table 4.1. The table arranges the accents in rank order for each of the three questions, and the mean scores on the scales are set out

Table 4.1. *Rank orders of accent evaluations with mean scores on three dimensions*

	Aesthetic content	Communicative content	Status content
1	RP (2.9)	RP (3.1)	RP (2.1)
2	French (3.4)	N. American (3.6)	Affected RP (2.9)
3	Irish (3.8)	French (3.8)	N. American & French (3.6)
4	S. Welsh (4.0)	Irish (4.0)	
5	N. England (4.2)	S. Welsh (4.2)	German (4.2)
6	Indian, Italian & Somerset (4.3)	N. England & Somerset (4.3)	S. Welsh (4.3)
7			Irish (4.6)
8		Cockney & Italian (4.6)	Italian (4.7)
9	N. American (4.5)		N. England (4.8)
10	Cockney (4.6)	Indian (4.8)	Somerset (5.1)
11 =	Affected RP (4.8)	Affected RP (5.0)	Indian (5.2)
11 =	German (4.8)	Birmingham (5.0)	Cockney (5.2)
13	Birmingham (5.1)	German (5.1)	Birmingham (5.3)

alongside each accent. It is important to remember that a score of 4.0 is the mid-point. Scores less than that are positive, and those greater are negative. Hence, the majority of these accents are evaluated negatively. Of the accents included, only RP, French-accented English and Irish English are seen as pleasant-sounding, only RP, North American English and French-accented English are judged as 'comfortable' from the point of view of interacting with speakers with these accents, and only RP, Affected RP, North American English and French-accented English are deemed to have social status. (What Giles referred to as 'Affected RP' can be seen as a more socially elite variety than general RP.)

The general patterns that emerge in the results are that two foreign accents – French and North American – are afforded relatively high prestige, and higher than any British regional accents, which themselves tend to occupy neutral to unfavourable positions (a mean score of 4.0 or higher). Giles also notes that the lowest prestige accents comprised town and industrial accents. The most conspicuous result is the position of RP, with relatively strong positive evaluations on all three questions. Standard language ideology in the UK context appears to show itself in this study in RP's dominance over other varieties (including Affected RP). The place of RP in English language attitudes is a recurring topic in this field, both within and outside the UK.

Methodological issues: scales and dimensions

There are one or two methodological issues to consider before looking at other studies. The three questions in Giles' study (pleasantness, status and comfort) are not viewed as exhaustive, of course. Respondents can be asked to rate the voices on all sorts of other qualities. And Giles himself found high correlations between the responses to the three questions, leading him to conclude that these three scales 'are best considered as three distinct variants of a single evaluative dimension' (p. 224). Since the time of Giles' study, however, research in the language attitudes field has identified more than one evaluative dimension along which people judge and differentiate. Zahn and Hopper (1985) pooled the labels employed on semantic differential scales in a large number of language attitudes studies and used them in a single study involving around 600 respondents. By putting the ratings through a factor analysis, they found that the scales loaded into three differentiated factors. They labelled these factors 'superiority' (which included scales such as educated/uneducated, rich/poor), 'attractiveness' (comprising scales such as friendly/unfriendly, honest/ dishonest) and 'dynamism' (for example, energetic/lazy, enthusiastic/ hesitant). From their findings, it would seem that these are the main three ways in which people evaluate language and speakers.

Semantic differential scales originated from the work of Osgood (e.g. Osgood, Suci and Tannenbaum 1957) and are the type of attitude-rating scales most typically used and associated with the matched guise technique. They need only involve using equidistant numbers on a scale (e.g. 1 to 7) with semantically opposing labels applied to each end (e.g. friendly/unfriendly). There is some inevitable variation in the design of these scales. Some researchers prefer to label more than just the two ends of the scale. In addition, some researchers prefer to use an even number of points on the scale, rather than an odd number. There are two reasons for this second preference. One is the standpoint that is not possible to have a 'neutral' attitude, and so respondents must be made to choose one way or the other. The other reason (which does not negate having a neutral attitude) is that the mid-point that is present when there is an odd number of points is ambiguous. It might indicate that the respondent holds an attitude located at that point on the scale (i.e. a neutral or neither-one-way-nor-the-other attitude) or that the respondent simply does not know.

One rationale for using semantic differential scales rather than Likert scales (in which respondents are given a statement to think about and are asked to indicate on a scale the extent to which they agree or disagree with it) is that they lend themselves more to more rapid completion. One advantage of that is to help to elicit snap judgements and minimise opportunities for mental processing, thus reducing the possibilities for the social desirability and acquiescence biases mentioned in chapter 3.

The use of these scales in language attitudes research, however, still has to be principled: that is, researchers still have to decide what the questions are that they want to ask their respondents. They have to decide what labels they will use on the scales (and how many scales and labels they need to use). This is generally done in one of three ways. One is to take labels that have been used in previous studies. Zahn and Hopper's (1985) factoring of previously used semantic differential scales to discover the three main dimensions along which language and speakers are evaluated was an important step in language attitudes research, and many researchers have since taken adjectives from their study to represent each of these three dimensions in their own studies. Another way is to elicit a pool of items from a preliminary group of comparable judges to see what sorts of terms they use when they consider and evaluate the language varieties concerned. Scales are then given labels arrived at in this way. From such spontaneously given items, there can be more confidence that the scale labels are meaningful to the respondents. A third approach is a mixture of these: that is, to take some previously employed labels and to supplement them with some arrived at from their own preliminary work (e.g. Nesdale and Rooney 1996).

The advantage of using labels from previous studies is that it can save a great deal of time, and allow a reasonable degree of confidence that one has covered the main evaluative dimensions along which respondents are likely to be making their judgements. It may also allow better comparability across studies. The difficulty with it is that it may lead to some circularity in which the same dimensions simply become better documented and so are assumed to be exhaustive. In early research into attitudes (not specifically language attitudes) using semantic differential scales, even though three main dimensions were identified, additional dimensions were found in some studies (Heise 1970: 238ff.). Hence the circularity involved in simply recycling previous labels can end up concealing other attitudinal dimensions that might be of interest. And it would be unwise for language attitudes research across many contexts, and with different populations, to base itself too strongly on the assumption that there is just one small set of universal dimensions. As we shall see later in the book, too, exclusive reliance on semantic differential scales (however the labels are arrived at) has other drawbacks.

OVERALL PROS AND CONS OF THE MATCHED GUISE TECHNIQUE

Before looking at other matched guise studies, we will consider some of the main advantages of, and controversies around, this method. The main strengths are:

> As an indirect method, it is a neat and rigorous design aimed at people's private attitudes. As we have mentioned, direct questioning can be less likely to elicit such private attitudes, and is more vulnerable to social desirability bias.
>
> It has led to a large number of studies internationally, many of these in multilingual and multiethnic contexts, and allowing a fair degree of comparability of findings, and the development of relevant theory.
>
> Researchers have been able to establish the main dimensions of language evaluation (prestige, social attractiveness and dynamism), thereby also contributing to our sociolinguistic understanding of language variation.
>
> It has led to a detailed demonstration of the role of language code and style choice in impression formation.
>
> It has provided foundations for research at the interface of sociolinguistics and the social psychology of language.

These are significant achievements. Nevertheless, the matched guise technique has attracted a great deal of controversy (see, for example, Giles and Coupland 1991; Garrett, Coupland and Williams 2003). It is important to bear in mind that all research methods have limitations and we need to be mindful of what these are for this method too. They are outlined together here, but will feature more in relation to specific studies and alternative methods as they are introduced through the book. To begin with, several issues have been raised around the vocal presentations of the language varieties:

> *The salience question*: it is argued (e.g. Lee 1971) that providing respondents with the repeated content of a reading passage presented by a series of voices may exaggerate the language variations and make them much more salient than they would normally be outside the experimental environment.
>
> *The perception question*: there are two issues here. Firstly, in most studies, one cannot be certain how reliably the respondents perceive the variables under investigation. For example, a non-standard accent might conceivably be misperceived as 'bad

grammar' rather than a non-standard accent (Bradac 1990), even if the text read out is the same for all varieties. We shall see examples of this in chapter 6. The second issue is one raised by Preston (1989) and concerns whether we can be sure that respondents identify each voice as representing the area that the researchers themselves believe it to represent. In some studies, this issue is addressed by playing the recorded speech samples to pilot respondents comparable to the respondents in the main study, to see if they 'validate' them. But Preston has suggested that, in the case of regional varieties (rather than, say, different speech rates), the respondents in the main study should be asked where they think the speaker is from.

The accent-authenticity question: in order to focus on the judgements of a particular variable (e.g. regional accent), other features (e.g. intonation, speech rate) are held constant in the voice recordings. But some of these may normally co-vary with accent varieties. For example, regional varieties may normally have different intonation patterns. Hence, one might question the authenticity of the varieties that the respondents are asked to evaluate: that is, whether the speaker really does represent the kind of speech that people would typically encounter in such speech communities.

The mimicking-authenticity question: in some studies, the audio-recordings are of just two varieties by bilingual or bi-dialectal speakers. But in studies where speakers produce several varieties, the accuracy of the renderings is likely to be reduced. As Preston (1996) has found, there can be many inaccuracies when people are asked to mimic accents, and even if respondents are able to 'validate' the voices, they might nevertheless perceive the voice to be 'odd' in some way (p. 65).

The community-authenticity question: it has also been argued that the labels used for the audio-recorded regional speech varieties in published reports could sometimes be more specific. For example, language attitudes studies in various locations in Wales have sometimes referred to audio-recordings representing 'Welsh English', and the findings therefore demonstrating attitudes to 'Welsh English'. Where studies have produced results that differ from those of other studies in Wales, some attention needs to be given to community factors such as the particular regional variety of Welsh English used in each study (since these do vary perceptually and descriptively, and could account for the different results), as well, of course, as which communities the respondents are drawn from (see Garrett *et al.* 2003).

The style-authenticity question: audio-recordings of the language varieties to be presented to respondents have often been produced by asking speakers to read out a written text onto tape in the different varieties. Labov (1972) employed reading aloud as a technique for eliciting a relatively formal style of language in order to contrast its linguistic features with those of more casual or spontaneous styles. The style implications of reading aloud for the preparation of speech samples for attitude studies has tended to be ignored or overlooked. It may not be wise to assume that more spontaneous speech will be evaluated in the same way.

The neutrality question: the texts that are read onto audio-tape are often described as 'factually neutral' (for example, a route from A to B, or a description of a building). Using such texts is intended to minimise the risk that respondents react more to some aspect of the contents of the text rather than to the speaker. One needs, however, to be mindful of the limitations to the effectiveness of this. Given the ways in which we interpret texts as we read them, drawing upon pre-existing social schemata, the concept of a 'factually neutral' text cannot be assumed to be unproblematic. In a study of attitudes to speakers of different ages, for example, Giles, Coupland, Henwood, Harriman and Coupland (1990) were unable to generate a text that was age-neutral. The same text was interpreted differently according to how old the speaker was perceived to be, and the speakers were judged differently. (More detail of this study is covered when we focus on the age variable in chapter 6.)

The matched guise technique has played a leading role in a great deal of language attitudes research since its development in the 1950s, and its prominence has undoubtedly, and indeed appropriately, led to considerable scrutiny and debate. But at the end of chapter 2, the point was made that researching language attitudes is always challenging, and so it is important to take a wide view and understand that any particular method will only be partially convincing. Research methods can only partially achieve the usual demands of reliability and validity. That said, it is important not to become uncritically entrenched in canonical methods, but to continue to explore innovations, and opportunities to study the same attitudes with more than one method.

OTHER 'INNER CIRCLE' CONTEXTS

Australia ▐▐▐

Ball (1983) conducted a series of small matched guise studies into attitudes to English accents present in Australia. The studies were aimed at addressing a number of issues, including how far it was advantageous to an immigrant into Australia to learn to speak in an 'authentically Australian manner' (p. 165). Each of the studies differed somewhat from the others. For example, they did not all investigate the same accents. However, included in one or more studies in the series were RP, East Coast American, Australian, French, Italian, German, Glasgow and Liverpool accents. Ball concluded that his study demonstrated the presence in Australia of a stereotype of speakers with a Liverpool accent from television programmes. While the Glasgow accent was judged neutrally, Liverpool was judged in terms of incompetence but warmth. French-accented speakers (less common in Australia at that time than German and Italian immigrants) were judged largely neutrally, except in terms of high attractiveness. Italian and German immigrants were much more numerous in Australia, with the Italians tending to occupy low positions in the socio-economic structure, and the Germans occupying more white collar and skilled positions. Italian-accented speakers were judged as highly sociable, but incompetent, unsure and somewhat unattractive. German accented speech evoked a stereotype of more attractiveness than RP speakers, and rather more competence than other non-Anglophones. Encouragingly, in the light of the above attitudinal differentiation, non-standard and non-local accents did not encounter any across-the-board downgrading in this study.

For the purposes of this chapter, the findings for RP, East Coast American and Australian are particularly noteworthy. The evaluative profile of RP aligns with studies elsewhere: that is, RP speakers are seen as high in competence but low in sociability. The profile of East Coast American is comparable to that of RP in this study, but we will see later that this is not typical. As regards the Australian voice, Ball summarises by saying that it 'appears to betoken a good-natured, but lazy and ineffective character' (1983: 163).

It is useful to draw upon the design of Ball's studies to illustrate some of the issues that researchers have to deal with and decisions and innovations that they make as they attempt to ensure that the data they collect represents people's real attitudes. Such issues are fundamental and will recur through this book just as they recur in conducting research. To begin with, and linking to a question raised earlier in this chapter, the semantic differential scale labels were largely drawn from an earlier study in the UK of London and Yorkshire accents by Strongman and Woosley (1967). In addition, a matched guise design was used in all four studies, in that one person produced all the varieties. It is worth noting that the person was always a male, and that we need to be open to the possibility that female voices might evoke different evaluations.

Beyond this, there were some differences in the four studies. In one of them, two 'dummy' voices were included amongst the others on the tape. These 'buffer' voices (female, in this case) were rated in the usual way by the respondents, but they were not included in the analysis. Researchers sometimes use this technique to minimise the risk of respondents realising that they are listening to one person producing all the accents under investigation. As mentioned earlier, there are pros and cons with any approach, and here a disadvantage can be that the whole task of the respondents hearing and judging the accents becomes longer, and can increase the risk of fatigue detracting from the value of the data. In some studies, researchers ask respondents at the end of the data collection whether they realised that they were listening to the same person each time, and this is something that Ball did in one of the other studies in this series instead of inserting additional voices. In the last of the four studies, two voices were used, both male and both covering the same accents, again in order to reduce the risk that respondents would realise they were listening to the same speaker, but again of course making the task longer. The findings showed that there were in fact some differences in the way that the accents were judged, according to which male was presenting them. But there was sufficient consistency to enable Ball to draw out some general findings. The fact that findings can vary according to who one gets to produce the accents (even if the same sex and age, reading the same text, etc.) is nevertheless an important factor.

A further noteworthy design feature in Ball's research was that in one of the four studies, in addition to the matched guise tapes, he also gave another group of respondents a list of ethnic labels and asked them to rate a typical member of each group. This conceptual approach is similar to that used by Giles (1970) alongside his matched guise work, as we mentioned in chapter 3. Giles found little difference between the two ways of presenting the accents. However, Ball found that attitudes towards the separate varieties were less differentiated with the ethnic labels approach, and that the stereotypes elicited were somewhat different too, leading him to wonder 'which method, if either, is the better one for detecting true ethnic attitudes' (p. 170).

New Zealand

Huygens and Vaughan (1983) investigated attitudes of New Zealanders to a range of speech styles that were commonly used in their country. The varieties were all English and consisted of British English, Dutch-accented, Maori-accented and Pakeha (white European New Zealand). Social class also featured in this study alongside ethnicity. To achieve this, the speakers were selected according to their positioning on a scale of occupational prestige, and placed in an upper, middle or lower category. The speakers were then rated on personality scales such as warm/cold and self-confident/shy, and on social scales such as highly educated/poorly educated; high status job/low status job.

The results showed significant ethnic differences amongst the British, Dutch and Maori, with social class differences affecting the judge-ments of the Pakeha speakers more. On the social scales, the British variety gained the most favourable associations, the Maori the least, with the Dutch between these two, at around the mid-point of the scale. The upper-class Pakeha speaker was favoured to nearly the same extent as the British. On the personality scales, the British, Dutch and upper-class Pakeha were all judged favourably, with the Maori speaker evaluated most negatively. There were differences amongst the par-ticular scales, with the British and upper-class Pakeha seen as the most self-confident, and the Dutch associated more with hard-working quali-ties. The Maori accented and lower-class Pakeha speakers were seen as the most warm. The general profile of British English in this study again aligns with other findings: that is, lacking in warmth, but high in social status.

This study differed in important ways from the 'standard' matched guise design. Most significantly, the voice samples were all produced by different speakers. There are two reasons for doing this. One is that it might not be practicable to find one individual who can realistically produce the range of varieties wanted for the study. The other is to avoid the accent and mimicking authenticity issues mentioned earlier in this chapter. Using 'authentic' speakers of each variety is likely to give more accurate representations. On the disadvantage side of the balance sheet, this can mean that the voices differ in more than just the accent variable under investigation and that differences in atti-tudes to the speakers might therefore be due to other features. In Ball's (1983) study above, we saw that two different speakers producing the same varieties can be judged differently. One way of compensating for this is to anyway use more than one person for each variety and then to merge the ratings for each variety on the assumption that the overall results will to some extent supersede individual differences between the speakers. In this study, too, the researchers employed both male and female speakers of each variety. The difficulty with using multiple speakers for each variety is once again the risk of fatigue effects. One way of offsetting this is to include fewer language varieties in the study, but Huygens and Vaughan's solution was to compile twelve audio-tapes, each with different subsamples of the various speakers. They then split their 120 respondents into twelve comparable groups of ten, each of which then heard and rated just one of the tapes. The technique of presenting the speech varieties to respondents by recording separate speakers of each variety is sometimes referred to as a type of 'modified matched guise' or 'verbal guise'. 'Verbal guise technique' is the term employed in this book for this design.

Huygens and Vaughan's study also took into consideration the salience and style-authenticity questions. Instead of asking all their speakers to read out the same text onto tape, they asked them to say how they would direct a foreign sailor in the city from the wharf to the public library. Hence a degree of comparability was maintained by keeping the topic constant, but allowing the speakers to talk more spontaneously in their normal speech. Although this then means that speakers differ in linguistic features other than accent (e.g. grammatical and lexical qualities), Huygens and Vaughan, through an examination of the transcripts, did not think that these other features accounted for differences in ratings of the voices.

USA

In the USA, Stewart, Ryan and Giles (1985) investigated attitudes towards RP and standard American English. This was a verbal guise study with two people (both males) reading the same text onto tape for each variety. The study also included a social class variable, although differently from Huygens and Vaughan. (We return to this variable in chapter 6.) Attitude rating scales covered social status traits (e.g. intelligent, ambitious) and solidarity (or social attractiveness) traits (e.g. sincere, friendly). The results showed RP speakers to be judged as having significantly more status than American speakers, but, again, with less social attractiveness. This striking reversal of the social and solidarity dimensions in the evaluative profiles of American and British English underlines the critical importance of assessing judgements on all the separate attitudinal dimensions. It is also worth noting that RP was afforded higher social status than the respondents' own accent despite the fact that RP was viewed as less intelligible, as arousing more discomfort, and as being spoken faster than American English. (In reality, the recorded samples were spoken at the same speech rate.)

Denmark

Whereas the studies reviewed so far have examined only the attitudes of native speaker respondents of English, Ladegaard (1998) investigated the attitudes of Danish respondents to verbal guises of a range of native speaker English accents: RP, American, Australian, Scottish and Cockney. Each variety was produced by one male speaker. They were of various ages but 'carefully selected for comparable voice qualities' (p. 256). They were given a speech that was part of an interaction with a fieldworker, and were invited to modify it so that it sounded natural to them, and to rehearse it. These various design features of the study, then, are directed at the salience question along with the accent-, mimicking- and style-authenticity questions.

Ladegaard's findings for RP were in accord with the findings in the Anglophone countries. The RP speaker was the most favourably evaluated for status and competence (intelligence, leadership, self-confidence, perceived social status and level of education) and for linguistic superiority (fluency, communicative efficiency, aesthetic quality, correctness and appropriate model of pronunciation), but he was downgraded on social attractiveness (e.g. reliability, friendliness, helpfulness). The Scottish speaker was the most favourably evaluated on friendliness and helpfulness. The Australian speaker was seen as the most reliable. The American speaker was viewed as the most humorous.

Regional standards

Weighing up the studies outlined above, US speakers emerge overall with a type of evaluative profile not dissimilar to those that Edwards and Jacobsen (1987) have termed 'regional standards'. In their Canadian study of attitudes to Canadian varieties of English, they found that Nova Scotian English attracted higher status and competence ratings than other varieties but without losing ground on solidarity and social attractiveness. By combining the evaluative profile of a regional variety (rated high on social attractiveness) with that of a standard (rated high on status and competence), Nova Scotian can be said to be operating, in terms of people's attitudes, as a regional standard.

Edwards and Jacobsen (1987: 370) refer to an earlier Australian study by Ball and Berechree, in which a 'Cultivated Australian' accent, analogous to RP, evoked high evaluations of both competence (compared to 'broad' and 'general' varieties) and attractiveness. Similarly, Gordon and Abell (1990: 46) found a 'Cultivated New Zealand' variety that vied with RP on social status and surpassed it on social attractiveness traits, although, in this case, it achieved a less favourable profile elsewhere in New Zealand (Bayard 1990). Within the United Kingdom, where, as we saw in chapter 1, the previously dominating position of RP is increasingly questioned, Garrett, Coupland and Williams (1995) have argued that, in terms of attitudes, a variety of English spoken in south-west Wales could be seen as a candidate for the regional standard for Wales. This notion that there might be more than one standard within a national context is arguably at odds with the general view of standard language ideology discussed earlier. There will be more occasions in this book when we consider this possibility.

Multiple contexts: Australia, New Zealand and the USA

We have considered a number of studies that have looked at attitudes towards these international native speaker Englishes. In each of these, respondents have been drawn from a single geographical context. A larger scale and more recent study by Bayard, Weatherall, Gallois and Pittam (2001) incorporated groups of respondents from the USA, New Zealand and Australia, and examined their attitudes towards American, Australian, New Zealand and English Englishes.

This was a verbal guise study, in which a text was read out by one female and one male speaker of each of the four varieties, so eight speakers in all. The text represented a short letter written by a student to his/her parents. The researchers made efforts to keep variables such as the reading speed and numbers of hesitations reasonably constant across all the voices, and played the voices to respondents to check that they were recognised as the varieties they were intended to represent. The voices were arranged in a different random order on four different tapes, and any single respondent would hear only one of these four tapes. This is a technique often used (especially when tapes contain a larger number of voices) to guard against fatigue effects. If respondents begin to tire in the rating task, the ratings of the last voices on the tapes might not be so reliable. Making more than one tape with voices in different orders is a way of evening out any such effect across the different voices. It is also used to even out ordering effects. Arguably, for example, a respondent might rate an Australian accent differently after hearing a New Zealand accent than after hearing an RP accent.

The respondents filled in twenty-two six-point rating scales in this study, in which 1 = not at all, and 6 = very. The results were factor analysed and they grouped into four dimensions. These, along with the labels of the scales they contained, were:

Power (dominant, controlling, authoritative, assertive, strong voice, powerful voice)

Competence (reliable, intelligent, competent, hardworking, educated voice, ambitious)

Solidarity (cheerful, friendly, warm, humorous, pleasant voice, attractive voice)

Status (education level, occupation, income, social class)

Table 4.2 illustrates the main results of their study (see Bayard *et al.* 2001 for more comprehensive results and tables). It is evident that the US female was judged in first position on nine out of twelve possible occasions (i.e. each of the three groups of respondents' ratings on the four dimensions (power, status, competence and solidarity), with the English male judged first on status on two out of the possible three occasions (and second on the other occasion). The Australian male was ranked highly, arguably more favourably than the US male, ranked in the first three accents on eight occasions compared to the US male's six. In terms of solidarity ratings, and in line with the earlier findings reviewed above, the RP speakers were rated consistently low by all three groups of judges. New Zealand and Australian respondents attributed higher solidarity to their own varieties over RP (albeit only for the female speaker in the case of the New Zealanders), and the US voices took first and second places for solidarity in all cases.

Bayard *et al.* draw particular attention to their finding that attitudes to RP in these countries may now be changing, compared with the findings in earlier studies such as those by, for example, Ball (1983), Huygens and Vaughan (1983) and Stewart *et al.* (1985), reviewed in this chapter. Bayard *et al.* (2001) note that 'the RP voices did not receive the higher rankings in power/status variables we expected' (p. 22). The US female voice 'was rated most favourably on at least some traits' by respondents from all three countries, 'followed by the American male'. The authors summed up by saying that 'overall the American accent seems well on the way to equalling or even replacing RP as the prestige – or at least preferred – variety'. The explanation for this change is seen in terms of the globalisation of the world media and the 'unceasing global media onslaught' (p. 44) in the form of American cultural models, programme content and American English.

A further finding concerns how each national group of respondents evaluated their own native varieties. Given that six-point scales were

Table 4.2. Rank ordered evaluations (with mean scores) for Australian, New Zealand, English and USA Englishes by Australian, New Zealand and USA respondents in Bayard et al. (2001)

	New Zealand respondents				Australian respondents				USA respondents			
	POW	STA	COM	SOL	POW	STA	COM	SOL	POW	STA	COM	SOL
	USF 3.869	EEM 4.204	USF 4.159	USF 4.286	USF 3.569	AUM 4.242	AUF 4.200	USF 4.493	USF 3.906	EEM/USF 3.698	USF 4.614	USF 4.802
	AUM 3.591	USF 3.895	EEM 4.091	USM 3.937	AUM 3.484	EEM 4.066	USF 4.157	USM 4.044	AUM 3.399		USM 4.132	USM 3.875
	EEM 3.474	USM 3.837	AUM 3.992	NZF 3.696	EEM 3.273	USF 3.864	EEM 4.148	AUF 3.890	USM 3.258	AUM 3.651	AUM 3.903	AUM 3.557
	AUF 3.390	AUM 3.671	AUF 3.829	AUM 3.486	USM 3.233	AUF 3.770	AUM 4.076	NZF 3.724	EEM 3.250	USM 3.528	AUF 3.884	AUF 2.995
	USM 3.379	AUF 3.390	USM 3.819	AUF 3.423	AUF 3.194	USM 3.604	USM 3.909	AUM 3.715	AUF 3.052	AUF 3.395	EEM 3.833	NZF 2.867
	NZF 3.080	EEF 3.388	NZF 3.719	EEF 3.146	EEF 2.266	EEF 3.082	NZF 3.667	EEM 2.879	NZF 2.662	NZF 3.236	NZF 3.553	EEM 2.786
	EEF 2.792	NZF 3.080	EEF 3.681	EEM 3.035	NZF 2.080	NZF 2.788	EEF 3.439	EEF 2.859	EEF 2.545	EEF 3.019	EEF 3.343	EEF 2.664
	NZM 2.153	NZM 2.153	NZM 2.679	NZM 1.978	NZM 1.931	NZM 2.419	NZM 2.569	NZM 2.047	NZM 2.404	NZM 2.769	NZM 2.919	NZM 1.799

Notes: AUM = Australian male, AUF = Australian female, EEM = English male, EEF = English female, etc. Ratings were made on six-point scales. POW = power, STA = status, COM = competence, SOL = solidarity.

used, if we take group mean scores of between 3.25 and 3.75 as a kind of neutral zone, we can see that the US respondents always rated their own speakers positively or neutrally (in fact, for status, even their highest ratings are quite neutral). The Australian respondents rate their voices positively for status, competence and solidarity, and neutrally (male) and negatively (female) for power (their highest rating on the power dimension is also only neutral). The New Zealanders contrast starkly, in that they never rate the New Zealand speakers positively. In six out of the eight instances, they rate them negatively. In the other two instances, they award neutral ratings (the female on both occasions). From this, then, there seems to be a great deal of linguistic deference on the part of the New Zealanders. This deference, or 'cultural cringe' (Bayard et al. 2001), perhaps echoes the earlier negative findings in New Zealand for 'Cultivated New Zealand' in Bayard (1990).

Differences in ratings for the two speakers of the same variety are not easy to place a secure interpretation on, especially if they are all reading the same text with controlled variation in other features such as speech rate. But one might anyway argue that something other than accent (if both speakers are representative of the same accent) can be at work. We have mentioned before that different idiosyncratic voice features of the individual speakers might trigger different attitudinal reactions, and in one of Ball's (1983) studies in Australia, two speakers who were both male and who both read the same text in the same variety received different evaluative reactions. But in Bayard et al.'s study, the two speakers are also of different sexes. Hence it might simply be that attitudes towards female speakers of a variety really can be generally different from those towards male speakers of the same variety, perhaps even linked to gender differences in the linguistic features of the variety. The case of New Zealand English in Bayard et al.'s study is of interest in this regard. They note that the New Zealand male speaker in their study, who is rated lowest across most traits with some consistency, and always well below the group-mean mid-point of 3.5, was noticeably monotonic in reading style compared to the other speakers in this study 'which may have accounted for the low ratings he received from all three groups' (2001: 27). Yet such a feature need not be specific to an individual, or unrepresentative of the variety itself. In New Zealand English, for example, Daly and Warren (2001) have found a difference in the speech qualities of males and females, with males using a significantly narrower pitch range and less dynamism in their speech than females.

CONCLUSIONS

In this chapter, we have reported some key matched guise and verbal guise studies on attitudes to English within the UK, and compared attitudes in Australia, the US, New Zealand and the UK. This has also provided a context for highlighting some of the main issues that researchers have to consider when they design and interpret their studies and exemplified some of the different sorts of solutions employed. In turn, this has allowed an appraisal of the matched guise and verbal guise techniques. The studies themselves have given a picture of attitudes towards varieties of English amongst these 'inner circle' native speakers, and shown how the varieties achieve distinctive profiles across a number of evaluative dimensions. In chapter 12, we will be referring back to some aspects of the studies by Giles (1970) and Bayard *et al.* (2001), when we look at more recent studies looking at many of these same English varieties. These more recent studies have used different research methods (that is, not matched guise or verbal guise), and we will consider the differences and similarities in the findings.

FURTHER READING ON CHAPTER 4

You might like to read the following two articles referred to in this chapter:

Bayard, D., Weatherall, A., Gallois, C. and Pittam, J., 2001, Pax Americana?: accent attitudinal evaluations in New Zealand, Australia and America. *Journal of sociolinguistics* 5, 22–49.
Giles, H., 1970, Evaluative reactions to accents. *Educational review* 22, 211–27.

QUESTIONS FOR CHAPTER 4

1. If you were designing a language attitudes study in which you would present audio-recorded voices to respondents, would you prefer to use a verbal guise or matched guise design? Say why.
2. Bayard *et al.*'s study looked at attitudes in Australia, New Zealand and the USA. If you yourself do not live in any of those three countries, do you think that attitudes in your country to these Englishes are likely to be similar or different? Say what you think they would probably be.
3. If you live in Australia, New Zealand or the USA, do you think those attitudes are likely to be the same today as they were when the study was carried out. (It was published in 2001.)

5 Matched and verbal guise research in more contexts

This chapter looks at further work within the matched guise/verbal guise tradition, embracing a greater range of contexts, languages and language varieties than chapter 4. It also continues to introduce and highlight methodological innovations and developments that have occurred within this approach, and also to point to some key theoretical issues relating to the language attitudes field. The significance of context is highlighted, as well as the related notion of ethnolinguistic vitality.

A SEMINAL STUDY: FRENCH AND ENGLISH IN CANADA

The seminal study in the matched guise tradition was conducted by Lambert, Hodgson, Gardner and Fillenbaum (1960) in Montreal: 'a community whose history centers in a French–English schism which is perhaps as socially significant for residents of the Province of Quebec as that between the North and South is for Southerners in the United States' (p. 44). Two groups of respondents, one English-speaking and the other Canadian French-speaking, heard audio-recordings of four bilingual speakers reading a passage in English and French. The respondents were reminded how we form impressions of people we hear on the telephone or radio, and were accordingly asked to rate the speakers on fourteen traits: height, good looks, leadership, sense of humour, intelligence, religiousness, self-confidence, dependability, entertainingness, kindness, ambition, character and likeability on a six-point scale. The main findings, for our purposes, were that the English Canadians evaluated the English voices more favourably than the French voices on most traits. Against expectations, the French Canadians also evaluated the English voices more favourably than the French voices. Moreover, they also evaluated the French voices less favourably than did the English Canadian respondents. Lambert and his colleagues, referring to earlier work that found that minority groups sometimes take on the stereotyped values of majority groups, interpreted this last result as evidence for a minority group reaction on the part of the French speaking respondents (*cf.* the 'cultural cringe' in chapter 4).

A few additional points are worth highlighting here. Lambert *et al.* (1960) also included direct questions about the respondents' level of bilingualism. A higher level of skill in the other group's language would allow more interaction and intergroup contact, and this might lead to smaller differences in ratings of the guises. But this 'contact hypothesis' proved not to be supported (see the section on social stereotypes in chapter 2).

A further feature is that, after the listening and rating task, the respondents were asked to rank the fourteen traits 'in terms of their desirableness in friends' (p. 45). The rationale for this was to provide a more personally relevant set of traits. This practice of asking respondents how much value they place on the various traits would seem to have high utility, especially if such values could differ across groups or contexts where, for example, 'honesty' might be seen as of more significance than, say, 'liveliness' in one context, but of less significance in another. A further issue that is raised in passing by the authors is *what* value might be placed on particular evaluations. They make the point that a high rating on a semantic differential scale for a particular trait does not necessarily indicate favourableness. A high rating for 'ambition', for example, need not imply a favourable attitude (p. 46n). Negative attitudes towards high ambition are not impossible. Essentially, this is making a distinction between a 'semantic differential' and what we might call an 'attitudinal differential'. These matters of 'what value' and 'comparative value' have not generally received a great deal of attention in subsequent research, but they will resurface later in this book.

With its tensions between the francophone and anglophone communities, Canada has been prominent in language attitudes research, and in 1989, Genesee and Holobrow published a replication of this pioneering study. Their purpose was to examine whether there had been any shift in these language-based stereotypes since those reported by Lambert *et al.* in 1960. The interim period had seen considerable socio-political change in Quebec, including the introduction of Bill 101 in 1977, which defines French (the majority language of Quebec) as the only official language in Quebec. In this study, respondents rated Canadian English, Quebec French and European French guises. Their findings were that respondents were giving higher solidarity (e.g. likeable) ratings than previously to their ingroup, but that both groups of respondents still downgraded Quebec French on the status traits (e.g. educated, ambitious). These status differences could not be explained by any actual socio-economic advantages for English speakers, and indeed similar differences were found with European French. This seems to be an instance of how stereotypes can be strongly resistant to change, and quite at odds with objective evidence. Genesee and Holobrow suggest that it may be 'easier to change perceptions of ingroup solidarity than perceptions of ingroup status, and that the former can be achieved through actions with high symbolic value, such as language legislation' (1989: 36).

FRENCH IN FRANCE

The notion of 'European French' is inevitably problematic in itself, of course. There has been some dispute over there being a standardised model for France. Paltridge and Giles (1984) refer to sources such as Désirat and Hordé (1976) denying that there is, and to others (e.g. Lerond 1980) suggesting that there is a neutral, de-regionalised standard. To this end, Paltridge and Giles (1984) set out to investigate whether the sorts of findings in Giles' work in the UK (reviewed in chapter 4) would apply to the French language in France. In this verbal guise study, respondents heard accents representing Paris, Provence, Brittany and Alsace, each of which was spoken by two people reading a text, totalling eight readers. Data was collected from respondents in each of these four regions of France, comprising three different age groups, one with mean age 12, one with mean age 30 and one with mean age 72. Data was collected from each of these groups in their usual everyday settings: respectively, school classrooms, work environments and retirement homes.

Respondents were given twenty scales, and analysis of the results reduced these to five factors. These factors were named 'professional appeal' (e.g. cultured, ambitious, quick-witted), 'social appeal' (e.g. likeable, sociable), 'steadiness' (e.g. methodical, conformist), 'power' (e.g. superior, politically committed) and 'accentedness' (e.g. accented). The first two of these factors can reasonably be seen as reflecting the superiority and social attractiveness dimensions seen in other studies and in line with Zahn and Hopper's (1985) dimensions, and in the statistical analysis these two dimensions (especially the first) were in fact found to be stronger than the others (i.e. accounting for more variance). With respondents of both sexes, of three age groups and from four regions judging four varieties of French, the results are somewhat complex, and so no more than one or two are reviewed here.

To begin with, all respondents (considered together) differentiated the four varieties in terms of accentedness, with Provence being seen as the most accented, followed by Alsace. Brittany was seen as less accented, and Paris the least. Paris-accented speakers were rated highest for professional appeal, with a definite hierarchy emerging amongst the accents on this factor (Paris, then Provence, then Brittany, then Alsace). The position of Provence shows that this hierarchy does not entirely match the levels of perceived accentedness, but rather seems linked to the social meanings of the accents. Paltridge and Giles noted that the Provence accent was sometimes employed in the persuasive context of broadcast advertising, for example, and that this was rare amongst regional accents. Alsace French was the most denigrated of the four varieties on these two strongest factors, and was indeed the only variety judged negatively on social appeal, with all other three varieties undifferentiated from each other at the positive end of the scale.

Apart from the valuable differentiated view of attitudes to French varieties that this study provides, there are three points to take away from this study for future reference in this book. The first is that the age of the respondents turned out to be a potent variable in this study, with some differences in attitudes on all the factors amongst the adolescents, young adults and elderly. For example, the elderly respondents seemed more generous in their judgements, and did not differentiate amongst the non-standard varieties in terms of professional appeal. The design of the study does not allow us to determine whether these more generous evaluations are just a feature of that particular generation, or whether they occur in everyone as they get older, or whether they are linked more to the fact that these respondents were retired and institutionalised. But the notion that attitudes vary with age is an important matter for which there is evidence elsewhere, as we shall see.

The second point relates to the issues raised in chapter 2 about the choosing of labels of semantic differential scales: in other words, choosing what qualities the respondents will be asked to judge. Paltridge and Giles chose their scale-labels by asking 249 pilot respondents (from the same regions and age groups) about what they saw as the main positive qualities and main shortcomings of 'Paris-accented people', 'Brittany-accented people' etc. Rather than simply taking labels from previous studies, or from Zahn and Hopper's (1985) lists, this was an effort to ensure that they would employ terms that were evaluatively meaningful to the respondents in the main study. The third point is that in our discussion of Zahn and Hopper's three dimensions (superiority, social attractiveness and dynamism) in chapter 2, we mentioned the importance of remaining open to the possibility of other, additional dimensions, especially with attitudinal work extending across so many linguistic, cultural and social contexts. In this study of attitudes in France to varieties of French, the statistical analysis generated five rather than three factors, and at that time Paltridge and Giles saw this as 'relatively unique in the voice evaluation literature' (1984: 81).

ATTITUDINAL HIERARCHIES

In some of the matched and verbal guise studies reviewed so far, one aspect that has emerged is that, although sociolinguists have tended to differentiate language varieties as either standard or non-standard, the distinction seems less categorical in terms of attitudes. As we have just seen in Paltridge and Giles' study, varieties can have different evaluative profiles, and hierarchies can exist amongst them. Such findings have also occurred in other contexts. In Egypt, El-Dash and Tucker's (1975) verbal guise study of language attitudes towards Classical Arabic, Egyptian Colloquial Arabic, American English, British English and Egyptian English found significant status differences. In terms of status-associated evaluations of intelligence, Classical Arabic speakers were seen as more intelligent than speakers of Colloquial Arabic, and British or American English. Egyptian English speakers were rated more intelligent than speakers of Colloquial Arabic. In addition, in terms of the status-associated judgements of leadership, Classical Arabic and Egyptian English speakers were deemed more suitable leaders than all the others. Also, American English speakers were seen as possessing more leadership qualities than British English speakers and Colloquial Arabic speakers. Hence, overall, results appeared to point to an Egyptian status hierarchy roughly along the lines of Classical Arabic and Egyptian English, then American English, and then British English and Colloquial Arabic.

In Japan, McKenzie's (2008) verbal guise study of attitudes towards Englishes included four native – inner circle – voices (Mid-west US English, Southern US English, Glasgow Standard English and Glasgow vernacular English), and two non-native – expanding circle – voices (moderately and heavily accented Japanese English). Japanese respondents' attitudes to these varieties revealed a significantly distinguished status hierarchy of US English, followed by UK English, and then moderately accented Japanese English, and finally, heavily accented Japanese English.

In Australia, Nesdale and Rooney (1996) studied attitudes towards strong and mild versions of Anglo-Australian, Italian Australian and Vietnamese Australian accents. The respondents were 10–12-year-old children at monocultural and multicultural schools. Again, a clear status hierarchy emerged from their judgements in the order of Anglo-Australian accents having significantly more status than Italian Australian accents, which in turn had significantly more status than Vietnamese Australian accents. Anglo-Australians are the majority and most well-established group in Australia, but Italian Australians are one of the largest established minority groups, especially in comparison with the smaller and more recently arrived Vietnamese Australian group. It seemed that these 10–12 year olds were aware of such differences at some level, and their attitudes were the same regardless of whether they were attending multicultural or monocultural schools.

Readers might question whether children of this age are too young to have developed stable attitudes towards language. There were in fact some differences in this study between the 10 and the 12 year olds in the way they judged the mild and strong accents, with only the 12 year olds viewing the mild accents as significantly more statusful than the strong ones (when they were not informed what the ethnic provenance of the accents were). But there is a body of research that suggests that children have developed attitudes at least towards the standard variety and their own non-standard variety a few years earlier than the students in this study: i.e. around about the time they commence formal education, even if they develop awareness of and attitudes towards other languages and varieties in the years after that (see Garrett *et al.*, 2003: 85ff.).

In the USA, Rodriguez, Cargile and Rich (2004) examined the attitudes of ethnic majority (Anglo-Americans) and ethnic minority respondents (African Americans, Asian Americans and Hispanics). Drawing scales from Zahn and Hopper's (1985) inventory, the researchers presented these listeners with verbal guises of what they referred to as Mainstream US English (MUSE) and strong- and mild-accented African-American Vernacular English (AAVE). Across all the respondents together, on status variables, an attitudinal hierarchy was revealed of MUSE, then mild-accented AAVE, then strong-accented AAVE.

Interesting methodological issues emerge from this study. The first concerns how the researchers sought to take exceptional measures to avoid social desirability bias in the responses. Insofar as social desirability bias requires a degree of conscious cognitive processing, there are two conditions necessary for this to occur: *motivation* and *opportunity* (or *ability*). In other words, respondents must first feel some need to replace their own privately held view with a more socially acceptable one, and must then be able to do that. Motivation might be attenuated, for example, by guaranteeing anonymity, so that respondents feel sure no one will know what each of them has said. Indirect methods such as the matched guise technique are one way of attenuating ability. Trying to minimise the time for thinking by forcing respondents to answer rapidly is another technique. Rodriguez et al. (2004) split each of their voices into several tiny segments (1–2 seconds) and played these one at a time. After each one, respondents filled in just one of the scales in a brief pause of about a second.

It is also notable that the researchers close their paper by drawing attention to two design features in order to underline the limits within which their results and claims may be generalised. They emphasise that the texts read onto tape, and the context in which the study took place, were academic in nature. They also stress that the voices were female. It is all too tempting at times to lose sight of the parameters of one's research design and to overgeneralise findings. As Rodriguez et al. rightly imply, perhaps results would be different with male voices and a more solidarity-focused text and context. That would be another study.

Some studies above have distinguished mild and strong accents and found different attitudes towards them. Other research has gone further than this to investigate to what extent respondents discriminate, perceptually and attitudinally, between more gradations of accentedness in the largest of all the bilingual minority groups in the USA – Mexican Americans. Ryan, Carranza and Moffie (1975) selected ten readings of a formal passage recorded by male bilingual students with varying degrees of accentedness, eight of which had been linguistically measured in a previous study (Brennan, Ryan and Dawson 1975). Amongst other ratings, the respondents had to evaluate each speaker in terms of how accented they thought they sounded, the likely eventual occupation (status) and the likelihood of the speaker being a friend (solidarity).

The results showed, firstly, that the respondents' perception of the levels of accentedness corresponded highly with the linguistically measured differentiation previously carried out: i.e. they distinguished them as finely as the linguists had done. Secondly, the degrees of accentedness correlated highly with the judgements of status and solidarity. The more Spanish-accent features the speaker produced, the more negative was the stereotype. Hence, a further hierarchy emerged, with status diminishing as accentedness increased. A subsequent study of Mexican-American accentedness by Brennan and Brennan (1981) produced similar findings regarding a status hierarchy, but found a categorical difference regarding solidarity. No solidarity differences were found amongst all but one of the accents. This one relatively unaccented voice attracted scores significantly lower than the others.

These studies have shown that attitude hierarchies have emerged in many contexts, then. However, this is not a clear pattern universally. Berk-Seligson's (1984) verbal guise study of attitudes towards Spanish varieties in Costa Rica is an example of an exception to such clarity. Berk-Seligson describes Costa Rica as relatively homogeneous, with an absence of sharply defined social groupings. Three Costa Rican speakers recorded a text. A number of phonological variables were pronounced either in their prestige forms, or in their stigmatised forms, or half in each. On two status-like scales (rich/poor and intelligent/ stupid), the three varieties are in fact significantly differentiated in the expected hierarchical direction, but overall findings are that, while the prestige speaker is judged more positively than the intermediate speaker, the intermediate and stigmatised speakers are not differentiated attitudinally.

In some instances, too, other sorts of attitudinal hierarchies occur. Gibbons (1983), for example, conducted a verbal guise study into attitudes amongst Hong Kong bilinguals towards Cantonese, English and code-mixing of these two languages. Code-mixing of Cantonese and English was taken to be disliked by its users, but it is nevertheless very common in conversational settings, and this incongruity between attitudes and behaviour was a main motivation for the study. To help ensure that the guises were appropriate to the situation, a genuine conversation in which code-mixing occurred was used a basis for the three texts to be recorded. The recordings were then played to a pilot group who judged how 'naturalistic' they sounded before they were used in the main study. On the status dimension, there was no hierarchy evident. Code-mixing and Cantonese were judged equally statusful, and both carrying less status than English. But there was a hierarchy for Westernisation, with English given the least Chinese cultural orientation, code-mixing awarded significantly more, and Cantonese significantly more again. There was a different hierarchy for the 'Chinese humility' factor, with Cantonese achieving the most, followed by English, and then code-mixing viewed most negatively. These relationships, some hierarchical, produced an overall pattern in which the use of English appears associated with status and Westernisation, the use of Cantonese with Chinese humility and solidarity, and the use of code-mixing with arrogance and antipathy, but with status equal to Cantonese, and as a neutral choice regarding Westernisation.

The authors suggest that these findings explain the mismatch between the common use of code-mixing on the one hand, and negativity towards it on the other. The antipathy towards it is tempered by its role as a marker of intermediate acculturation between Chinese and Western and its perhaps holding a degree of covert prestige within the community (Gibbons 1983: 145). Empirical studies of attitudes towards code-mixing and codeswitching are comparatively scarce (but see Fitch and Hopper 1983; Akbar 2007), and, given these kinds of complexities, appear to warrant more attention.

ALTERNATIVE MEASURES OF ATTITUDES

The utility of semantic differential scales has been well demonstrated through the many matched and verbal guise studies reviewed so far. Despite some of their limitations, which will be given closer consideration later in this book, they are conducive to snap responses, and in this sense seem particularly suited to studies where indirect methods are preferred. In addition, the use of a suitable range of scale labels permits the investigation of an array of personality traits, for example, to illustrate social connotations and stereotypes, and allow comparisons amongst these for the various language varieties. However, other measures have also been used in matched and verbal guise studies, and to the extent that respondents are not aware of the purpose of the investigation, these too can be said to constitute part of indirect research designs.

Ireland

How much respondents can recall of a spoken message has been taken as one attitudinal measure. Cairns and Duriez (1976) used this approach in a study of schoolchildren (mean age 10.8) in Northern Ireland during the period of disturbances there between Catholic and Protestant communities. Half of the children were from Protestant schools and half from Catholic schools. After a preliminary test to establish the comparability of comprehension abilities across the respondent groups, each group was played a text read in either middle-class Belfast (Northern Irish) or middle-class Dublin (Southern Irish) English or in RP, after which they took a factual test and answered questions to assess national identity ('Which country do you live in?' and 'What is the capital of your country?').

Significant differences were found in their recall scores. When they heard the text in RP, Catholic children scored significantly lower than the Protestant children. And in fact, they also scored lower than the Catholic children who heard the Belfast voice. When the Protestant children heard the Dublin accent, they scored even less than the Catholic children did with the Belfast accent.

National identities also diverged markedly. In response to the question 'which country do you live in?', 'Northern Ireland' was the reply for 83 per cent of the Protestants and 42 per cent of the Catholics. 'Ireland' was the reply for 14 per cent of the Protestants and 58 per cent of the Catholics. And replies to 'what is the capital of your country?' were 'Dublin' for 70 per cent of the Catholics and 3 per cent of the Protestants, and 'Belfast' for 97 per cent of the Protestants and 30 per cent of the Catholics. Overall, then, these Catholic children in Northern Ireland clearly had a closer affiliation with the Republic of Ireland. Cairns and Duriez (1976: 442) suggest that their negative attitudes to RP are likely to be part of a generally negative orientation to 'things English', as a complement to Irish national identity. Although recall data itself does not fill out the attitudinal dimensions stereotypically associated with speakers (status, social attractiveness, etc.), it does perhaps point to the overall orientation in language attitudes. Generally negative attitudes in these contexts might lead to less attention and so less retention.

Denmark

A further measure that has been employed is co-operative behaviour. Here, then, there is reliance upon a link between behaviour and attitudes. Kristiansen (1997) studied attitudes to varieties of Danish in the naturalistic setting of a cinema. He created an audio-recorded message that was played to various cinema audiences in the cinema foyer and theatre just before the start of the film, asking them to complete a questionnaire about their cinema-going habits and their views on the film programme, with a few added questions asking for information about their age, sex, occupation, area of residence and work location. They could pick up the questionnaires from the stage at the front of the cinema. The message was recorded in four varieties of Danish, only one of which was played on each film-showing. These varieties were Standard Danish, Copenhagen Danish, and mild and broad varieties of Zealand Danish.

Both Copenhagen and the cinema location (Naestved) are situated on the island of Zealand. Naestved is a middle-sized Danish town about 50 miles south of Copenhagen, but there are differences in the varieties of Danish spoken in these places. Copenhagen Danish is traditionally associated with its urban working class. However, features of this variety have spread amongst young people all over Denmark in recent years, and it is now heard more in the national broadcast media. In contrast, the Zealand variety is more localised and is associated more with older people in the countryside, and few of its features are now heard in young people. Standard Danish is traditionally associated with high social status and correctness, and is considered the media norm and promoted in schools all over Denmark. Kristiansen's goal was to investigate whether the mild local variety (Zealand) was dying out or whether it had a future, and whether its use was considered appropriate only in private settings such as the family and friends, or also in public contexts like cinema announcements.

The study was a verbal guise design, with each variety produced by a different person. Behavioural co-operation was measured by counting completed questionnaires as a proportion of the total ticket sales for each film. The data was collected from the audiences of five different films: *Cry Freedom*, *The Last Emperor*, *Three Men and a Baby*, *Dirty Dancing* and *Wish You Were Here*. The overall results for all audiences considered together were that Standard Danish received significantly more co-operation (about a quarter of audience members) than the other three varieties (a fifth or sixth), which themselves did not differ from each other. The Standard seemed to represent the kind of language that audiences in general expected to hear making public announcements in the cinema, and no hierarchy was found amongst these other varieties on this measure. Copenhagen speech, along with Zealand (whether mild or broad), all appeared to be seen as less suitable, regardless of the age, occupation, etc., of the respondent.

However, interesting patterns emerged when looking at the results for each individual film, and these allowed some insights into language change in Denmark. For *Cry Freedom*, the audience was the most serious and intellectual, consisting mainly of adults working in education or healthcare. This audience co-operated the most and responded to all the varieties equally. Hence, they can be regarded as a social group that is tolerant of diversity and variation in language. In the case of the other films, the level of audience co-operation with Standard Danish was about the same for all four. But results for the other varieties differed, with audiences in some cases co-operating more than they did with Standard Danish and in other cases less so.

The Last Emperor, the second most serious film, attracted a broad adult audience from a greater range of occupations than *Cry Freedom*. Although the audience showed no strong geographical affiliation to Zealand, they nevertheless co-operated significantly more with the Zealand-accented speech than with Copenhagen or Standard (to which they did not differ in their responses). Kristiansen interprets their pattern of co-operation as defending or upholding local values against the intrusion of those of the larger society.

Three Men and a Baby was the most entertaining of the films and the best attended, primarily by students and occupational trainees. But the level of co-operation to the requests was the lowest, and they were negative to non-standard Danish. These mainly young people seemed to be showing negativity to the use of non-standard varieties in public places.

Dirty Dancing was also a light film, attracting an occupationally similar large young audience, but this young audience came more from the local region. On a par with Standard Danish, they responded more to the broad Zealand variety, reflecting their greater affiliation with their countryside locality, and they responded less well to the Copenhagen and mild Zealand varieties, as if rejecting these as town accents.

Wish You Were Here was ranked a mid light–serious film. The audience was not broad, and, though young, was older and more in employment than the other young audiences. This young adult audience came predominantly from the local town itself, and it is striking how they co-operated least with the broad local 'countryside' Zealand variety, but their responses to their mild local variety were on a par with Standard and Copenhagen Danish.

In terms of the sociolinguistic situation in Denmark, Kristiansen draws several conclusions from this study. For young people overall, the Copenhagen accent is seen as roughly equivalent with the local dialect, but both the local and Copenhagen varieties are downgraded compared to Standard Danish. Also, looking at the audiences overall, Kristiansen finds that co-operation with the local voices came more from older than younger audience members, and that co-operation with Copenhagen voices came more from the younger adults. But turning the focus to young people in the town of Naestved itself, the young people showed a more positive orientation both to Copenhagen Danish and to the mild Zealand variety, rejecting only the strong variety associated with local rural life. They appear as both a 'spearhead of the Copenhagen dialect advance' and a 'regional centre' that might 'secure a future for a mild local accent' (Kristiansen 1997: 304).

In terms of research methodology, Kristiansen compares his results with those of direct approach studies carried out previously, in which respondents were aware of the purpose of the study. In these earlier studies, results had been quite different; young people evaluated the Copenhagen dialect more negatively, for example, and gave more general support to the traditional local dialect. In contrast, the results of his cinema study matched more accurately what was actually going on in the Danish sociolinguistic environment in terms of language behaviour and linguistic change. The naturalistic setting and the assessment of attitudes through the indirect approach of comparing levels of co-operation seemed a more productive and valid approach to the study of language attitudes in this context.

Wales

Kristiansen's cinema study design was inspired by an earlier pioneering study by Bourhis and Giles (1976) in Wales, in which attitudes were also assessed as the ratio of questionnaire completion in a local cinema theatre. Bourhis and Giles' study differed from Kristiansen's in a number of ways. The primary difference was the nature of the setting: Wales is a bilingual context in which the Welsh language had for some time been in decline but had recently begun a revival. In Wales as whole, the proportion of bilingual Welsh speakers at the time was about 26 per cent, and just 8 per cent in Cardiff, the research location. However, there had been a recent marked increase in adults attending Welsh language classes. Another difference is that no details are given, or analysis reported, for the various subgroups in the audiences (age, area of residence, etc.). The main focus is on the audiences in terms of whether or not they were bilingual Welsh speakers. The announcements in this study were either in RP, or in broad or mild south Wales accented English for middle-class audiences attending films in English ('Anglo-Welsh' audiences who were assumed to be monolingual), with the addition of the Welsh language for Welsh–English bilingual audiences attending a play in Welsh. The study had a matched guise design, with all recordings made by the same male bilingual speaker.

Bourhis and Giles suggested that Welsh audiences would probably react more favourably when the request to complete questionnaires was in a speech variety symbolising their own ingroup rather than an outgroup. Hence, as a reflection of language attitudes in this bilingual context, they hypothesised that a predominantly English-only speaking Welsh audience would co-operate more with a plea in Welsh-accented English than in RP. Their findings, however, did not entirely match this prediction, since RP and mild accented Welsh English met with equal co-operation, and the broad accent was significantly less effective. It is possible that for these Anglo-Welsh listeners, despite any emotional distancing from RP in this intergroup context, this formal public setting triggered powerful social norms relating to the use of prestige speech in this formal theatre setting, and that these offset any potential biases against outgroup speakers employing a standard RP accent. In contrast, the broad Welsh-English speech might have sounded inappropriately informal and so received about half the response rate.

For Welsh-speaking audiences, more co-operation was anticipated with a request in the Welsh language than in English, and then more with one in a Welsh-English accent than in RP. This expectation was largely confirmed. Bilingual Welsh speakers virtually ignored the RP request. The Welsh-language plea was the most successful, followed by the Welsh-accented Englishes, but the mild and broad accents were not attitudinally differentiated. Language appeared to be the most salient dimension of Welsh identity for these bilinguals, and these findings supported those in a contemporary study by Giles, Taylor and Bourhis (1977), in which Welsh bilinguals viewed themselves more similar to English people who spoke Welsh than to a Welsh people who spoke only English. Also, it may be that requests in Welsh English were perceived as coming from Welsh people who could not speak their own ethnic language, and moreover in the setting of a Welsh-language play where public announcements might be seen as only acceptable in Welsh.

Bourhis and Giles (1976) noted that 'it would seem that the importance of the status or the ethnicity of a speaker as symbolised by his speech style may be attenuated or accentuated depending on the purpose, setting and topic of a particular interpersonal or intergroup exchange' (p. 16). One cannot assume, for example, that a standard variety such as RP, even if it might have strong support from standard language ideology, will afford advantages throughout the UK in all contexts. The way in which language can take on different social meanings in different contexts is an aspect of the multidimensional nature of attitudes. Multidimensional qualities will be considered on more occasions in this book.

ETHNOLINGUISTIC VITALITY OF CONTEXTS

An important component of the context for Bourhis and Giles' study, then, was the socio-political backdrop around the Welsh language itself, at a time when momentum was growing amongst some sections of the population in Wales towards revitalisation of the language. The concept of ethnolinguistic vitality developed at this time (Giles, Bourhis and Taylor 1977). This comprised a three-dimensional model of sociostructural factors intended to sum up a language's strength at a particular time, and was primarily aimed at minority language contexts. The three dimensions are *demography* (the speaker-base of a language in terms of numbers, spread, concentration, patterns and degree of migration, etc.), status (the community's economic wealth, social status, socio-historical prestige and the status of its language) and institutional support (e.g. the degree to which the community is able to use their language in institutions such as the home, schools, local government, church, business, media). The vitality of an ethnolinguistic group is 'that which makes a group likely to behave as a distinctive and active collective entity in intergroup situations' (Giles *et al.* 1977).

In Catalonia (another competitive language environment), Woolard and Gahng (1990) captured changing attitudes as the political back-drop changed after the granting of autonomy in 1979. During the time of Franco, despite the suppression, Catalonia had enjoyed some success in its economic development. One effect of this was to draw in Castilian-speaking immigrants from the south of Spain, and by 1979 less than half of the Catalonian population was of Catalan-speaking descent. In terms of ethnolinguistic vitality, then, Catalan was arguably losing some of its vitality on the demographic dimension.

Woolard and Gahng (1990) compared the language situation in 1980 with that in 1987. During that period, most demographic, economic and other social structures in the Barcelona region did not change much. However, there was considerable political change, with Catalonia's new government attempting to bolster the position of Catalan with a number of new initiatives. In such natural environments, it is generally difficult to claim with certainty that particular policies have been the cause of sociolinguistic changes. That notwithstanding, Woolard and Gahng felt that political change was the most significant aspect of the context that could enable the creation of new sociolinguistic meanings which changes in ethnolinguistic vitality might bring. Significant new initiatives had been launched in the educational sphere with a require-ment that all primary and secondary teachers should know both Catalan and Castilian, along with the greater use of Catalan as a medium of instruction in some subjects. In addition, a wholly Catalan-medium television channel was established in 1983. Other changes included a legal charter for the full official co-use of Catalan in govern-ment, the judiciary, public signage, plus government financial support for Catalan language activities. In terms of ethnolinguistic vitality, then, the sociostructural context changed. These political initiatives were instances of additional institutional support for Catalan, and in social domains that were likely also to strengthen the status dimension.

The 1987 study followed the same procedure as the 1980 study (reported in Woolard 1989), and also used the same matched guise voices. Texts were read in Catalan and Castilian by four bilingual females. Two were Catalan-dominant, one urban and one rural in accent, and both with Catalan accents in their Castilian. The other two were Castilian-dominant, one with an Andalucian accent and markedly non-native Catalan, and the other with standard Castilian and slightly non-native Catalan. Castilian and Catalan respondents completed a range of six-point attitude rating scales.

Comparing the findings from 1987 with those from 1980, it was clear that the relative statuses of the two languages had not changed a great deal, but that there were differences in the solidarity findings. This supports Genesee and Holobrow's (1989) suggestion, mentioned earlier in this chapter, that actions of high symbolic value, such as new political initiatives, are likely to impact more on the solidarity than the status dimension. Woolard and Gahng found that Catalan continued to carry significantly greater status than Castilian in the Barcelona area, irrespective of the ethnic background of the speaker or listener (although this relationship had become somewhat more marked in 1987). The Castilian speaker from Andalucia was still particularly stigmatised, regardless of whether she was speaking Catalan or Castilian.

In terms of solidarity, the most favourable attitudes in both 1980 and 1987 were towards members of the respondents' own ethnolinguistic group using the ingroup language. However, while in 1980 these same co-members were downgraded for using the outgroup language, they were no longer so heavily penalised for this in 1987. So, for example, Castilians disapproved of Castilian speakers when they learnt and used Catalan in 1980, but in 1987 there were fewer such sanctions. A further difference was that, in 1980, respondents were indifferent to the language choice of the other ethnolinguistic group. In 1987, however, respondents were reacting favourably to members of the other ethnolinguistic group if they used their (i.e. the respondents') language. So the Andalucian speaker and the standard Castilian speaker now received better solidarity ratings from the Catalan respondents when they used Catalan. It no longer seemed to matter so much to Catalans who spoke Catalan just as long as it was spoken. In terms of the vitality of Catalan, there were potential demographic gains in the sense that Castilians could now learn and use Catalan with fewer sanctions from other Castilian speakers and with more solidarity rewards from Catalans.

From these results, it seems that the Catalan language policies were followed quite rapidly by significant changes in language attitudes. Catalan was already a language with vitality in that the numbers and the socio-economic status of its speakers were notably high. It appears that, under such conditions, the addition of institutional support can be effective (Woolard and Gahng 1990: 326). The findings also suggest that the link between language choice and ethnic identity needed to be weakened for the use of Catalan as a second language to become widespread (p. 327). In this regard, one might argue that the resulting increased vitality of Catalan was a vitality of a milder *ethno*linguistic nature.

The notion and model of ethnolinguistic vitality has experienced considerable development and critical appraisal since its proposal in the 1980s. It has been noted that such vitality can be studied not only objectively in terms of the 'concrete socio-political reality' but also in the subjective terms of how people perceive the language situation (e.g. Bourhis, Giles and Rosenthal 1981). Such subjective study, then, may also provide insights into people's attitudes to language and their relations with other ethnolinguistic groups, and their aspirations for the future, since 'people react to their *perceived* environment' (Gould 1977). Comparing the subjectivities of competing languages can reveal how groups may have quite different subjective views of the same shared ethnolinguistic backdrop. To illustrate, Pierson, Giles and Young (1987) found that Western and local Cantonese students in Hong Kong held quite different vitality perceptions of the same objective vitality situation. Prior to the Sino-British treaty of 1983, each saw their own group has having more ethnolinguistic vitality than the other group, while each nevertheless viewed the other group as having more power and control. After the treaty, despite the objective situation remaining the same, Chinese subjective vitality increased, while Western vitality decreased.

Coupland, Bishop, Evans and Garrett (2006) have noted how the model of ethnolinguistic vitality can be problematic in some contexts. Ethnolinguistic ingroups and outgroups can be hard to specify. For instance, ethnic identities in Wales may be linked either to the Welsh language or to Welsh varieties of English (see also Garrett, Bishop and Coupland 2009 on Welsh and Welsh identities in the Welsh diaspora in Argentina and North America). We will return to such matters later in this book.

CONCLUSION

We have looked at matched and verbal guise studies in a range of contexts. Alongside the findings of the studies themselves, we have considered how studies differ in their design and methodology in response to the specific research questions and language situation, and also in response to the pervasive difficulties involved in trying to ensure that the data really does represent people's attitudes. Along the way, too, there has been mention of some complexities. For example, attitudes cannot be seen as having monolithic uniformity, but may vary amongst age groups, occupational groups and localities (Kristiansen 1997), according to accent strength (Ryan, Carranza and Moffie 1975), setting and contextual backdrop (Bourhis and Giles 1976) and ethnolinguistic vitality. Chapter 6 covers some of these variables in more depth.

FURTHER READING ON CHAPTER 5

For a useful review and discussion of ethnolinguistic vitality, see:

Bourhis, R., El-Geledi, S. and Sachdev, I., 2007, Language, ethnicity and intergroup relations, in A. Weatherall, B. Watson and C. Gallois (eds.), *Language, discourse and social psychology* (pp. 15–50). Basingstoke: Palgrave Macmillan.

Mann, C., 2002, Reviewing ethnolinguistic vitality: the case of Anglo-Nigerian pidgin. *Journal of sociolinguistics* 4, 458–74.

QUESTIONS FOR CHAPTER 5

1. Summarise the main features of ethnolinguistic vitality theory, and apply this to any minority language context with which you are familiar.
2. Do you live in a country where there are laws to protect languages? If so, how do various groups in the society feel about such laws?

6 Attitudes to speech styles and other variables: communication features, speakers, hearers and contexts

Much of what we have looked at so far has concerned attitudes to 'whole' languages (e.g. the French and English languages in Canada) and to social and regional accents within a language. In places, findings showed that such attitudes can vary amongst people of different ages or from different regions, or depending on the situation in which language is used. Moreover, language also comprises more features than regional or social accents, and people have attitudes towards these too. It is also reasonable, as such a field of research develops, for people to ask 'does it make any difference if X?', or 'surely it will depend on Y.' Communication processes are complex. In this chapter, we look at evaluative reactions to some other components of communication, and to some of the relationships between, and relative potencies of, some of these components. Matched and verbal guise techniques, along with the use of scales enabling the use of inferential statistics, have been particularly prominent and productive in attempts to examine relationships in this area. While coverage cannot be exhaustive here, in this chapter I seek to give a reasonable overview of some of the main work regarding communication features, speaker variables, hearer variables and contextual variables.

COMMUNICATION FEATURES

Lexical provenance

Against the backdrop of research showing how people react evaluatively to the accent in which a message is delivered, Levin, Giles and Garrett (1994) compared the effects of the vocabulary used. They refer to earlier research showing how the use of higher relative frequencies of Latinate vocabulary in English led to favourable evaluations in terms of formality and intelligence compared to when there was a higher incidence of Germanic vocabulary, which led to favourable judgements in terms of informality and trustworthiness. If standard accents, then, triggered perceptions of formality and intelligence and non-standard accents were linked with social attractiveness, which had the stronger effect? For example, would a non-standard accented speaker using Latinate vocabulary be rated at the same level on the status dimension as a standard-accented speaker employing more Germanic vocabulary?

In this study, UK respondents heard recordings of a bi-dialectal speaker of RP and south-east Wales English describing a house. One version was constructed in formal (Latinate) and the other in informal (Germanic) style. The respondents were randomly divided into four groups, each of which heard only one of the four recordings (i.e. either the Germanic text in an RP guise, or the Latinate text in a south-east Wales English guise, etc.). They rated the speakers on eighteen scales concerned with personality traits (trustworthy, intelligent, etc.), and fourteen related to communication features (e.g. did the speaker use simple grammar?). Significant differences were found in twelve of the fourteen communication feature scales, and in eight of the eighteen personality trait scales. Accent accounted for far more of these than lexical qualities. For example, on the personality traits, lexical formality had effects on only two traits. Germanic speakers were seen as more flexible and more helpful than Latinate speakers. In contrast, accent had effects on seven traits. RP speakers were judged as being more intelligent, dominant, formal, ambitious and a greater source of advice than south-east Wales English speakers. South-east Wales speakers were seen as more sincere and more flexible than RP speakers. An interesting indicator of the potency of accent compared to lexis in this study is that listeners perceived that the RP speakers were speaking less colloquially, and using longer and fancier words, even though they were in fact reading exactly the same two texts as the south-east Wales speakers. (See the parallel misperception in Stewart, Ryan and Giles 1985, in chapter 4.)

Lexical diversity

Lexical diversity is viewed in terms of 'vocabulary richness' or high 'type-token ratios' (Bradac, Cargile and Hallett 2001: 142). A direct relationship has been found between lexical diversity and evaluations of competence and status (Bradac, Bowers and Courtwright 1980; Bradac, Mulac and House 1988). Evidence has been found, for instance, that a communicator using low lexical diversity may be seen as less suitable for employment requiring technical expertise, and more suited to low-status employment (Bradac 1990).

Bradac and Wisegarver (1984) studied the attitudinal effects of lexical diversity in their complex-design study of attitudes to variables that included standard American English and Mexican-accented English. For high-status jobs, a Standard American speaker communicating with high lexical diversity was seen as significantly more suitable than a Standard American speaker with low diversity, or than Mexican-accented English with any level of diversity. These latter three combinations were judged equally less suitable. For ratings of intelligence and competence, there was a three-stage hierarchy of Standard American with high diversity, then Mexican-accented English with high diversity, followed by both low-diversity combinations. There are certainly indications in this context that lexical diversity impacts on judgements by accent, and to a more extreme extent in the case of standard speakers.

A UK study by Giles and Sassoon (1983), however, compared RP and Cockney speakers delivering either high or low lexically diverse messages and found that lexical diversity had no effect on listeners' evaluations on either status or solidarity traits (p. 309). Accent carried more potency than lexical diversity. Giles, Wilson and Conway (1981), in a simulation eliciting judgements of speakers as potential candidates for a range of jobs in the UK, found that low lexical diversity was evaluated more highly than in previous work in the USA. These differences suggest that there is much to be explored still in this area, from study methods (e.g. how levels of lexical diversity are operationalised in the speech samples) to further contextualisation (e.g. judging speakers in a broader range of simulated contexts). Notably, too, there has so far been no research into whether the use of lexical diversity can change people's attitudes (Hosman 2002).

Speech rate

Research into the rate at which people speak has had at least some fairly consistent findings. Assessments of a speaker's competence increases as speech rate increases (e.g. Brown 1980). Social attractiveness evaluations, however, only increase up to a certain point, and then even out or decline. Hence, while low speech rates lead to downgrading on both solidarity and status, high speech rates lead to downgrading only on solidarity and upgrading on competence. However, this inverted 'U' relationship for solidarity occurred in US findings but did not occur in the UK study by Brown, Giles and Thakerar (1985). They found that, while status ratings again increased linearly with speech rate, solidarity ratings also linearly concurred with speech rate, but negatively so: i.e. decreasing as speech rate increased.

Without a good number of studies, it can be difficult to interpret such differences. It is tempting to attribute them to the most obvious difference between the studies: that is, a cultural difference between the UK and the USA. But Brown *et al.* (1985) rightly consider other differences between the studies. One is that, while each of the respondents in other studies listened to several voices and rated each one in turn, each respondent in the UK study heard only one of the voices (i.e. there were several comparable groups of respondents, each only judging one of the voices). This is another important methodological consideration. The argument for this was that in everyday life we do not usually make comparative judgements of several people saying the same things, or answering the same questions, but we instead hear just one speaker and make comparisons and judgements against an internal standard. Hearing just one voice helps address the salience question in chapter 4. It also arguably raises the authenticity and validity of the study. To attempt to resolve the question as to whether the differences in results are attributable to cultural differences or to study design, one might conduct the study both ways in the same context (e.g. either in the USA or in the UK).

Other communication features have also received some research attention. These include politeness (see review in Wilson 2002), syntactic complexity, language intensity, equivocal language, and powerful and powerless speech styles (see review in Hosman 2002).

SPEAKER VARIABLES

Physical appearance

Most of the empirical studies of speech evaluation that have so far been reviewed have entailed respondents evaluating audio-recorded voices, sometimes with some background information provided, such as details of the social class of the speaker. One might question whether the speaker's appearance (e.g. what they are wearing) might affect attitudes towards the speaker more than accent. Not all communication takes place out of view, as it does over the telephone, radio, audiotapes, public announcement systems, email, etc.). Giles and Farrar (1979) explored this issue in a field study in which a researcher called at houses on a middle-class housing estate in the south of England, posing as someone conducting a survey on people's attitudes to the economic situation. Women residents were asked to complete a questionnaire asking about how inflation was affecting their households in terms of food, clothing, recreational activities, etc. At each house, the researcher would state her standard request, in either RP or Cockney, wearing either smart or casual dress, and then return half an hour later to collect the questionnaire.

No attitude scales were used in this study, but instead, as in the case of Bourhis and Giles (1976) and Kristiansen (1997) in chapter 5, a measure of co-operation was used. Attitudes were inferred from the number of words each respondent wrote, with an additional measure of whether they wrote in a formal or informal style (defined by a number of variables, including sentence length and frequencies of adverbs).

The number of words written was significantly higher in response to the RP requests than the Cockney. Dress style was not significant either on its own or in interaction with either of the accents (i.e. it was not found to have an effect with one accent significantly more than the other). On the co-operation measure, then, accent eclipsed dress style. For the communication style, the RP request made in smart dress generated very formal style, and in casual dress generated very informal style. Dress style made no difference in the case of the Cockney speaker, and the level of formality was mid-way between the two extreme levels of judgements of the RP speaker (echoing the pattern found in Bradac and Wisegarver's 1984 findings for lexical diversity and accent). Overall, then, on the measures used in this study, accent appears a more potent variable, and any disadvantages pertaining to dress style appear to incur greater losses for standard speakers than others.

Elwell, Brown and Rutter (1984) approached the question of the presence of visual information in a more laboratory style matched guise study. Respondents judged a Standard British-accented speaker and an Indian-accented speaker in a simulated job interview. Some respondents saw the speaker on video as he spoke, and others only heard him. The standard accent received higher ratings than the Indian-accent on almost all variables. The presence or absence of visual information made no difference to these effects.

A Quebec study by Aboud, Clément and Taylor (1974) looked specifically at the matching and mismatching of appearance and accent in a rather different way from Giles and Farrar. This was a matched guise study in which standard Quebec French, a familiar conversational French-Canadian style, and Joual were presented to respondents along with photographs, ostensibly of the speakers, and these audio and visual materials were designed so as to give clues about social class. Respondents preferred 'incongruous' combinations as friends or work mates (i.e. a middle-class-looking person speaking Joual French, or a working-class-looking person speaking standard French). The authors considered the interpretation that such incongruities might be seen as indicating social flexibility, and that this might be a valued characteristic for friendships, since friendships imply a range of interactional domains. Such solidarity ratings were maximally low when a standard French was used by a speaker ascribed with high social status, and when Joual was used by a speaker ascribed with low social status.

However, with superiors and subordinates in the workplace, the respondents preferred the use of Standard French, suggesting the operation of specific norms. Besides this, though, people identified as working class were judged more extremely than those identified as middle class. That is, it was found that the style of speech of middle-class people in these superior and subordinate positions did not affect evaluative reactions as much as it did in the case of working-class people. More specifically, those who spoke more standard than their expected level were evaluated more positively than those who spoke at their expected level, who in turn were evaluated more positively than those who spoke at below their expected level. One interpretation considered by Aboud *et al.* (1974: 249) was that, while middle-class people might be expected to command less formal styles of French in appropriate contexts, working-class people are not expected to command a more formal style in more formal contexts. Expectations certainly have an important place in people's evaluative reactions in communication contexts (see, for example, Burgoon, Denning and Roberts 2002).

Social class

We have seen earlier in this book how Mexican-American speakers were downgraded on the status dimension (Ryan, Carranza and Moffie 1975). Ryan and Sebastian (1980) considered whether this would occur in a situation where listeners were already certain of the status (in terms of the social class) of the speaker. Middle-class Anglo respondents heard both standard American and Mexican-American English voices, and were given information that each speaker was either lower class or middle class, or were given no such information at all. The results showed that, overall, Standard English speakers received relatively favourable ratings compared to Mexican-accented speakers, and speakers with middle-class backgrounds were preferred to those with lower-class backgrounds. The least favourable ratings were given to a speaker with a Mexican accent who was known to be of a lower-class background. Information about social class made a greater difference on almost all measures to those with Mexican-accented speech than it did to the standard American speakers. Giles and Sassoon (1983) noted that these results raise the possibility that the many findings regarding attitudes to standard and non-standard accents may dissipate quite considerably when we already have such secure information about speakers, given the inter-dependence between accent and social-class information found in this study.

Ryan and Sebastian's (1980) findings were not replicated in the UK study by Giles and Sassoon (1983), using Cockney as the non-standard variety, rather than an ethnic minority variety. Giles and Sassoon's finding was that when a speaker was known to be working class or middle class, non-standard speech still evoked a lower rating on status traits in comparison with RP. That is, accent was still found to be the more powerful variable. Bradac and Wisegarver (1984), this time with Mexican-American accents, also found that speaker status was unimportant, compared to accent and lexical diversity, on judgements of intellectual competence.

From these individual studies, with their varying designs and prior-ities, one or two patterns are at least suggestible, even if they are not uniform across all the findings. In terms of status findings, several studies indicate that people believed to be of high social status who speak with standard accents attract very high ratings, while people believed to be of low social status who speak with non-standard accents attract very low ratings (e.g. Giles and Sassoon 1983; Ryan and Sebastian 1980). In terms of solidarity findings, on the other hand, low ratings are likely when people believed to be of high social status speak a standard language variety, and when people believed to be of low social status speak non-standard varieties. In contrast, high ratings for solidarity are likely when people believed to be of high social status speak non-standard varieties (in the case of Ryan and Sebastian 1980), and when speakers believed to be of low social status speak a standard variety (Aboud et al. 1974; Giles and Farrar 1979; Ryan and Sebastian 1980). (See Bradac and Wisegarver (1984) for a more detailed review of this research.)

Sex and age

There are also some findings regarding the effects on attitudes of the sex and age of speakers. For instance, Gallois, Callan and Johnstone (1984), in their verbal guise study of standard Australian English and Aboriginal Australian English, found that on solidarity ratings white Australians and Aborigines judged male Aboriginal speakers as more friendly, trustworthy and gentle than standard Australian speaking males. In contrast, however, Aboriginal females were rated less favour-ably than Standard Australian speaking females. Regarding speaker age, Ryan and Capadano (1978) found that both male and female speakers were seen as comparatively inflexible when they were older.

Older female speakers were also seen as more reserved, passive and 'out of it' than younger women.

COMMUNICATION/SPEAKER INTERACTIONS

Matched guise studies, with their use of scales and appropriate statistical analysis, are well suited to exploring effects of more than one variable. Some studies reviewed above have, for instance, looked at the relative effects of accent and a further variable, such as physical appearance, lexical diversity or social status. Other studies have investigated several variables in one design (e.g. Gallois *et al.* 1984 included Aborigine, white rural and white urban respondents judging male and female Aborigine and Australian English speakers in two different contexts). The sex and age variables, reviewed above, have also been explored further in such studies to investigate their relative effects on judgements, and provide a more detailed understanding. Street, Brady and Lee (1984), for example, compared the effects of speaker sex and speech-rate variables. Both male and female speakers were seen to have greater competence when they increased their speech rate. For solidarity, there was a sex difference in the findings for speech rate; they found that speech rate affected attitudes towards male speakers but not females. Males were judged more socially attractive with moderate to fast speech rates than if they spoke slowly.

The age variable was pursued further by Stewart and Ryan (1982), examining the attitudes of 18–21-year-old respondents to speaker age and speech rate. They found main effects for each of these on the competence dimension; fast and medium speakers (compared to slow speakers) were seen as more competent. Younger speakers were rated more competent than older speakers, too. On solidarity measures, the speech rate made a greater difference to younger speakers than it did to the older speakers. Young slow speakers were judged significantly more negatively than young fast speakers. Stewart and Ryan suggest this division of the young speakers might be a disconfirmation effect (viz. a disconfirmation of a stereotype that young people speak fast), and raise the question of whether there would be a corresponding disconfirmation effect for the older speakers (stereotypically expected to speak slowly) if a similar study were run with older respondents.

In a more complex matched guise study incorporating speaker age (a study that drew attention to some important fundamental issues in language attitudes research), Giles, Coupland, Henwood, Harriman and Coupland (1990) looked at interactions between accent, age of speaker and speech rate. Respondents heard a male speaker talking about his car either in RP or in a Lancashire (north-west England) accent, at slow, medium or fast speech rates, and sounding either young (early twenties) or older (early sixties). Attitude scales ratings were found to group into ten factors in this study. Main effects were found for each of the three variables: speaker age, accent and speech rate. For accent, RP was found to be more statusful, but carry negative solidarity and less integrity. For age, the elderly speakers were rated as more old fashioned, frail and vulnerable. On the competence factors, however, neither the speaker's accent nor age had any significant effects (i.e. traits such as ambitious, intelligent, forgetful, indecisive). Speech rate had the highest number of effects of these variables, leading Giles *et al.* to suggest that it can be a more potent factor than accent and age. In summary, fast talking was associated with more drive and dynamism, but less social attractiveness.

But there were several interactions in the results that qualify these broad patterns. When using RP, the elderly speaker was perceived to be more aged, while the opposite was the case for the young speaker. Importantly, whereas younger speakers were seen as less vulnerable when they spoke the non-standard variety, elderly speakers were judged as less vulnerable when they spoke RP, if they spoke it fast. And in fact, the one rated most vulnerable speaker of all took the shape of an elderly, slow-talking non-standard speaker. It seems that, for the elderly, fast RP speech can mollify ageist assumptions, but not without some social costs, such as being perceived as unfriendly, selfish, etc.

After the completion of rating scales in this same study, respondents had to explain why they had rated the speakers as they had done. There was a great deal of negativity in these explanations, but they varied in nature according to accent and age. To illustrate, for RP, the young speaker was seen as arrogant and selfish, and the older speaker was viewed as egocentric, talking of trivia, and living in the past. For the non-standard variety, the young speaker was viewed as trying to impress, while the older speaker was seen as stupid, and losing his grip. When asked to point to parts of the spoken text to justify their comments, respondents would often point to the same spoken utterances to express very disparate views. Respondents were also given statements from the discourse and asked why the speaker had said them. For 'I didn't know what to think', they felt that the young speakers were withholding judgement, but they thought the older speakers were confused.

The importance of the responses to these open-ended items is that they provide examples of how language attitudes cannot be seen as 'passive reactions to blocks of vocal sounds' (Giles *et al.* 1990: 55). Rather they can be seen as very much part of an interactive process responding to text and context. At one level, this relates to the neutrality question (see chapter 4), demonstrating the argument that texts cannot be factually neutral. And this can also be seen as an instance of the multidimensionality of language attitudes, as if attitudes are a set of resources that we access and apply variably across contexts, even if there is some consistency in the attitudinal responses that surface as social groups do this. The collection of open-ended data alongside the completion of rating scales allowed insights into this multidimensionality, providing richer data with which to interpret the quantitative patterns identified in the attitude scale ratings.

In some of the studies reviewed earlier that have researched two or more variables together, some findings have been interpreted with reference to 'incongruities' and 'disconfirmations', to some extent alluding to the violations of language expectancies referred to in chapter 1 (Burgoon 1995; Burgoon, Denning and Roberts 2002). Researchers have also directly designed assumed incongruities into studies, for example between message content and accent. Powesland and Giles (1975) conducted an attitude-change focused study in the UK in which a message arguing either for or against trade union reform (the Industrial Relations Act) was presented in either RP or a Bristolian regional accent. The Act itself was assumed to be regarded as a politically conservative or right-wing argument, and RP was seen as its congruous accent. Regionally accented speech was assumed to have left-wing connotations, and therefore congruous with argument against the Act. Having sought the views of the respondents on the Act some days before the main study, the researchers then played one of the four speech versions to each matched subgroup of respondents to see if and under what conditions attitude change occurred. They found that RP speakers incurred more attitude change towards their own position when they argued in defence of the trade unions rather than against them. Bristolian speakers changed attitudes more when they argued against the unions rather than in their support. The incongruity appeared to make the speaker more persuasive, mediating the effects of accent alone. A similar study was conducted in the USA by Giles, Williams, Mackie and Rosselli (1995). This time the debate concerned the English Only controversy, which includes arguments for and against issues such as the assimilation of minorities, bilingual education and making English the official language in the USA. Pro- and anti-English Only arguments were presented in either Anglo or Hispanic accents to US west coast Anglo undergraduates. The assumption in designing the study was that the two congruous conditions were the Hispanic-accented speakers arguing against and Anglo-accented speakers arguing in favour of English Only, matching their stereotypical group stances. Results echoed those of Powesland and Giles, showing that the congruous versions were not influential, but the incongruous ones were.

One possible explanation for these findings is that in the congruous condition the listeners perceive a 'knowledge bias' in the speaker when they identify standardness and non-standardness in the accent: i.e. they assume the speaker has a biased point of view. Incongruity could lead them to afford the speaker more credibility and so increase the possibility of persuasion (for a summary, see Perloff 2008: 227ff.). It is also suggested that the incongruity can provoke more cognitive engagement (systematic processing) with the message (see, for example, Chaiken 1987).

HEARER VARIABLES

The authors of both the previous two studies refer to the limitation that the respondents represented the majority groups (RP speakers and Anglo-speakers). The characteristics of the respondents are obviously important in determining whose attitudes one has investigated and how far they might reasonably generalise. But they are also particularly important as one attempts to interpret and explain results and build theories. It is to the characteristics of the respondents that we now turn. In a few studies referred to so far, listener variables have been referred to primarily in terms of standard social dimensions (e.g. the different age groups in the study of varieties of French by Paltridge and Giles 1984, and the different film audiences in the cinema study by Kristiansen 1997, in terms of occupation, age, sex, area of residence, place of work). Other types of hearer variables, including traits and states, have also been investigated, however.

Ethnocentrism

One of the first studies to turn attention to personality differences in listeners was carried out by Giles (1971), and focused on ethnocentrism, an orientation towards regarding one's own group as being the most important. Giles identified ethnocentrism as a trait that might make some people much more negative and less liberal towards regional accented speech, seen as outgroup language. Ethnocentrism might be reduced through the experience of a more diffuse social environment. In his study, respondents completed an ethnocentrism scale in the first stage of the study so that two groups could be selected for the second stage, one group with high ethnocentricity scores, and the other with low scores. These respondents then heard audio-recordings of RP, Birmingham, Somerset, Northern English, Irish and Southern Welsh accented speech, and filled in scales for pleasantness, status and communicative comfort (*cf.* Giles 1970). The study provided an empirical demonstration of a tendency for highly ethnocentric listeners to rate regional accents less favourably than less ethnocentric listeners across all three of the measures in this study. In contrast, highly ethnocentric listeners also rated RP significantly more favourably (although both groups showed communicative comfort with RP speakers).

McKirnan and Hamayan (1984) extended this research to the USA, examining the impact of ethnocentrism and exposure to outgroup members on attitudes to Hispanics and the Spanish language among lower-middle-class white Anglophone elementary schoolchildren. The school setting contained a Spanish bilingual programme in which Mexican-American students were withdrawn from several hours of regular classes each day to receive mother tongue tuition. The study showed that the greater the adherence of the respondents to the speech norms of Standard English, and the more sensitive they were to intrusions from Mexican English (particularly those concerning Spanish lexical items and phonemes), the more negative their attitudes were to Hispanics and their language.

Mood

Given that, as we noted in chapter 2, affect can be viewed as an integral component of attitudes, one would anticipate that the affective state of hearers can also have an impact on their evaluative judgements of others. Yet, as noted by Cargile *et al.* (1994) and Cargile and Giles (1997), this area has received relatively little research attention. But on the basis of the little work done, and the research into emotions in the persuasion field (e.g. Dillard and Meijnders 2002; Nabi 2002), it is possible to draw out one or two patterns here as regards the influence of mood. Here, then, we consider whether judgements of speakers are likely to vary according to whether the judges are in a good or bad mood. For example, if one is collecting language attitudes data from students in an undergraduate lecture, and they have all just had a bad experience or good experience (perhaps relating to the quality of the previous lecture), might this affect the data? We take as a starting point here that the source of the mood is unrelated to the actual research task itself.

At the general level of forming judgements of people, people in good moods are likely to form more positive impressions of others, and positive moods can influence a host of processes, such as evaluations, expectations and behaviour (Isen, Shalker, Clark and Karp 1978). But there is less consistency in the case of bad moods. These have been found to lead to more negative evaluations of others (Forgas and Bower 1987), or to lead to more positive and prosocial outcomes (Isen, Horn and Rosenhan 1973).

We might delve a little further in relation to persuasion-focused studies of the kind we have summarised by Powesland and Giles (1975) and Giles *et al.* (1995). One of the most influential theories in the persuasion field is Petty and Cacioppo's (1986) Elaboration Likelihood Model (ELM), which (necessarily simplified here) says that people process communications through two distinct routes: central and peripheral routes. In the former, people weigh up arguments thoughtfully, distinguishing strong from weak arguments. In the latter, people tend to look at the message relatively quickly, or focus on simple cues, unrelated to the core of the message itself, to work out whether to accept or reject the message. Such simple cues might include the simple quantity (rather than quality) of arguments made, the physical attractiveness of the communicator, their speech features, background music or how much credibility they feel the communicator has. Taking the central route will depend on factors such as motivation (how important this issue is to them) and ability (how complex the issue is, how much time they have, for instance). Following this theory, one might argue that in such persuasive contexts, where people are highly motivated on the matter and able to engage with the pros and cons to reach their own decision (e.g. about whether they agree with the English Only movement, or with new trade union legislation), the accent, speech rate, lexical diversity, age, sex, physical appearance of the speaker would play a weaker role as they weigh up the core issues.

Bless, Bohner, Schwarz and Strack (1990) explored how positive and negative moods might affect the likelihood of people using central or peripheral routes when confronted with a message containing strong and weak arguments. They found that people in a good mood were less likely to take the central route, regardless of the strength of the arguments (unless they were actually instructed to give the matter serious thought). In contrast, people in a bad mood were more likely to take the central route, engage with the strong arguments in the message, and change their attitudes. These findings could mean that speech features would have less influence on attitude change when people are in a bad mood. Wegener, Petty and Smith (1995) take a more anticipatory look at mood. They found that if people anticipated that the message they were about to receive concerned something positive to them, they were more likely to engage with it carefully, whereas if they thought it concerned something negative, they would tend to take the peripheral route. It seems that if people are in a good mood, they prefer to stay in it. People in a negative mood were more likely to take the central route, since they had less to lose. So one could speculate that if speech features are peripheral cues, these would be more likely to have an impact in such persuasive contexts amongst people in good moods who are not convinced that the message will enable them to stay that way.

Extrapolating this from the ELM, although plausible, is nevertheless only speculative, and in need of empirical work to test such conjectures. Nevertheless, there is enough evidence from the work of Isen *et al.* (1973, 1978), for example, for Cargile *et al.* (1994) to conclude in their summary of mood that listeners' moods can influence their evaluations of speakers, even if we need to know more detail. This is a field much in need of more research. In addition, there is arguably a need also to look at discrete emotions, rather than confining the focus to the broader notions of positive and negative mood (see, for example, Cargile and Giles 1997; Nabi 2002).

Expertise

Expertise of listeners may also affect the extent to which language attitudes come into play. In terms of the ELM once again, listeners with efficiently organised background knowledge of the message–topic have the freed cognitive capacity to weigh up the arguments, and are likely to do this if they have the motivation and ability. Those with less expertise or without motivation or ability would be more likely to rely on peripheral cues such as language attitudes. Similarly, lack of experience of particular social encounters (e.g. with people from new social groups) may also lead to increased reliance on available cues such as language attitudes. (See Cargile *et al.* 1994 for a summary.) Inevitably, there are some complexities, such as whether there can be instances where, for example, intergroup factors mean that a speaker's accent motivates listeners to engage with a message more, and even to build expertise. Indeed, an accent might become an argument in itself. (See Perloff 2003: 142ff. for other examples of such complications.) Again, this is a relatively open research field.

CONTEXT

Brown *et al.* (1985) noted how a slow speech rate, though generally evaluated negatively, can be evaluated differently when listeners perceive it to be helpful to understanding. As Cargile *et al.* (1994: 225) note, 'attitudes towards a speaker's slow rate of speech would be different in the context of a nuclear physics lecture than during introductions at a cocktail party'. Features of language behaviour, then, may be evaluated differently in different situations.

We have already seen how context can be seen at different levels, including the more immediate level in which language attitudes data is collected. For example, chapter 2 referred to some instances where the characteristics of the researchers themselves, or the language used during data collection in a bilingual context, had effects on the attitudes expressed by the respondents (Price *et al.* 1983; Webster 1996; Bellin *et al.* 1999). The actual sociolinguistic comparisons designed into the study can also create their own context. Abrams and Hogg (1987) found that when they asked their Scottish judges from Dundee to evaluate audio-recorded speakers from Dundee and Glasgow, they expressed more favourable attitudes to the Dundee speakers on both status and solidarity than to the Glaswegian speakers. However, when they were asked to judge the same Glaswegian speakers alongside standard English speakers, they rated the Glaswegian speakers much higher on both dimensions, and indeed much higher even than they had rated their own ingroup (Dundee) speakers in the earlier comparison.

While studies have found attitudinal judgements extending along status and solidarity dimensions, Carranza and Ryan (1975) designed status and solidarity stressing contexts into their study. Bilingual Anglo- and Mexican-American respondents rated Standard American-English and Mexican-Spanish speakers. The speakers were either representing the home domain (a mother preparing breakfast in the kitchen for her family) or the school domain (a teacher giving a history lesson to her class). The findings showed that the students evaluated the Spanish speaker more favourably in the home context than in the school context, and rated the English speaker more favourably in the school context than the home context. There is also a body of language attitudes research into a range of other contexts, including medical, legal, educational and employment contexts. We have touched on these in one or two studies (e.g. judgements of employment suitability in Bradac and Wisegarver 1984, and in Giles, Wilson and Conway 1981), but these applied contexts are given greater coverage in chapter 8.

Other contexts, referred to as 'cultural' (Cargile *et al.* 1994: 226), comprise the political, historical, economic and linguistic contexts, including the nature of language ideologies in any particular cultural context (for example, the tendency proposed by Milroy 2001 for language ideology to be focused on social class in the UK, but on race in the USA), and ethnolinguistic vitality, as we saw in Woolard and Gahng (1990). Kristiansen (2005) looked at the different ideological climates in seven Nordic countries in relation to the linguistic influence of English. Marked differences were found in the attitudes to English in those seven countries, with Denmark showing the most positivity and Iceland the least. The pattern of attitudes was found to relate to the power of traditional ideological differences in these contexts, varying with their distinctive 'linguistic climates' arising from their different histories and language policies.

In reviewing Lambert *et al.*'s (1960) study in chapter 5, reference was made to their question asking respondents how much importance they attached to various traits speakers were rated on. Boninger, Krosnick and Berent (1995) conducted a series of studies into the sources of attitude importance. Attitudes holding importance are seen as those that are more resistant to change, having more stability over time, having an impact on cognition (e.g. selective exposure to and better memory of attitude-relevant information), and impact on behaviour (e.g. writing letters of complaint or support, choice of friends and partners, the use of one language rather than another). Three origins of attitude importance were established in their study. These were social identification (e.g. with social groups), value relevance (values such as individualism, free enterprise, equality) and self-interest (e.g. avoiding costs, pursuing rights, lifestyles, material benefits). Boninger *et al.* underline the likelihood that the comparative magnitude of these three origins varies both diachronically across different historical periods, and also synchronically across different cultural contexts, especially in the case of values and self-concepts. Mutonya (1997), for example, found evidence that the label 'proud' carried a negative cultural value amongst respondents in Kenya, whereas in many other contexts, a high rating for 'proud' would have been assumed to carry approval. Unless we are confident of the cultural values placed on attitudinal labels, it is difficult to view them as positive or negative attitudes to speakers. This is a further aspect of the multidimensionality of language attitudes, and a further way in which context is so significant in language attitudes research. These issues will resurface later.

FURTHER READING ON CHAPTER 6

For its important findings with regard to the interaction of text and context in language attitudes, it is valuable to read in the original the following study that was reviewed in this chapter:

Giles, H., Coupland, N., Henwood, K., Harriman, J. and Coupland, J., 1990, The social meaning of RP: an intergenerational perspective, in S. Ramsaran (ed.), *Studies in the pronunciation of English: a commemorative volume in honour of A. C. Gimson* (pp. 191–211). London: Routledge.

For a concise review of language expectancy theory:

Burgoon, M. and Siegel, J., 2004, Language expectancy theory: insight to application, in J. Seiter and R. Gass (eds.), *Perspectives on persuasion, social influence and compliance gaining* (pp. 149–64). Boston: Pearson.

Concise reviews of the Elaboration Likelihood Model and of credibility can be found in:

Benoit, W. and Strathman, A., 2004, Source credibility and the Elaboration Likelihood Model, in J. Seiter and R. Gass (eds.), *Perspectives on persuasion, social influence and compliance gaining* (pp. 95–111). Boston: Pearson.
Petty, R., Rucker, D., Bizer, G. and Cacioppo, J., 2004, The Elaboration likelihood model of persuasion, in J. Seiter and R. Gass (eds.), *Perspectives on persuasion, social influence and compliance gaining* (pp. 65–89). Boston: Pearson.

A brief overview of mood can be found within the following chapter:

Dillard, J. and Meijnders, A., 2002, Persuasion and the structure of affect, in J. Dillard and M. Pfau (eds.), *The persuasion handbook: developments in theory and practice* (pp. 309–27). Thousand Oaks, CA: Sage.

QUESTION FOR CHAPTER 6

If someone's speech style leads them to be judged as 'clever', 'ambitious', 'highly educated', 'assertive', 'eager', 'high class', 'enthusiastic', 'determined', 'polite', 'funny', to what extent would you say that each of these is a favourable evaluation?

7 Communication accommodation theory

So far in this book, language use has taken a relatively immobile form, although there have been some glimpses of mobility in the treatment of a few areas such as speech rates, codeswitching and degrees of accentedness. Accommodation theory foregrounds the dynamic communicative shifts that can occur as we respond in communicative interaction. The study of language attitudes needs to take account of these, since the psycho-social processes that attitudes research deals with are also those that inform choices that we make in interaction. Making adaptations as we communicate with others may be (or may be seen as) a behavioural signal of our own attitudes, and these adaptations may themselves also evoke attitudinal responses in our communication partners, as well as bystanders, eavesdroppers, members of wider audiences etc. Hence communication accommodation theory can also be seen as the implementation of attitudes in discourse.

As a sociolinguistic theory, it is also a counter to the more deterministic view of style that Labov employed in his seminal sociolinguistic research, in which styles covering different levels of formality were elicited from speakers by giving them different tasks (reading lists of words, talking about their own experiences etc.). Giles points to the absence of information of the interviewer's accent or speech style during Labov's sociolinguistic interviews (e.g. Giles and Powesland 1975: 171), and raises the question of whether the style features of the interviewees' speech in his research might have been influenced by the interviewer's speech features rather than by the task alone.

BASIC NOTIONS

The basic notions of communication accommodation theory (speech accommodation theory in the original formulation by Giles 1973) are 'convergence' and 'divergence'. (In practice, 'converging' is also expressed as 'accommodating'.) Convergence refers to a strategy of reducing dissimilarities in the communication features used with communication partners, and divergence refers to a strategy of accentuating differences. Maintenance (i.e. not shifting in either direction) is also a strategy. These strategies can involve a wide range of features, from the language that is used, to phonological variants, accentedness, speech rates, levels of lexical diversity, gestures, posture, smiling, the use of humour, pause frequencies and lengths, and so on. Where such communication variables map onto societally valued forms and stigmatised forms, these shifts are seen in terms of being 'upward' and 'downward' respectively.

Further distinctions are also made. Convergence and divergence do not necessarily involve all levels of communication features at once, and indeed both strategies may in some instances co-occur across different features. Bilous and Kraus (1988), for example, found that females converged towards males on some dimensions (e.g. utterance length and interruptions), but diverged on others (e.g. laughter). In addition, convergence and divergence need not be symmetrical. An example of asymmetrical convergence was found in American–Japanese interactions by White (1989). Within their respective cultures, Japanese speakers engaged in more backchannelling (e.g. 'uh-huh', 'mmhm') during conversations than Americans. In cross-cultural interaction, Americans converged by backchannelling more, but the Japanese participants maintained their usual high level, rather than reciprocating by backchannelling less.

OPTIMAL LEVELS

Research has also pointed to optimal levels of convergence. In Street's (1982) work on speech rates reported in chapter 6, he found that differences of up to fifty words per minute between interviewer and interviewee were acceptable, but that beyond that, observers downgraded the speaker. Giles and Smith (1979) investigated attitudes towards a Canadian speaker converging in pronunciation, speech rate and message content, and they found that listeners were positive towards convergence on each of these three levels, but were negative towards the speaker when he converged on all three at once. The optimum was found to be convergence on speech rate and either pronunciation or content. From this idea of an optimum, then, we can also infer notions of overaccommodation (sometimes referred to as hyperaccommodation) and underaccommodation. The magnitude and dimensions of shifts have an impact on attitudinal responses.

MOTIVATIONS

Why should such shifts occur? We have mentioned in previous chapters the importance of motivation and ability in human activity. The motivations in this case have been identified as communication efficiency, as a desire to gain social approval, and also a desire to maintain positive social identities. Putman and Street (1984), for example, found that interviewees adapted their speech rate and the duration of their turns as they sought to create favourable impressions and communicate effectively with the interviewer.

The reference to the maintenance of positive social identities requires reference here to social identity theory (Tajfel and Turner 1979), which argues that an individual's self concept relates in part to their membership of social groups. These social groups emerge from the psychological process of social categorisation (e.g. into ethnicities, age groups, social classes, professional groups, students, etc.). Tajfel and Turner posit that we make comparisons between our own group's position and the positions of other groups, and in so doing we strive to distinguish our own group in a positive light. Divergence from members of other groups, for example, can be very much a part of this process of distinguishing. Where social identities become dissatisfying, group members typically resort to various strategies to re-establish positivity, such as by redefining what is valued about their group in relation to others, or by seeking membership of an alternative group. Convergence, then, to an outgroup member can be part of the process of aspiring to a new and more valued social identity in the other group.

In some work reviewed in previous chapters, it has been noted that RP tends to attract high ratings on prestige and competence, but that regional varieties achieve higher ratings on social attractiveness. Bourhis, Giles and Lambert (1975) examined these patterns in an accommodation environment. Respondents heard simulated radio interviews with a Welsh athlete who, they were told, had recently come seventh in an international diving competition. They heard an interviewer speaking in either RP or mild Welsh-accented English. With the latter, the interviewee responded in a mild Welsh accent, but with the RP speaker he either maintained his mild accent, or he converged to RP or he diverged to a broad Welsh accent. South Welsh respondents judged him to be more intelligent when he converged to RP and least intelligent when he diverged to a broad accent. But RP convergence also meant he was seen as less trustworthy and kindhearted, whereas diverging to a broad Welsh accent led to higher ratings on these same two scales. Hence, evaluations of competence and social attractiveness also pertained through shifts to these accents. Maintaining or stressing one's perceived nationality or ethnicity by means of language in this kind of intergroup setting appears to be a valued tactic for asserting cultural identity, in line with social identity theory. Communication accommodation often operates as a way of negotiating salient social category memberships.

A further example is found in Bourhis (1977), in which two Welsh-accented speakers play the role of two suspects by either converging to an RP-accented English policeman or diverging through broadening their Welsh-accented English. Respondents rated the diverging speakers higher on social attractiveness traits and as more nationalistic, but lower on competence-related traits. In this study, though, the suspects were also rated as less guilty and deserving of a lighter sentence when they diverged. It appeared that the intergroup salience of this scenario meant that listeners were rewarding the suspects for upholding their Welsh identity in such a threatening context. Convergence and divergence, then, can be seen in terms of rewards and costs (Homans' 1961 exchange theory is generally invoked in this regard in the accommodation literature). Convergence towards the RP-accented English policeman might be seen as offering the best chance of a positive or less negative outcome, for example, but could be seen as incurring costs to the suspect's social identity. Divergence placed social identity ahead of legal repercussions.

CONSTRAINTS

One might also see some types of intergroup encounters in terms of constraints. Group membership can bring powerful expectations to stay within the confines of certain norms. Milroy (1987: 60), for example, refers to a Belfast youth who was mocked, shouted at and punched when he diverged from the vernacular speech norms in the presence of his friends. This resulted in his immediately converging back to them. Here, then, we see the importance of ability or opportunity in social activity, and how some contexts may restrict or effectively eliminate these.

Even if accommodation theory was in part a response to the situational determinism embodied in Labov's sociolinguistic interviews, the theory needs to take account of constraints. Attitudes to speakers are likely to differ when there are recognised restrictions on communication mobility. Constraints come in many forms, including straight forward explicit instructions. In this regard, a significant early development in accommodation theory was demonstrated in a study by Simard,

Taylor and Giles (1976). In this study, French Canadian listeners heard an audio-recorded English Canadian speaker describing a route on a city map. The listeners had to trace the route on a blank map. Later, they were given a map with a new route traced on it, which they themselves then had to communicate to the English Canadian speaker in either English or French, as they preferred. They also had to complete a questionnaire which elicited their perception of the speaker's language abilities and his effort to bridge the cultural gap, as well as their own abilities as they themselves described a route to the English Canadian.

Each respondent heard one of six conditions in the study. The voice was either in English or French, and was preceded on each tape by an interaction between the researcher and the speaker, in which the researcher gave the speaker one of three instructions. In one instruction, the researcher was heard telling the reader to describe the route to a French-speaking student, who would be tracing it on an unmarked map. In another, the researcher also added that the description should be given in French, or that it should be given in English. And in the third, the researcher included in his interaction with the English Canadian speaker that although he knew the latter could speak French, he was free to use either of the two languages in the recording.

The findings confirmed the basic tenets of accommodation theory in the condition where the respondents were aware that the speaker could speak French and that the speaker was free to speak either language. But revisions were required to the theory to explain other findings in this study. When the speaker spoke French because he was told to, he was judged less favourably in terms of bridging the cultural gap than when it was left up to him to decide which language to use. In other words, external pressure made a difference to the way that convergence was evaluated. In addition, the speaker who did not use French when he was told to was evaluated more favourably than when he was not told to. This suggested that French Canadian speakers, unless they had information suggesting otherwise, simply assumed that non-accommodation in an English Canadian was due to a lack of adequate competence in French.

In sum, attitudes varied as follows. When a speaker was heard to converge, listeners reacted most favourably when they attributed this to the speaker making an effort, and less favourably if listeners knew that it was merely due to external pressure. When a speaker did not converge, listeners' attitudes were the most negative when they knew that this was simply due to lack of effort, and less negative when they were able to put it down to lack of French language proficiency or to external pressure. From these results, then, it is clear that a core feature in how people judge accommodating and non-accommodating communicators is causal attribution. Causes are generally attributed to factors of ability, effort and external factors (see, for example, Hewstone 1989, or the summary in Pennington, Gillen and Hill 1999).

Constraints are not always stated explicitly, however, and may simply reside in the expectations or norms associated with particular situations. Recall, for instance, the preferred use of standard French with subordinates and superiors in the study by Aboud *et al.* (1974) in chapter 6. We are in principle free, of course, to break communication conventions. O'Keefe (1988) has set out different types of beliefs about communication (design logics), and suggests that some people work with a rhetorical design logic, which means that they tend to operate on the basis that context can be created by communication as much as the other way around. Nevertheless, in some contexts, important outcomes may depend on the attitudes and decisions of others who do not share such beliefs in that particular norm-focused situation. Ball, Giles, Byrne and Berechree (1984), for example, examined accommodation in the context of an employment interview. The job interviewer spoke in either a refined or a broad Australian accent. The respondents first heard the interviewee outside the interview (in order to gauge how he usually spoke) and then had to judge him in the interview, in which he either maintained his usual speech patterns, or diverged upwards or downwards from the interviewer, or converged upwards or downwards to the interviewer. Ball *et al.* found that the respondents valued adherence to sociolinguistic norms, rating him more competent, eager and determined when he used the refined accent, irrespective of upward or downward convergent or divergent shifts. In terms of causal attributions again, speech behaviour was viewed as determined by external factors (the situation) rather than factors internal to the communicators (effort, ability). People's shared beliefs about what they should and should not do in different contexts are important to investigate and take into account in understanding language attitudes (see also Gallois and Callan 1991).

Accommodative mobility can be more strongly restricted at times, then. The presence of explicit directives and shared beliefs about norms can prescribe or delimit accommodative shifts but, in addition, speakers who identify strongly with a salient ingroup are more likely to maintain their normal communication patterns or diverge from outgroup members to send out clear signals about their identity and loyalties. This was also demonstrated in Welsh learners in the language laboratory in the study by Bourhis and Giles (1977) reviewed in chapter 1. (See also Gallois, Franklyn-Stokes, Giles and Coupland 1988.)

OBJECTIVE AND SUBJECTIVE ACCOMMODATION

However, in other contexts, the picture is much more fluid and much more open to variable subjectivities. Communicators can be much more reliant upon their impressions of what features they themselves are producing in their communication, and of what their communication partners are producing, too. In other words, in the flow of communication, we need to consider how well we identify accommodation. It is, in some instances at least, possible to track and measure independently and objectively how features change during interaction in terms of convergence and divergence. However, in the course of our interactions, we are likely to make adjustments according to how we believe or perceive others to be shifting, and this may be quite different from the objective view. In media contexts, of course, speakers have to work on the basis of their beliefs about their audiences. Bell (1991) refers to 'audience design' in which newsreaders converge towards a common style of speech aimed at their audience. The same newsreader delivering news on two different stations shifts to a different style for each station with the aim of accommodating to the different assumed audiences. In a speech evaluation study, Thakerar and Giles (1981) found that speakers who were believed to be relatively competent were perceived to be more standard accented than they actually were. In a study of accommodation in job interviews, Willemyns, Gallois, Callan and Pittam (1997) measured both objective and subjective accommodation by the interviewees to broad and cultivated Australian accents. Overall, they found that both males and females had broadened their accents by the end of the interviews. But, reporting on their own perceptions of how they had performed, the respondents themselves disagreed that their accents became broader (with the females disagreeing more than the males).

Hence there is an important distinction to be made between objective and subjective accommodation, since, as has been mentioned earlier in this book, people react to their perceived environments. Platt and Weber (1984) show how we cannot always be confident that judgements based on subjective impressions will lead to appropriate outcomes. They point out that the motivation to converge is connected with some notion of what it is one is trying to move towards. Mismatches between the goal and the accommodative communication itself may make the resultant communication adaptations difficult for the recipient to interpret. Platt and Weber point to the particular difficulties in the case of interaction between speakers of native and nativised varieties of a language, between native speakers and immigrants acquiring that language, as well as between different groups within a native variety (e.g. different social classes).

MISMATCHES AND PSYCHOLOGICAL ACCOMMODATION

Platt and Weber (1984) identified a range of mismatches in Singapore, where Singapore English speakers interact with English native speakers from North America, Britain, Australia and New Zealand. They point to cases where a desire to accommodate was fulfilled either only partly or not at all. Some mismatches arose from a lack of sufficient familiarity with stylistic variations and sociolinguistic practices within the other speech community. For example, they point to some educated expatriates trying to speak colloquial basilectal Singapore English, when Singaporeans only use this in certain situations with close friends, fellow workers, family members, etc., and regard its use by expatriates as inappropriate, as well as inaccurate. While the expatriates in Platt and Weber's study appeared to use such adaptations for communicative efficiency (e.g. 'to get a better rapport'), the Singaporean respondents had no positive reactions at all to such use, and regarded it at best with amusement and at worst with annoyance. Here, then, what might be a case of an expatriate making a well-intentioned effort to accommodate can be met with entirely different causal attributions amongst those on the receiving end, with annoyance perhaps arising from the communication behaviour being attributed to rather different internal causes, such as paternalism or a tendency to patronise.

Difficulties in interpreting communication adaptations can also arise simply because their status as convergence or divergence is highly ambiguous for recipients either objectively or subjectively, again because of a lack of familiarity with cultural practices. Ross and Shortreed (1990) investigated the attitudes of Japanese students to the use of convergence and divergence by Japanese native speakers in conversation with non-native speakers of Japanese. The students heard audio-recorded conversations with non-native speakers who were of either high or low proficiency in Japanese. The native speakers responded either in standard Japanese, or in English or with foreigner talk (a register than includes features such as a slower rate of delivery – see Long 1983). All of these three response-types are interpretable variably, as either convergence or divergence. For example, the use of foreigner talk could be perceived as convergence (to facilitate communicative effectiveness) or as divergence (mimicking inadequacies). Replying in English could be seen as convergence to an outgroup member perceived as having comparatively limited ability in Japanese or as an overt rebuff of the speaker's attempts at converging towards Japanese linguistic norms and culture.

The respondents were asked to rate the native speakers on a number of scales that included 'internationally minded', 'highly educated', 'polite' and 'sincere'. They rated responding in English as the most international strategy and symbolic of higher educational attainment. Interestingly, too, with the non-native speakers who were best able to speak Japanese, replying in English was also seen as polite. So although responding to an approach in Japanese by using English could be seen in objective terms as divergence, there was much goodwill attached to this, and so it could be seen as a form of convergence at a psychological level. Responding in foreigner talk was viewed as the most polite option regardless of the level of proficiency of the non-native speaker. Replying in standard Japanese was seen as the least empathetic response, even with high proficiency speakers of Japanese. Ross and Shortreed's own interpretation of these attitudinal reactions is in terms of language competition, in which both groups are attempting to converge simultaneously towards one another.

The notion of psychological accommodation in their study has also emerged elsewhere in accommodation research and is another important distinction to make, especially in instances where the objective communication behaviour opposes the psychological motive. There is arguably a distinction to be made also between subjective accommodation and psychological accommodation. The former can be said to relate more to the extent to which objective communication adjustments are perceived by interactants (for example, the interviewees in Willemyns *et al.*'s 1997 study whose perception was that they broadened their accent much less than they had done in objective terms). An example of psychological accommodation is provided by Giles, Coupland and Coupland (1991: 33): males and females with initial romantic interests in each other might diverge to 'prototypically strong and soft communicative patterns respectively in many communities where traditional sex role ideologies abound'. But the romantic motivations suggest this is better interpreted as complementarity, or psychological convergence, rather than labelling it only as divergence on the basis of the descriptive communication features.

Platt and Weber (1984) underline the fact that miscarried accommodation attempts are by no means limited to native and non-native speaker contexts such as Singapore. Such incomplete accommodation (underaccommodation) and inappropriate accommodation (misaccommodation), as well as overaccommodation (hyperaccommodation) also occur within the same native speaker variety between speakers from, for example, different age groups. Earlier, too, we referred to the multidimensionality of accommodation motives – social approval, communication efficiency, social identity issues – and these can be fulfilled or not fulfilled quite independently of each other.

An exploration of such issues, as well as the role of subjectivities, was carried out by Gould and Dixon (1997) in the important professional context of healthcare for older adults. The background to their study is that older adults are often unable or unwilling to comply with the drug regimens they are given by their physicians. Somewhere between 30 per cent and 40 per cent of older adults are estimated not to follow their drug instructions, and this can result in serious medical problems for this age group in particular. An important factor for this age group can be their cognitive abilities, and whether they are actually able to comprehend and recall the instructions they receive verbally from physicians. Some linguistic features have been found to assist recall, in young adults at least. These include the use of simple words and sentences, concrete rather than abstract statements and the stressing of important words.

This study looked at effects of overaccommodative speech (explained below) on the grounds that health professionals may view this kind of communication adjustment as necessary for successful communication with older adults. The hypothesis was that such adaptations in speech were a potentially facilitative way of presenting complex medical information to older adults, particularly those with lower working memory ability.

There were three groups of respondents in the study in order to allow the required comparisons. All were female. There was a younger group (mean age 21) and two older groups (mean age 71), of which one had high working memory and the other had low working memory. Each group heard a person delivering (fictitious) medical instructions. The design was matched guise with a video-recorded speaker presenting one set of instructions as if to a patient in their forties and another set of instructions to a patient in their eighties. This second version was composed with many features of overaccommodative speech: careful and exaggerated intonation, simple and repetitive sentence structures, more common words or explanatory phrases, more redundancy and explicitness, more directives and comprehension checking questions. The respondents had to do the following: recall the ideas, rate the speaker (e.g. kind, dominant) and the speech (e.g. clear, helpful), say whether they preferred the way either of these doctors gave instructions to the way their own doctor gave them, and say how likely it was that they would want one of these doctors to be their own.

The finding for recall was that the only group to benefit from overaccommodation was the older respondents with high working memory. There was no gain for the younger respondents, presumably because they were already performing at a high level. Most importantly, though, there was no benefit for the older people with low working memory, arguably the main target for these speech adjustments. Gould and Dixon note that it is possible that overaccommodative features such as repetition make the message longer and so may be more taxing on cognitive abilities.

In terms of the ratings, all groups had similarly negative reactions to the overaccommodative speaker, but nevertheless rated his overaccommodative speech features more highly. And in terms of instruction preferences, 42 per cent preferred their own doctor's instructions to those of the neutrally speaking one, and 82 per cent preferred their own doctor's instructions to those of the overaccommodative one. Similarly, they were more likely to prefer to have the neutrally speaking doctor as their own than to have the overaccommodative one. Both the older and younger respondents found the overaccommodative speaker patronising and demeaning. Hence, even if the communication style increased the memory performance of some of the older patients, it was nevertheless the least acceptable to them. As Gould and Dixon emphasise, if a positive doctor–patient relationship is important in gaining high levels of compliance with medical regimens, as many health researchers have claimed, then these kinds of speech adjustments can be of some significant detriment (1997: 66).

DISCOURSE DEVELOPMENTS

Acccommodation theory and research has undergone some significant developments since the original formulation in the 1970s. Much, though not all, of the work reviewed above, for example, has been experimental in design, with a focus on the receptive side of accommodation, with variables often highly controlled, and with evaluations of generally monologic accommodative shifts recorded on audio-tape. Countering this, Coupland (1984) argued for more discursive approaches alongside such studies, in order to ascertain and examine how communication is accommodated in real social interaction. 'Sociolinguistics', he points out, 'is acutely aware of the possible gap between elicited and (unknowingly) observed speech, between controlled and uncontrolled data' (p. 52).

His study examined conversations between a travel agency assistant and fifty-one clients, all of whom, including the assistant, were natives of the city (Cardiff) in which the study took place, and had some degree of locally accented speech. It was presumed that, for the assistant, communication efficiency and social approval were relevant criteria for success, and that arguably such assistants are employed to ensure that these occur.

In his sociolinguistic analysis, Coupland tracked and quantified the use of four phonological variables that reflected social and stylistic variation in Cardiff English. The pattern that emerged was that the assistant did appear to be attempting, consciously or unconsciously, to match the speech features of her interlocutors and to reduce speech dissimilarities. However, Coupland offers an alternative interpretation to the assistant's speech behaviour, suggesting that the 'matching' socio-linguistic product is only incidental. She can be seen as not simply attempting to reproduce the levels of standardness and non-standardness she identifies in her interlocutors, but as trying to project a persona that is similar to those of her interlocutors by trying to reduce dissimilarities in social images, while also trying to project one that is suited to her contextual role. Since this explanation proposes that there is a set of interpretive procedures between reception and production (rather than simple matching), it can be seen as an interpretive formulation of accommodation theory.

An important issue here is that the accommodation studies reviewed above have not adequately considered the differences between a whole range of speech features. As much of the language attitudes research reviewed in this book has shown, phonological behaviour carries regu-lar and specific social meanings in a speech community (such as intelli-gence, competence, level of education, social class, trustworthiness, kindness) in a way that is unlikely with some other features studied in accommodation research (e.g. utterance length). Coupland argues that the assistant could be seen as trying to position herself at various points between the poles of standardness and non-standardness in order to be perceived as trustworthy and competent, and certainly to avoid being perceived as incompetent or untrustworthy. Such judge-ments are of course receiver-based, and her sociolinguistic accommo-dation can be seen as attempts to indicate to interlocutors that she deserves to be awarded such attributes. As Coupland notes, the accom-modation motivation of 'desiring social approval' does not capture the way in which attitudinal dimensions (social attractiveness, compe-tence, etc.) profile independently with different phonological varieties. Interestingly, he points to one instance in his data where the assistant shifts to produce a succession of non-standard phonological variants before shifting back again to a more standard style. This succession cannot be seen as a 'matching' response to non-standard patterns in the interlocutor's speech. But her shift to non-standard forms coin-cides with the clients considering leaving work early in order to get to the airport in time for their flight, and so she appears to be projecting the role of a co-conspirator. Having in this way emphasised social attractiveness (e.g. trustworthiness, goodwill), she then reverts to more standard forms to emphasise once more her efficiency and competence. A shift to non-standard variants that constitutes linguistic divergence can be viewed here as psychological convergence. Competence, trustworthiness and goodwill, as primary dimensions of credibility (e.g. McCroskey and Young 1981), are likely to constitute critical social images in such service encounters.

Coupland's interpretive approach to accommodation has been pursued in a great deal of recent work in this field. Ferrara (1991), for example, has pursued this approach analysing therapy sessions. There are many tokens of individual phonological variables in a single utterance, and so accommodation to these can occur almost instantly in encounters with strangers, as in Coupland's study. However, features of other levels of language occur less frequently and so are unlikely to be accommodatable until later stages (where there are later stages). Ferrara examined series of therapy sessions with clients over a period of time to see how these other levels of language were accommodated. In this professional context, therapists have to tread a careful path between projecting high competence and high benevolence. Amongst her findings was the significant discovery that, in the sessions from clients and therapists who had worked together over a two-year period, there were frequent instances of discourse collaboratives (e.g. the completion of sentences begun by another), as well as echoing and mirroring (repetition of another's utterance in an adjacent utterance). These types of discursive accommodation facilitate the rapport about the beliefs and actions of the client and are motivated towards the ultimate wellbeing of the client (p. 216). Ferrara's study highlights the value of longitudinal studies in contexts of sustained interaction, and the value of investigating a range of specific professional contexts.

Collaboratives, echoing and mirroring are examples of 'discourse attuning strategies', and these constitute an important elaboration of communication accommodation theory to incorporate a broader range of 'addressee foci'. These include such phenomena as giving attention to the addressee's conversational needs and role relationships. For example, a speaker may try to facilitate a conversation partner's participation by offering a turn (and perhaps foregoing one's own), working to redress face threats, eliciting disclosable information and providing encouraging backchannelling. These can all be regarded as psychological convergence. Conversely, speakers may overattune or underattune. Overaccommodation and underaccommodation would fall under these rubrics, processes that have been identified in many areas of research (see, for example, Yaeger-Dror 1992), including a great deal of work in intergenerational and lifespan communication (see, for example, Coupland *et al.* 1988). It may well be that high attuning of various kinds is a core and positive component of many kinds of supportive encounters (Giles *et al.* 1991), but sometimes evoking negative attitudinal responses and having unintended detrimental effects.

QUESTIONNAIRE-BASED INTERGENERATIONAL RESEARCH

Such discursive accommodation strategies have also been built into questionnaires with rating scales to elicit quantitative evaluations of intergenerational communication. Some larger scale surveys have used such materials to examine perceptions and evaluations across cultures (e.g. Giles, Makoni and Dailey's 2006 comparison of perceptions of communication and ageing among young adult Ghanaians, South Africans and North Americans), and across ranges of age groups within a culture. Williams and Garrett (2002), for example, collected data from 490 adults in the UK aged between 20 and 59, who evaluated their communication experiences with elderly adults (65–85 years), young teenagers (13–16 years), and their own age peers. Overall, communication from the elderly adults was viewed as non-accommodative (e.g. closed-minded, complaining about life and health, talking down to others). This was most marked in the evaluations given by 20–29 year olds, while older respondents had a more positive view of communication with the elderly. Young teenagers were generally viewed as less accommodative in their communication (e.g. less supportive, less complimenting, less attentive), more non-communicative (e.g. giving short answers, drying up in conversation) and self-promotional (e.g. trying to impress, cheeky, acting superior, talking about their own lives).

Williams and Garrett (submitted) also employed multiple regression statistical analysis on data from young teenagers (aged 12–16) to establish what kinds of communication qualities were associated with what the respondents saw as 'good communication'. They found that the teenagers' satisfaction with their interaction with the oldest age group was affected by the degree to which those older people seemed overbearing (e.g. talked down to them, gave unwanted advice), and the degree to which the teenagers themselves felt able to find and talk about topics of conversation more relevant to the older person's needs, and whether or not the teenagers tended to perceive the interaction in intergroup terms (e.g. they were aware of age differences, felt and acted like a typical younger person).

Teenagers' reported communication satisfaction with their peers was linked to the degree to which their peers were accommodative (e.g. gave useful advice, were kind and helpful, listened), low in non-communicativeness (i.e. they kept the conversation going), and the degree to which they themselves felt they could find common topics that they enjoyed. Their communication satisfaction with young adults (20–25 years) was related to how accommodative they found the young adults and how far the teenagers themselves felt they could adjust their communication and the topic to their conversation partner, as well as the degree of discomfort they felt in these conversations.

These results show that these young teenagers feel that topic accommodation (i.e. their finding common and enjoyable topics) is important with conversational partners across all these age groups. It implies that the teenagers strive to find common ground when they converse with others and the more success they have with this, the more satisfied they feel. This is perhaps part of the development of communication skills as teenagers mature into young adults. Beyond topic accommodation, though, it is notable that a standard view on what constitutes good communication (an assumption of most communication skills training programmes) does not emerge. For the teenagers, what constitutes good communication depends on which age groups are involved. For example, it was only in communication with the older people that the teenagers found intergroup salience to be significant. It was not a factor for them in their communication with young adults. Interestingly, this is not reciprocated by the young adults themselves; Williams, Garrett and Tennant (2004) found that, in their conversations with teenagers, the young adults saw intergroup salience as a barrier to satisfaction, suggesting that young adults are more likely to discriminate between themselves and teenagers in intergroup terms than vice versa.

CONCLUSION

Communication accommodation theory, then, has developed considerably, originating as a socio-psychological model for understanding bilingual and accent shifts in interactions, and moving to 'an interdisciplinary model of relational and identity processes in communicative interaction' (Coupland and Jaworski 1997: 241). As we have seen, much communication accommodation research has addressed important professional contexts, some even involving (over the longer term) issues of 'life and death' (Giles *et al.* 1991: 47). Research drawing upon and developing accommodation theory has improved our understanding of a good range of such fields. These include, as we have seen above, lifespan and intergenerational communication (for a comprehensive review of this field, see Williams and Nussbaum 2001), health contexts (see also Hamilton 1991; Street 1991), second language encounters (see also Zuengler 1991) and employment interviews, but research extends to other domains too, such as courtrooms (e.g. Linell 1991), police–civilian encounters (Giles, Fortman, Dailey, Barker, Hajek, Anderson and Rule 2006) and organisations (e.g. Bourhis 1991).

Communication accommodation theory has drawn our attention, then, to the dynamic and interactive nature of communication and our motivations in its process, including effective communication, attitudinal responses and our social and personal identities. It also helps us to understand why such motivations are not wholly, or not at all, fulfilled at times. Attitudes and motivations feature not only in our perceptions, evaluations and attributions as we encounter such adjustments and attunements; they are also components of our own communicative competence that underpin, consciously or unconsciously, our moment-to-moment deployment of linguistic, non-verbal and discursive resources to achieve our communication goals.

FURTHER READING ON CHAPTER 7

There is a useful chapter on accommodation theory in:

Giles, H. and Coupland, N., 1991, *Language: contexts and consequences.* Buckingham: Open University Press.

And a valuable collection of papers on a range of professional contexts in:

Giles, H., Coupland, J. and Coupland, N. (eds.), 1991, *Contexts of accommodation.* Cambridge: Cambridge University Press.

The following chapter contains discussion of accommodation theory in relation to multilingual communication:

Bourhis, R., El-Geledi, S. and Sachdev, I., 2007, Language, ethnicity and intergroup relations, in A. Weatherall, B. Watson and C. Gallois (eds.), *Language, discourse and social psychology* (pp. 15–50). Basingstoke: Palgrave Macmillan.

QUESTIONS FOR CHAPTER 7

1. In your own words, summarise the differences between objective, subjective and psychological accommodation.
2. Think of occasions on which you have been conscious of accommodation processes during conversations: for example, where there has been noticeable divergence, as you or someone else has tried to maintain a distance from an interlocutor. Or where accommodation has 'misfired' in the way that Platt and Weber found. Were any accusations made? If so, what were they?

8 Language attitudes in professional contexts

In the four professional contexts considered in this chapter – legal, health, education and employment – communication at all levels is of paramount significance. Life opportunities, life quality, and indeed life and death can depend on it, from courtroom examinations to employment interviews, to patient–doctor exchanges to teacher–student interaction. Some areas are also sites of much controversy regarding discrimination (see, for example, Roberts, Davies and Jupp 1992; Lippi-Green 1994; 1997). Researching them is essential, but at the same time fraught with difficulties, such as the confidentiality of authentic data, the need at times to rely on simulated (rather than real-life) events, assembling people working in the respective fields to participate in these. At the same time, each of them is multifaceted. Legal processes, for example, cover many areas, from police investigations to jury verdicts to parole boards. Courtroom factors alone include characteristics and behaviour of lawyers, jurors, defendants, plaintiffs and victims, and courtroom messages include *voir dire* messages, opening and closing statements, direct and cross examination, and judges' instructions. Inevitably, research is uneven across areas in these fields, with some still relatively unresearched, and with small clusters of studies in some areas allowing us to see more patterning in the data.

LAW

Given the scope of the field set out above, there are many points at which language attitudes could play a role, and findings in one such area (e.g. judgements of guilt) might not apply in another (e.g. sentencing). (See Danet 1990; and Reinhard 2002 for overviews.) Language attitudes work has tended to focus on evaluations of (at least simulated) police interviews with suspects, and of courtroom testimonies. Recent research directions have included the study of police communication in the community, and the study of how voices are described to police in cases where victims or witnesses hear the voice of, but do not see, the person committing the crime.

Law enforcement

Giles *et al.* (2006) investigated public perceptions and evaluations of the police and law enforcement in California. The more accommodative the police were seen to be in their communication with the public, the more positively they were regarded. This was essentially the same for all three groups of respondents: English-speaking adults, Spanish-speaking adults, and university students. Accommodation was even a stronger factor than trust, and also than socio-demographic variables such as age and ethnicity. Giles *et al.* conclude, 'given that it is commonly estimated that 97 per cent of police work is related to or communicating with the public and their issues . . . accommodative practices can be enormously important in this regard'. Similar results for accommodation and the police have been found in Russia and the People's Republic of China (Giles, Hajek, Barker, Anderson, Chen, Zhang and Hummert 2007).

Communication in courtrooms

Bell and Loftus (1985) reviewed research on vivid testimonies in courtroom scenarios and concluded that vividness can affect jurors' judgements of guilt. They considered vividness in terms of the degree of detail of events described in testimonies. Research into persuasive effects of vivid language generally (i.e. not limited to legal contexts) has produced some very mixed findings, in part because of varying operationalisations of vividness across studies, but also because effects may depend on a range of conditions, such as the credibility of the speaker or whether the communication is face-to-face or in print (see Hamilton and Hunter 1998 and Hosman 2002 for overviews). In the legal setting, Bell and Loftus suggest that vivid testimony may have more effect than pallid testimony when there are contradictory testimonies.

Lind and O'Barr (1979) investigated the effects of 'simultaneous speech'. Respondents heard tapes of male witness and male lawyer interaction during testimony either with no simultaneous speech or with three different degrees of perseverance with simultaneous speech on the part of the attorney. Respondents judged simultaneous speech to indicate the lawyer's loss of control over the interaction; the more he persevered, the less fair he was seen to be to the witness.

Far more attention has been given to investigating the effects of powerful and powerless speech in courtrooms. O'Barr and Atkins (1980) examined transcripts from 150 hours of trials in a North Carolina court to see if the features of Lakoff's (1975) 'women's language' were in fact more attributable to powerlessness rather than to gender. Features investigated (see also O'Barr 1982; Conley and O'Barr 1998) included:

Hesitations (e.g. *well, uh*, yes, *um*, that's correct)
Hedges (e.g. *sort of, I guess*)
Intensifers (e.g. I *really* agree with you . . . *very* much.)
Superpolite forms (e.g. would you please, I'd really appreciate it if)
Tag questions (e.g. it's cold, *isn't it?*)
Disclaimers (e.g. I know this is *a stupid thing to ask*, but . . .?)
Deictic phrases (e.g. That car *over there* is the one that hit the garden wall.)

O'Barr and Atkins' conclusion was that these features correlated with powerlessness, regardless of gender. Whether powerless language cuts across sexes or is essentially women's language is still disputed (e.g. Coates 2004). Nevertheless, the features referred to as powerless language have attracted much research attention. Burrell and Koper (1998) conducted a meta-analysis of twenty studies on the effects of powerful language, of which thirteen were framed in legal settings, and overall, powerful language was perceived as more persuasive than powerless language, and to lead to increased credibility.

Hosman (2002) notes that there have been two approaches to investigating powerful language. One examines it as a cluster of features, but the other is a molecular approach giving attention to individual components. This second approach has revealed some differences amongst the features. Bradac and Mulac (1984) found that, while hedges and hesitations were associated with less credibility, attractiveness and dynamism (i.e. powerlessness), politeness was perceived as powerful. Wright and Hosman (1983) found hedges and intensifiers working differentially in the testimonies in their study, with hedges affecting judgements of both credibility and social attractiveness, but intensifiers affecting only the latter. Hosman (1989) found that intensifiers were perceived as powerless when used in combination with hesitations and hedges, but powerful when used on their own. This molecular approach seems important in research looking at different professional contexts. For example, features suggesting uncertainty (such as hesitations) might carry more, or a different, significance in a courtroom than elsewhere (see Haleta's 1996 educational study below).

Accent and accommodation in suspects

Seggie's (1983) Australian study investigated effects of accents: RP, broad Australian and Malaysian Chinese. The inclusion of the latter was motivated by a significant increase in immigration during the

1970s, along with a growth of trading and cultural links. Three groups of respondents each read details of one of three crimes: a crime of violence against a middle-aged man, a crime of violence against property and a non-violent crime of embezzlement. The respondents were told that police had interviewed a large number of people, and they would hear recordings of three of them, one of whom they had now charged with the crime. Respondents had to rate each speaker on their probability of having committed the crime. In a second stage, they were asked to imagine that the trial had taken place and to recommend the appropriate type and duration of punishment they regarded as appropriate: imprisonment or prison with hard labour.

The broad-accented Australian speaker was judged more likely to be guilty of the crimes involving violence. The RP speaker was seen as more likely to be guilty of embezzlement. The Australian and RP speakers were viewed as more likely to be guilty of these respective crimes than the Asian speakers were to be guilty of any of these crimes. There was no difference between the speakers in the punishments recommended for the different crimes. Seggie notes that the uniformity in punishment recommendations may have been due to the design of the study, since respondents heard all three voices when they made their recommendations, and simply had to imagine that each of them was guilty in turn, so the task lacked some verisimilitude. He also suggests the low probability of guilt for the Asian speaker as probably a reflection of there not being a highly formed and widely applied stereotype of such speakers in Australia at that stage, at least in the context in which the study was conducted. The study is also of interest in that it provides some indication that legal context can eclipse the social judgements of trustworthiness and sincerity that we have seen awarded to non-standard speakers in so many other studies. Seggie points to the implication that 'such social judgements might therefore be subject to relatively easy extinction' (p. 204).

A similar study, this time involving accommodation, was conducted in South Africa by Dixon, Tredoux, Durrheim and Foster (1994). White English-speaking South Africans, also competent in Afrikaans, listened to audio-recordings of an exchange between a middle-aged male English-speaking interrogator and a young male suspect with a Cape Afrikaans accent, pleading his innocence. The suspect either responded in English (convergence) or with lapses into Afrikaans (partial divergence) or only in Afrikaans (complete divergence). The respondents had to rate his likelihood of guilt, and fill in scales for the usual evaluative dimensions. There were two crime types: violence against a person, and passing fraudulent cheques. In line with Seggie's results, Dixon *et al.* found that the suspects were more likely to be viewed as guilty when they were accused of blue collar crimes than of white collar crimes, regardless of how they accommodated. Hence, it seemed that raters saw the speakers more as members of a social category than individuals. In line with Dixon *et al.*'s predictions from accommodation theory, the suspects who converged into English were rated significantly less guilty than those who diverged into Cape Afrikaans, but this occurred regardless of the type of crime. In terms of the three attitudinal dimensions (superiority, social attractiveness and dynamism), although the divergent speakers were rated lower on superiority, social attractiveness ratings seemed not to be related to the guilt attributions of these White South African respondents. This lack of relationship between social attractiveness and attributions of guilt provides some support for Seggie's suggestion that the commonly found link between non-standard varieties and social attractiveness may be eradicated in these kinds of legal contexts.

Dixon, Mahoney and Cocks (2002) conducted the same type of study in the UK, with black and white suspects with RP and Birmingham (Brummie) guises. In chapter 4, we saw how Brummie-accented speakers were particularly downgraded in the study by Giles (1970). It was assumed that a Brummie speaker would be associated with a working-class culture. The study again involved blue collar and white collar crime (armed robbery and cheque fraud). The Brummie suspect was rated significantly more guilty than the RP speaker, regardless of the type of crime. But an interaction in the data showed that black Brummie-speakers were the most highly associated with committing the blue collar offence. In this study, in terms of personality traits, both the superiority and the social attractiveness dimensions were associated with guilt. These findings, then, contrast with those of Seggie (1983) and of Dixon *et al.* (1994) just reviewed. In this context, at least, it seemed possible that the Brummie-speakers might be seen as less assured and more associated with 'shiftiness' than the RP speakers. In any event, the role of the social attractiveness dimension, given the differences in these three studies, merits further research in this applied setting and in other contexts.

It is important to note that in none of these legal context accent studies so far was there any evidence included. Dixon and Mahoney (2004) investigated whether there would still be accent effects when there was evidence to be considered, and whether accent would have more impact when the evidence was weak rather than strong. Apart from the inclusion of evidence, the design of the study was similar to the previous one, with Brummie and RP as the two accents. In this study, however, Dixon and Mahoney found that the suspects' accents did not affect how guilty they were thought to be. The strength of the evidence itself affected perceptions of guilt, as well as the likelihood of being accused of a crime in the future. It would seem from this study that just weak evidence is enough for mock jurors to base their appraisals of guilt on the facts of the case rather than on the suspect's accent. One possible explanation, applying the ELM (see chapter 6), is that evidence can provide a focus for central processing; without this, accent might function as a peripheral cue. Nevertheless, certainly accent had some significance in this study; the Brummie-accented speakers were seen as more typically criminal and more likely to be accused of a future crime than the RP speakers.

There are certainly some questions about many of the studies conducted into mock juror judgements, whether focusing on accent or on other variables such as physical attractiveness. Respondents in these studies generally make their own individual judgements, for instance, whereas real-life juries engage in social interaction and deliberation. In addition, the scenarios in the studies are very brief, and this might exaggerate effects of extralegal factors. (See Mazzella and Feingold 1994 for a review of such matters.) Nevertheless, these last studies still show that, estimates of guilt aside, accent, as with other social variables (Mazzella and Feingold 1994), may influence evaluations on dimensions that have legal significance. This points to a need for more studies, of varying designs and in a greater range of contexts.

A new direction: an 'audiofit' for voice descriptions from earwitnesses

A new forensic initiative in the language attitudes field has been pursued by Griffiths (2009). The background to his research direction is that, in cases of serious crimes where there are eyewitnesses (or victims themselves) who are able to provide descriptions of the physical appearance of perpetrators, the police have long used techniques to produce graphical representations of the perpetrators' faces from descriptions which people have been able to give them from memory. Such techniques have ranged from the use of trained artists to the use of interchangeable templates of the various facial features (e.g. 'Photofit' in the UK, and 'Identi-Kit' in the USA), and more recently the use of computer software (e.g. E-Fit in the UK, and FACES in the USA). These techniques, then, allow the police to organise and exploit these physical descriptions into a format that is more usable in their investigations.

In many crimes, though, the victims themselves are not able see the perpetrator, and there are no eyewitnesses either. Perpetrators may cover their faces, for example, or they may attack someone in darkness, or in some other way prevent the victim and anyone else from seeing them. However, in some cases, the victim or witnesses hear the person speak, and are able to provide a voice description, and this might be the main clue to the identity of the person concerned. Griffiths (2009), drawing upon the language attitudes field and its focus on how people perceive, describe, comment on and evaluate the speech of others, was interested in whether it might be possible to develop a 'forensic audiofit', a voice-description to provide a 'sibling' (p. 307) to the visual techniques referred to above. Was there some way of organising these kinds of 'non-expert' (or non-linguist) voice descriptions to produce something more usable in investigations?

His research involved respondents commenting on audio-recordings of supposed 'suspects' being interviewed in police stations in relation to particular crimes such as sexual assault and mugging. The suspects in the audio-recordings spoke in various British accents. The respondents were asked to complete a number of tasks, which gathered a range of quantitative and qualitative data about the speakers (including folklinguistic data – see chapter 11). From his analysis of the responses, Griffiths concludes that there is the potential to obtain quite specific descriptions of voices from non-linguists, and sets out a prototype audiofit.

His audiofit framework comprises three stages, and Griffiths also points to the importance of sequencing and types of questioning within the framework as a whole. The three stages are geo-social referencing, physical speech characteristics and comparative social associations. In the geo-social referencing stage, questions are asked about the geographical or social associations that the earwitness makes when they hear the voice. By this is meant finding out such things as whether they recognise the accent, whether they associate it with any region or with any social group, whether they noticed anything distinctive about the voice. In the second stage – physical speech characteristics – there is discussion of possible voice characteristics, including scaled characteristics such as pitch, speech rate, confidence, loudness, and also some qualities that lend themselves less to scaling, such as the presence or absence of speech impediments, and qualities such as 'rough', 'whispery', etc. Earwitnesses are also invited to add any other remarks of their own. The third stage – comparative social associations – asks earwitnesses such things as whether the voice sounds like or reminds them of anyone or anything.

Griffiths underlines that this is an initial exploration to investigate potential and feasibility, and he also says that the audiofit 'is unlikely ever to play as significant a role in the investigative process as its visually-oriented sibling' (p. 307). Even so, it is clearly more than just a new avenue to pursue in the language attitudes field; its applied focus may have the potential to make a significant difference in the forensic context in time.

EDUCATION

A great deal of language attitudes work relates to educational issues. Teachers' and students' attitudes to language issues are frequently investigated, and implications sought for pedagogical and curricular matters (e.g. Winford 1975 on teachers' attitudes to speech varieties in Trinidad; Chandler, Robinson and Noyes 1988 on students' attitudes to classroom use of grammatical terminology; Llurda 2005 on non-native foreign language teachers). Significantly, various facets of language attitudes are key components in social psychological and cognitive approaches to motivation in second language acquisition. In Gardner and Lambert's work, for example (e.g. Gardner 1985), attitudes to learning the language and to the second language group are features influencing learners' orientations in second language learning, which in turn guide their motivation towards certain goals such as instrumental (e.g. getting a better job) or integrative goals (e.g. interacting with members of the second language community). More recent developments, such as Williams and Burden's (1997) framework, maintain the view that attitudes constitute a critical internal factor in second language motivation. For a brief overview, see Dörnyei (2000).

Studies looking at evaluative reactions to speech features can be divided into school studies and college/university level studies, which we cover in that order. As Edwards (1982) argues, 'schools represent the single most important point of contact between speakers of different language varieties' (p. 27).

Evaluative reactions to speech features in schools

In previous chapters, we have referred to Harari and McDavid's (1973) study of stereotypical associations of pupils' names and how these appeared able to influence assessment (see also Adler, Rosenfeld and Towne 1995), and to Cairns and Duriez' (1976) study of recall when children in Northern Ireland received spoken passages in Belfast, Dublin or RP accents. Choy and Dodd (1976) also looked at the learning implications of using different language varieties in schools. Specifically, they studied 10–11-year-old pupils who were either dominant in Hawaiian English (HE) or in Standard American English (SE), and who were studying in a school in Hawaii where learning and testing were conducted through SE. Choy and Dodd measured comprehension and the degree of processing required (by measuring reaction times) when these pupils heard a story in SE and HE. The teachers were also given a questionnaire in which they were asked about their expectations of the pupils' likely performance in school subjects. Choy and Dodd found that the HE students performed better with HE materials and the SE students did better with SE materials. Similarly, HE students needed more processing time when listening to SE materials, while SE students needed more time for HE. Several implications are drawn from such findings, one of which is that measuring pupils' verbal skills in a dialect that is not their own is arguably detrimental (p. 191). There were also significant differences in the teachers' evaluations of the SE and HE speaking students, with HE students seen as performing less well in language arts and non-language arts related subjects. Choy and Dodd point to the possibility of this leading to differential treatment and expectations of the two groups. Good performance on HE material by HE students was not linked to better teacher attitudes towards the HE students in mainstream academic areas. Such findings are important if teachers' attitudes and expectations are seen as playing a role in pupils' academic success or failure.

Seligman, Tucker and Lambert (1972) focused on whether language attitudes affect student assessment. Each respondent (students at a teacher-training college in Canada) received a photograph of a pupil, then heard a recording of a pupil reading a passage, and then saw a drawing and composition, all ostensibly from the same 8–9-year-old student. They were asked to integrate this information into a composite evaluation of the student. There were seven such students, all hypothetical, since the drawings, compositions, voices and photographs were components mixed from different (real) students. (Hence this was a verbal guise study.) The components used in the study had been evenly balanced through pilot work. Half the compositions used had been previously assessed as poor and half as excellent. Voices had been rated for a range of qualities too (e.g. on scales for 'in/articulate', 'sounds un/intelligent'). Speech style was found to play an important part in the respondents' assessments, and it seemed therefore that their evaluations of the children's academic ability did not rest entirely on relevant information.

A subsequent and similar study by Granger, Mathews, Quay and Verner (1977) tried to identify what it might be about the speech features that affected judgements. While task quality was matched (as in Seligman *et al.*'s compositions and drawings), the audiorecorded children were of middle or low socio-economic class, and black or white.

The findings showed that both race and class had effects. Teacher evaluations were negative for lower-class students, with no difference according to whether they were black or white. On the other hand, middle-class white speakers were evaluated significantly better than middle-class black speakers. Again, then, it was found that evaluations of the students were based more on speech features than on school performance.

Beyond these three significant school studies from the 1970s, Boyd (2003) investigated the judgements by school principals and teacher trainers of the professional suitability of foreign-accented teachers in Sweden. Analysing through phonological, grammatical and lexical measures the Swedish proficiency of the teachers, and comparing these with the respondents' own judgements of the teachers' skills in Swedish and their suitability as teachers, Boyd concluded that the respondents' judgements of the teachers' accentedness were influencing their perceptions of other aspects of their language proficiency (cf. Levin et al. 1994 in chapter 6) and, most importantly, their suitability for teaching.

Tertiary education

At university level, research has tended to focus on the evaluative responses of the students to various communication characteristics in teachers. Andersen, Norton and Nussbaum (1981) investigated student reactions to a range of verbal and non-verbal communication behaviours that included teacher immediacy (behaviours to increase non-verbal interaction and reduce distance, physically and psychologically) and communicator style (verbal behaviours evaluated as 'animated', 'dramatic', 'dominant', etc.). These were found to enhance students' perceptions of teacher effectiveness and likeability, and students' intentions to enrol in more courses, but no relationship was found with actual student learning.

At a more explicitly linguistic level, Haleta (1996) examined the effects of teachers' use of powerful or powerless language in university classrooms, in terms of the presence or absence of hesitations. Use of the powerful variant led to higher scores on dynamism, credibility and status. Students reported feeling more uncertainty when teachers used a powerless style, and expressed concerns that the teacher seemed unprepared and lacking organisation, and they questioned the teacher's ability and whether the teacher would be delivering the right information.

In a similar vein to Boyd's (2003) work, Rubin and Smith (1990) addressed the issue of the presence of many international teaching assistants in US universities, and the frequent claim by students that the assistants lack adequate English language proficiency. In fact, they found in their study that 40 per cent of the students avoided these classes. Rubin and Smith asked undergraduates to evaluate audio-recorded non-native English speaking teaching assistants (in this case, Chinese) delivering short talks on a humanities or a science topic with moderate or high levels of accentedness. Measures of comprehension were also taken. They found that comprehension was the same for both levels of accentedness, as designed in this study. (Interestingly, too, in Gill (1994), while students recalled most information when delivered by North American teachers, there was no difference in recall when listening to information delivered in British or Malaysian English.) As in Boyd's study, Rubin and Smith found that the higher the level of perceived accentedness, the lower the teaching ratings received by the teacher.

Listening comprehension scores in Rubin and Smith were found to correlate with students' previous experience of courses taught by international teaching assistants, and Rubin and Smith suggested an interpretation that 'North American undergraduates need to be trained to listen to accented English' (p. 350). However, in a further study by Rubin (1992), two lectures by an American native speaker of English were audio-recorded. While listening to these, the undergraduates saw a picture of either a Chinese or a Caucasian woman. Even though all students heard exactly the same lectures in standard American English, they understood less when they saw the Chinese photograph. This suggested, then, that even if assistants were able to engage in pronunciation training that enabled them to achieve standard American English speech, there could still be an ethnicity bias amongst the students.

In Rubin (1992), undergraduates were asked to attend lectures taught by international teaching assistants. However, this was not found to increase listening skills, and even made some more critical of the assistants' performance. Other studies, too, have found negative or less positive attitudes resulting from experience with assistants (e.g. Matross, Paige and Hendricks 1982; Bailey 1984; Plakans 1997). However, other methods to improve attitudes and comprehension have been proposed and tested by Derwing, Rossiter and Munro (2002). Their approach comprised training in cross-cultural awareness with some explicit instruction on the nature of an L2 accent. Although no advantages were detected in comprehension, there were improvements in the students' confidence in their communication with L2 speakers, and more favourable attitudes towards accented speech. It does, then, seem possible through intervention to change these negative attitudes.

HEALTH

'Communication patterns have important effects on patient comprehension, recall of information, compliance to treatment regimen
and satisfaction with care' (Hinckley, Craig and Anderson 1989: 520).
Hence it is unsurprising to find a strong focus on how communication
can impact on patients' attitudes and compliance with a focus on the
prevention and cure of illness. But as we saw in chapter 7 in the study by
Gould and Dixon (1997), effects of communication patterns can
be multidimensional and complex. There is also evidence that stereotypes about certain patient groups are as prevalent amongst healthcare
professionals (Dryden and Giles 1987) as anywhere else, and effects have
been shown in a number of investigations (e.g. Platt and Weber 1984).

Verbal forms

Some research attention has been given to attitudinal responses to medical jargon. Such terminology may be used to establish a physician's
authority, to symbolise 'expert power' and establish credibility, and
to determine role relationship with patients. Different social (e.g. socio-
economic) groups may have different preferences for the amount of medical jargon used, although this has yet to be shown empirically. Bourhis,
Roth and MacQueen (1989) studied medical and everyday language in a
Canadian hospital from a communication accommodation perspective.
Doctors and patients held competing perceptions as to whether they were
converging to each other. Each group believed they themselves were doing
so, but this was disputed in each case by the other group. The nurses, on the
other hand, reported playing a 'communication broker' role, converging
to the doctors' medical language and to the everyday language of the
patients (and this was corroborated by the doctors and patients). Doctors,
patients and nurses all viewed everyday language as more appropriate
than medical language for communication with patients, but they also
felt that an equal mixture of the two was an acceptable compromise.

Other work on verbal forms has included question-asking. This
has provided at least some agreement that patients tend to have more
positive attitudes to their medical care when they are encouraged
to ask more questions (Hinckley *et al.* 1989: 524). In addition, the
use of swearwords has been investigated in counselling interactions.
Counsellors' inclusion of swearwords in conversation is likely to lead
to less compliance by clients, and to decrease the likelihood that they
will seek advice (e.g. Kottke and MacLeod 1989; Kurklen and Kassinove
1991; Sazer and Kassinove 1991).

Speech rates

Speech rate also evokes differing attitudinal responses in specific contexts. Ray, Ray and Zahn (1991), for example, found that when a physician was delivering a message about a highly serious illness, moderate speech rates led to the highest ratings of professional competence, while fast speakers were judged as less professionally competent. This was not a study of doctor–patient interaction, however, since there was no interaction involved, as Ray *et al.* point out, but simply the delivery of a message. In addition, the respondents were undergraduates, and in this context, that may limit generalisability to some key social groups. Buller and Aune (1988), for example, found that optimum speech rates may depend on factors such as the encoding ability of the sender and the decoding ability of the receiver.

Positivity and negativity

Some research has focused on various sources and measures of positivity and negativity in medical interactions. In an early study of intonation qualities, Milmoe, Rosenthal, Blane, Chafetz and Wolf (1967) recorded the voices of Chief Medical Officers (CMOs) who were responsible for the diagnosis and referral of alcoholics. A section was then taken from their responses to the question 'what has been your experience with alcoholics?' Undergraduates had to rate the excerpts in filtered form (in which only intonation was audible) and normal unfiltered form on measures of anger, irritation, professionalism, etc. It was then possible to see how each CMO's excerpt was rated to see if any particular qualities patterned with the CMOs who in practice had been most successful in their referrals. Milmoe *et al.* found that the voices of the most successful CMOs were those judged less angry in the intonation-only condition and more anxious in the normal condition. This combination of avoiding anger and showing concern seemed likely to be the most successful combination. Roter, Hall and Katz (1987) also put speech samples through a filter to isolate intonation patterns. In their study, patients reported the highest satisfaction ratings when they heard intonation patterns judged to be 'negative' in combination with supportive message content.

In some areas of healthcare, treatments need to extend over a very long period, and may involve considerable lifestyle changes. Rates of adherence to such regimens decrease markedly with time. Reinforcement Expectancy Theory (RET), reviewed in Klingle (2004), addresses how physicians can use verbal and non-verbal strategies to stave off negative attitudes in patients and increase their perseverance over time.

As we have just seen, patients appear to have a need for both approving and supportive messages from others. RET identifies three types of communication choices. The following examples are taken from Klingle (2004: 301):

> positive regard strategies (e.g. 'I know that changing one's eating habits is very difficult, but you're the kind of person who can do it')
>
> neutral regard strategies (e.g. 'You need to change your eating habits')
>
> negative regard strategies (e.g. 'You can't keep fooling around with your diet – a responsible person would know that now is the time to take charge').

People prefer to avoid negative communication and to maintain positive communication over time. Put simply, the theory proposes a mixture of positive and negative communication rather than only using one type of strategy. Research has shown different outcomes, however, for male and female physicians. During initial stages, male physicians can use both positive and negative types, but when females use negative strategies, these are less effective, and so they are limited to positive and neutral ones. However, further into the treatment period, when relationships are more established, male and female physicians have equal success switching between positive and negative strategies (Klingle 2004).

Positivity and negativity is also a factor in how messages are framed in public health campaigns. Messages can stress potential gains: for example, 'Using the right sunscreen can protect you against harmful rays.' Or they can be loss-framed messages: for example, 'If you don't use the right sunscreen, you will have no protection against harmful rays.' Gain-framed messages have been found to generate more positive attitudes towards prevention behaviours, such as sunscreen use, healthy diets, etc. Loss-framed messages have been more successful in promoting early detection checks, such as getting tested for sexually transmitted diseases, breast cancer, etc. (See Salovey, Schneider and Apanovitch 2002 for an overview.) Such a pattern might lead one to question the relative effectiveness of loss-framed messages such as 'smoking kills' on cigarette packets.

Accent studies

Fielding and Evered (1980) looked at diagnostic interviews during which patients report their symptoms to their doctor and the doctor arrives at a diagnosis to prescribe or recommend treatment. This is a critical stage in the process of medical care, and the outcomes can be of great personal significance to patients. This was a matched guise study in which medical students heard an interview between an RP-speaking doctor and a 'patient' speaking in either RP or a south-west England rural accent, describing a set of ambiguous symptoms that could signify a heart disorder. Symptoms included anxiety and tension, relationship problems and alcohol. With the RP accent, the symptoms were diagnosed as more likely to be psychosomatic than if they were presented in the regional guise. The RP speaker was also rated as having a more sophisticated vocabulary and using better grammar, even though the audio-recorded texts were identical for both guises (*cf.* Stewart *et al.* 1985; Levin *et al.* 1994; Boyd 2002). Of interest too is that the RP speaker was seen as more emotional than the regional speaker, while in so many other studies opposite judgements are found, with reserve and coldness associated with the middle-class standard. Additionally, the RP speaker was downgraded on certain competence traits relative to the regional speaker. These trait patterns might appear for RP speakers only in such specific contexts (such as seeking help through medical disclosure) and again point to the importance of contextualised studies.

Rubin, Healy, Gardiner, Zath and Moore (1997) take as their background the fact that increasing numbers of North Americans come into contact with healthcare providers originating from other countries, and they study whether linguistic stereotyping in this context affects patients' reactions and compliance with physicians' directives in the specific context of AIDS prevention messages. The messages were purportedly presented either by a male South-Asian physician with highly accented or moderately accented speech, or by a male Anglo-American. While listening, student respondents saw a photograph of either a South Asian or an Anglo-American 'doctor'.

As in the earlier mentioned studies by Rubin and Smith (1990) and Rubin (1992), the respondents did not evaluatively distinguish the two non-standard accents (high and moderate). This aside, though, when they perceived the ethnicity and accentedness of the Asian physicians, they judged them to be cold and unfriendly. However (and in contrast to Rubin 1992), the ethnicity of the speaker (operationalised through the two photographs) made no difference to what they recalled of the message. Recall was the same regardless of ethnicity and accent. In some ways, this is reassuring, but recall rates were actually rather low (well under 20 per cent of the propositions in the message), perhaps because the students assumed an unjustified familiarity with the AIDS prevention topic already (Rubin *et al.* 1997: 364). Nevertheless, intention to comply with the message, which was also unaffected by the accent or ethnicity of the speaker, was 'uniformly high'. Rubin *et al.* see room for some guarded optimism in these results, insofar as the accentedness of doctors did not appear to present barriers to patients' reactions to health advice.

EMPLOYMENT

Language attitudes studies in the employment domain have, with few exceptions, been limited to job interviews, a context fraught with complexities quite apart from social discriminatory issues (see Smith 1982). Largely, this has been on the role of accent in judgements of employment suitability. Exceptions tend to be thinly spread over a number of specific issues. For example, a study into letters of reference looked at the use of vivid language, and in contrast to the findings of Bell and Loftus (1985) in witness testimonies, found no effects on the evaluation of candidates (Ralston and Thameling 1988).

In addition, Rubin, DeHart and Heintzman (1991) examined how subordinates rate managers' communication styles. Rubin *et al.* wanted to compare reactions to styles in terms of influence strategies identified with Japanese managers (relying on altruism, duty, counsel and favour) and with American managers (direct request, reference to contractual obligations, and threat). Accent was also included. Although accent was found to be only a secondary factor, it contributed in the same direction as the influence strategies. Essentially, the subordinates preferred managers who in reality used a Japanese style but whom they erroneously perceived to be using an American style, revealing a bias that Rubin *et al.* refer to as a 'chauvinistic phenomenon' (p. 280). The study also underlines the importance of recognising that actual speech patterns and perceived speech patterns can have quite divergent effects on attitudes.

Employment selection

Although most language attitudes work on employment selection has focused on accent, a number of studies have looked at other features. Speech rates have been investigated by Street, Brady and Putman (1983), who found that listeners associated moderate to faster speech rates with more competence and social attractiveness than slower speech rates. Listeners also preferred speakers with rates similar to or marginally faster then their own. The two contexts included in their study (ordinary conversation and employment interviews) made no difference to this, although respondents felt that slow rates were more acceptable in job interviews than in conversational settings. A further feature, offensive language, has been researched by Powell, Callahan, Comans, McDonald, Mansell, Trotter and Williams (1984). They found empirical confirmation that its use by applicants in job interviews created negative impressions.

Parton, Siltanen, Hosman and Langenderfer (2002) researched the use of powerless features in simulated employment interviews. They found powerless features (here, hedges and hesitations) resulted in lower attributions of competence and employability. It is worth noting that there were two groups of respondents: undergraduates and professional interviewers. The undergraduates gave higher overall evaluations of speech styles and distinguished less between them, while the professionals evaluated the powerful style as significantly more competent than the powerless style. This raises a question about who the respondents are, or should be, in these professional studies, and we return to this at the end of the next section.

Accents in employment selection

The first comprehensive study of language attitudes in employment interviews was conducted by Hopper and Williams (1973). Employment interviewers in Texas rated recordings of males responding to questions representative of those used in job interviews. The interviewees used varieties described as standard English, Black English, Spanish-influenced English or Southern white dialect English. Apart from rating the speakers on a range of scales (designed in collaboration with the employers), the listeners also indicated the likelihood that they would hire the speakers for each of seven job categories varying from manual labour to executive positions. Analysis showed that the best predictor of hiring decisions was the rating of each speaker for intelligence and competence, especially for jobs involving executive or leadership skills. Ethnicity (Anglo-like/non-Anglo-like) was not found to be related to employment decisions.

In a second phase to this study, using only white and black speakers, competence was again found to be the best predictor of hiring for the executive positions, but, as job status decreased, the predictive power decreased. Differences due to race were apparent only for the executive position, where the standard speaker was preferred.

In a follow-up study, Hopper (1977) included more variables: race of speaker (black or white, indicated to raters on a background information sheet), standard versus non-standard accent, and qualifications. Employment interviewers rated each 'candidate' on a range of scales, including their perceived suitability for positions of salesman, supervisor and technician. Ratings of competence and likeability were the two main predictors of hiring decisions. Most significant, though, in this study, was the finding that the black speaker with a standard accent was favoured over the others for the top (salesman and supervisor) positions but not for the technician position.

Cargile (1997) conducted a matched guise study, in which a bi-dialectal native Chinese speaker presented a fictional interview response in Chinese-accented English and in Standard American English. Undergraduates (Asian and non-Asian) completed attitude scales and employment suitability scales for each of four jobs of differing status. Accent made no difference to the judgements of the two speakers, whether for suitability for the four jobs or regarding their social attractiveness, status and dynamism.

In these three studies, then, ethnicity alone arguably did not lead to any strong discrimination. However, other studies have found quite different findings for ethnicity. Rey's (1977) study in Florida had white American, black American and Cuban national candidates speaking with minimal, medium or heavy Spanish accents. White speakers were deemed the most suitable for all of the seven jobs except for manual labourer. They were seen as more suited to the executive position even by the black and Cuban judges. Black speakers were generally seen as more suitable for most jobs than the Cubans, especially if the latter were heavily accented. Similarly, de la Zerda and Hopper (1979) looked at Mexican Americans in Texas, with either Mexican-accented or standard speech. Standard speakers were seen as appropriate for high status jobs and inappropriate for the low status ones, while accented speakers were judged more suitable for low-status jobs and less so for high-status ones.

This 'double discrimination' (Kalin 1982) has also been found in several other studies, in Canada by Kalin and Rayko (1980) and Kalin, Rayko and Love (1980), comparing English Canadian speakers with a range of speakers with foreign accents (e.g. Greek, West African. South Asian), and in the UK by Giles, Wilson and Conway (1981), comparing RP with South Welsh English speakers. The generally held conclusion is that such discriminatory findings are the norm, and that there is a consensual status hierarchy of accents as well as occupations, with speakers with specific accents viewed as appropriate or inappropriate for given job levels. Linguistic deficiency is often cited as a reason for job discrimination (i.e. an individual's speech is viewed as a hindrance to communication with others), but we can see in this data that speakers with standard accents have been considered to be unsuitable for low-status jobs, and in such cases it is difficult to see how communication would be impaired (see Lippi-Green 1997). Another possible interpretation tendered by Kalin (1982: 160) is that apparent mismatches might lead to some anticipation of interpersonal friction and lack of co-operation in workplaces. (See also Atkins' 1993 direct approach questionnaire study of judgements of Appalachian and Black English by employers, with a focus on specific dialect features.)

Finally, an accent study by Seggie, Smith and Hodgins (1986) had a slightly different focus, researching effects on recommendations for training programmes in Australia. They studied the attitudes of two groups – small businessmen and female suburban shoppers – towards speakers of standard Australian English, broad Australian English, German-accented English and Asian-accented English. The respondents had to judge their suitability for training programmes for high and low status occupations (accountant and storeman respectively). Each group of respondents was also provided with identical details of background and qualifications for each guise. Each respondent heard only one guise. For the accountancy course, the businessmen judged the broad Australian speaker as the least suitable, and the other varieties as equally suitable. They saw the standard and Asian voices as equally suitable for either programme. However, there were significant differences between the businessmen's attitudes and those of the shoppers. The shoppers viewed the standard speaker as less suitable for the storeman programme, an outcome closer to the double discrimination identified by Kalin (1982). Intriguingly, too, in the light of Cargile's (1997) later findings in the USA, the Asian speaker was also judged differently. The businessmen saw him as equal to the standard speaker in suitability for the accountancy course, whereas the shoppers saw him as unsuitable and on a par with the broad Australian speaker. Seggie *et al.* (1986) attribute this to the businessmen's greater awareness of the Chinese community's considerable success in business in the large cities of Australia.

These accent studies throw up two issues. One is that, although the general attitudinal pattern appears to be the double discriminatory one, attention needs to be given to the relations specific to communities and groups. The diverging findings in Hopper and Williams (1973) and in Hopper (1977) suggest that black/white American ethnicity was not a critical determinant in employment interviews in Texas (although Ball and Giles 1982: 105 express some reservations). Cargile (1997; 2000) himself emphasises that judged suitability seems to some extent to take account of the images and achievements of the group in question (the Chinese community in the USA). Seggie *et al.*'s (1986) findings appear to demonstrate this insofar as the businessmen were more familiar with the business image of the Chinese community in Australia than the shoppers were.

The second issue concerns the respondents used in these kinds of studies. University students usually constitute the most convenient of all convenience samples for research conducted in universities, but the view is sometimes heard that one cannot always assume such findings can be generalised to wider populations. Ultimately, this is an empirical question, although there seems to be a dearth of studies that have addressed it. Bernstein, Hakel and Harlan (1975) noted that there had been a good number of studies into employment interviews that had included both employment interviewers and college students as respondents. Reviewing a number of these studies, covering such areas as accuracy of stereotypes, processing information and forming impressions of the content of CVs, Bernstein *et al.* concluded that there were no important findings to suggest that generalisability from student respondents is limited, beyond a tendency for them to be more lenient than employment interviewers. Nevertheless, Bernstein *et al.* encourage researchers who rely on student respondents in research into other areas of social psychology to run systematic comparisons of populations to establish comparability. Some of the studies reviewed above did in fact include employer-respondents, and some differences were found between the judgements of employers and non-employers such as students or shoppers (see also Barr and Hitt 1986). From the opposite perspective, Cargile (1997) found that while his student sample did not discriminate between standard American and Chinese-accented speakers in an employment context, they did so in their class-room context. Although, as Cargile (1997: 441) notes, attention has been given in language attitudes work to contextual factors such as formality/informality and status stressing/solidarity stressing, there may also be differences due to the personal relevance of the context and task, and indeed this is a key variable in the ELM. There are certainly signs here, then, that in certain professional contexts in particular there may be advantages, where practicable and depending on research questions, to include respondents working 'close to the coal face'.

CONCLUSION

This brief coverage of these important professional fields makes salient the scope and the complexity not only of the fields themselves but also the task of researching them to an extent that enables us to achieve robust findings. As we have seen, pockets of studies in specific areas do enable us to see some general patterns emerging and improve our understanding. In his summing up of these applied settings nearly three decades ago, Kalin (1982) concluded 'the complexity of the problem . . . combined with the fact that most of the territory to be explored is still uncharted, makes the prospects of exploration both exciting and challenging' (p. 163). Despite the many studies in these areas since that time, and our growing understanding of language attitudes in these contexts, the vastness of the field means that Kalin's conclusion is echoed here too.

FURTHER READING ON CHAPTER 8

Lippi-Green's book contains a lot of material on language attitudes and discrimination in professional contexts, including the courts and education:

Lippi-Green, R., 1997, *English with an accent: language, ideology, and discrimination in the United States.* London: Routledge.

Although not having an exclusive focus on language attitudes matters, the following chapter contains a good summary of persuasion factors in legal contexts:

Reinhard, J., 2002, Persuasion in the legal setting, in J. Dillard and M. Pfau (eds.), *The persuasion handbook: developments in theory and practice* (pp. 543–602). Thousand Oaks, CA: Sage.

QUESTIONS FOR CHAPTER 8

1. What are your own views on the use of jargon in communication with the public in professional contexts: e.g. the use of medical and legal terminology in medical and legal contexts?
2. While reading this chapter, were there any particular results from studies in these professional contexts that you were particularly concerned by? If so, are you able to think of possible remedies?

9   Societal treatment studies

Societal treatment studies tend to receive less attention in contemporary discussions of language attitudes research. Nevertheless, it is certainly a significant approach for gaining insights into the relative values and stereotypical associations of language varieties. Broadly speaking, the approach is seen in terms of the 'treatment' afforded languages and language varieties within society, and to their users. Studies that are gathered together under this heading include observational, participant observation and ethnographic studies, and studies of many sources in the public domain. Chapter 3 included reference to one or two societal treatment studies examining letters to editors, etiquette books and language use in cartoons, for example. Other published studies have looked at government and educational policy documents and their view of languages in school systems (e.g. Mitchell 1991; Cots and Nussbaum 1999), the use of dialect in novels (Rickford and Traugott 1985) and differences in English usage in newspaper style books (Metcalf 1985). There is indeed much diversity amongst the studies placed in the societal treatment category. In this chapter we pick out two themes where there has been sufficient focus of attention to create a body of work, albeit still a small one. One topic is the use of languages in consumer advertisements, and the other concerns recent work on linguistic landscapes.

LANGUAGE USE IN CONSUMER ADVERTISEMENTS

Consumer advertising has provided an informative source of societal treatment material. Studies of bilingual or multilingual advertisements can highlight how different languages convey cultural resonances in a particular culture. Advertisers exploit these resonances in order to imbue their products with the (stereotypical) qualities and values with which a given language and language group is commonly associated. In other words, audiences are assumed to associate the different languages with particular sets of connotations. Studying such values and associations in a particular society can tell us a great deal about assumptions and ways of thinking within that society. Thus, language choice within advertising becomes a powerful 'tool in the construction of social identity, be it national, racial or class identity' (Piller 2003: 173). Three studies of language use in consumer advertisements are reviewed below, each taken from very different contexts, and demonstrating very different social meanings.

Advertisements in Japan

A seminal study on advertisements was conducted by Haarmann (1984, 1989), who investigated the role of ethnocultural stereotypes in language use in Japanese television commercials. Haarmann noted that many adverts in the Japanese media made use of foreign languages that audiences would not be expected to understand. It was not necessary for the audiences to comprehend a given language for the language to convey stereotypical associations.

English and French were used in these advertisements as potential communicational means along with Japanese, whereas other languages were generally applied only in connection with product names (as well as background music and settings). Haarmann (1989) estimated at the time of his study that Japanese television was unique in monolingual countries in that it produced multilingual commercial texts (e.g. English–Japanese, French–Japanese or English–French–Japanese) along with monolingual Japanese, French or English. The bilingual verbal strategy of Japanese advertisements had no equivalent in Japanese everyday social interaction. It should be noted, too, that 95.4 per cent of his sample of advertisements were for Japanese products, rather than for products from countries where these languages originated. In the advertisements, Haarmann saw Japanese as neutral with respect to stereotype or prestige functions, but all other communicational means as linked to those functions. Foreign languages were strategically selected by advertisers for their specific associations in the context of specific products. Study of these stereotypical associations would give insights into language attitudes.

Table 9.1 gives some examples of the language use with particular types of advertisements in Japan, and the stereotypical associations that the inclusion of these languages could be assumed to be aimed at. Thus, French has ethnocultural associations with 'high elegance, refined taste, attractiveness, sophisticated lifestyle, fascination and charm' (Haarmann 1989:11; see also Kelly-Holmes 2000 for similar findings in the European Union), and it is used to advertise items such as perfume, watches, food and fashion. English, in comparison, is seen

Table 9.1. *Languages and their stereotypical features in Haarmann's study (based on Haarmann 1984)*

Language used	Stereotype features	Product attached to stereotype
English	International appreciation	Alcoholic drink, tennis racket
	High quality	Television set, hi-fi
	Confidence	Tape-recorded, cassette
	Practical use	Sportswear
	Practical lifestyle	Motor scooters
French	High elegance	Fashion, watches, biscuits
	Refined taste	Coffee, sweets, tasty food
	Attractiveness	Cars, handbags
	Sophisticated lifestyle	Home furnishings
	Fascination and charm	Make-up, cream, perfume
Italian	Appreciation for speed	Sports cars
	Simple elegance	Motor scooters
Spanish	Features of male culture (masculine charm)	Perfume
	Features of female culture (wild tenderness)	Cars
German	Commodity	Kitchens
	Pleasantness of rural life	Cheese

as a marker of 'international appreciation, reliability, high quality, confidence, practical use, practical lifestyle' (Haarmann 1989: 11), and is employed to associate products such as cars, televisions, sportswear and alcohol with these qualities. The languages 'provide the background or the associational bridge for evoking stereotypes about the corresponding communities. Foreign language use implies features that are likely to be received positively by audiences. The impression of "modern fashionable style" makes their use acceptable (despite not necessarily understanding them), and their prestige value allows audiences to feel like members of a modern cosmopolitan society' (Haarmann 1984: 110; see also Piller 2001 for similar findings in bilingual German–English advertisements).

Haarmann (1984; 1989) underlines the negative consequences that are concomitant with the use of such stereotypes. For example, they can reinforce roles of males and females (as, say, respectively company director and housewife). There were no images of Japanese women having high-ranking positions. And the reproduction of foreign (French, Spanish, English, etc.) stereotypes does not contribute anything to understanding other cultures and societies. This is not to say, of course, that people can and do not oppose the messages in advertisements (e.g. see Morley 1980 regarding 'lively and active' audiences), nor that products cannot be used to enhance human/personal life, but the socio-cultural ambience created by such advertisements within a consumerist social order should not be underestimated.

Advertisements in Switzerland

Cheshire and Moser (1994) looked at language use in print advertisements in Switzerland, and focused just on the use of English. Although Switzerland can be regarded as a multilingual country (German, French, Italian and Rumantsch), Cheshire and Moser point to the majority its inhabitants being monolingual in just one of these languages (notwithstanding the small proportion of Rumantsch speakers, who are bilingual in Rumantsch and German, and also the complex diglossic character of German-speaking Switzerland). The position of English is quite different from its position in Japan, lying somewhere between foreign language status (as in, say, Japan) and second language status (as in, say, India).

Cheshire and Moser took advertisements from two magazines: *L'Hebdo* and *L'Illustré*. The content of *L'Hebdo* was more focused on politics, the economy, social issues and news, and *L'Illustré* was pitched at a more popular level, with people, events, sport, gossip, etc. They found that English occurred in about a third of the advertisements. Of these, about 7 per cent contained only English, 20 per cent had only the product name in English and about 73 per cent contained a mixture of English and another language, usually French. In these latter, English was usually very prominent: for example, as the slogan or 'signature line' (Leech 1966) and in its position and font size. Given the different types of readerships of the magazines, and the presence of for the most part basic vocabulary combined with the presence of puns, Cheshire and Moser conclude that English would function differently from how it did in the Japanese context of Haarmann's study, in which it worked primarily as a cultural symbol. Amongst the Swiss, it could be used as 'language display' (Eastman and Stein 1993), laying claims to the attributes associated symbolically with speakers of English. However, it could also be used to convey referential meaning, with the exception of the puns in the case of some readers, and also with a flattering effect for those with the sophisticated knowledge required to understand the puns.

Several themes emerge from Table 9.2. Firstly, English is used more for products characterised by transient fashions (clothes, cars, etc.) rather than more everyday products (insurance, household equipment,

Table 9.2. *Proportions of advertised products using English (based on Cheshire and Moser 1994)*

Products	Percentage using English	Products	Percentage using English
Credit cards	100	Beauty	33.3
Cigarettes	84.4	Schools	30.9
Hi-fi equipment	77.8	Household equipment	18.9
Cigars	75.0	Sport and leisure	18.2
Computers and communication	70.8	Holidays and hotels	15.0
Cameras	53.3	Telephone chatlines	14.3
Air travel	51.9	Furniture	9.7
Alcohol	50.8	Insurance	4.7
Shoes and clothes	46.4	Banks	0.0
Watches	45.3	Medicine	0.0
Cars	41.2	Clairvoyance	0.0
Motorcycles	40.0	Soft drinks	0.0
Perfume	37.5	Others	31.0
Music	35.0	Whole sample	31.4

etc.), and this seems very much in line with Haarmann's (1989) findings in Japan regarding 'typical consumer goods'. Secondly, the international appreciation connotations of English found in Haarmann's study also feature here, albeit in terms of English as the language of international travel and tourism (extending to the advertisements for credit cards), and also as a lingua franca in science and technology, explaining its use in adverts for communication, computers and hi-fi equipment, and other advertisements foregrounding technical expertise. Alongside this international appreciation, though, Cheshire and Moser point to some advertisements carrying clear connections with English-speaking countries themselves associated with the products (Scottish sportswear, American cigarettes, etc.). Two other (related) themes are associations with sport and competition, perhaps extending to the language itself a common association between the USA and competition and winning.

A further striking feature of Cheshire and Moser's data was that, although about 36 per cent of the advertisements using English were for brands from English-speaking countries, 32 per cent were advertising Swiss products (and to a French-speaking readership), including Swiss watches (a principal industry and a significant component of the Swiss cultural stereotype). Cheshire and Moser attribute this use of

English to a problematic Swiss national identity, or the 'Helvetic malaise'. Switzerland can be viewed as a geographical entity comprising four ethnic groups with a turbulent history, who have been largely held together by dissociation from their neighbours, with a period of exceptional national unity in the face of fascism and the Cold War from the 1930s through to the late 1950s. The current absence of such immediate external threats, it is argued, seems to have led to a shift of focus to internal divisions within the country. With the growth of tourism, there is also, however, a tourist image of Switzerland – a kind of 'romantic gaze' (Urry 2002) – as a beautiful, peaceful and harmonious country with a courteous and efficient people (Cheshire and Moser 1994: 467). Cheshire and Moser argue that the use of English in advertising seems to be a solution to the national identity problem through allowing the Swiss 'to construct a self-image that is consistent with the favourable image that they present to tourists' (p. 467).

In the studies by Haarmann and by Cheshire and Moser, then, we have seen the use of English in two very different contexts, one where it is external to the country, but where its use brings to Japanese social identity a sense of added involvement in the wider contemporary world, and one where English is more familiar and not external, and whose associations reflect a satisfying Swiss 'tourist' identity back to the Swiss. 'English can serve as an open reservoir for symbolic meanings', argue Cheshire and Moser (p. 468). Sometimes it triggers associations with national and international domains where it is used, but new symbolic meanings can also be evoked, and variably according to different contexts.

Welsh advertisements in North America

This third study (Bishop, Coupland and Garrett 2005a) has its primary focus on the use of a minority language (Welsh) over a period of 150 years in a North American newspaper: *Y Drych* ('The Mirror'). *Y Drych* was founded in 1851 in New York City to serve the expatriate Welsh community, and was published continuously until 2003, when it merged with another North American Welsh-focused newspaper called *Ninnau* ('Us/Ourselves'). At the outset, it was an almost exclusively monolingual Welsh newspaper, but in the main body of text (i.e. non-advertising) there was a rapid transition from Welsh to English between the 1920s and 1940s, and the Welsh language arguably began to function largely in terms of language display, a process of change charted and analysed in Coupland, Bishop and Garrett (2003).

CYMERADWYAETH.

UTICA, N. Y., Mehefin 15, 1888.
FONEDDIGION! Pleser i mi yw dwyn tystiol-
aeth i effeithiolrwydd eich Meddyginau Poblog-
aidd ac Ymddiriedol. Bum yn dyoddef yn iawr
oddiwrth y Grydcymalau am flynyddau, a'r gan-
af diweddaf yr oedd poen mawr yn un o'm hael-
odau. Ar ol cymeryd dwy botelaid o'ch meddyglyn, yr wyf wedi cael llwyr wellhâd. Nid \ fi
yn teimlo dim oddiwrth fy hen anhwylder er
pan gymerais eich meddyglyn.
                                    LEWIS R. EVANS.
Ar werth gan y CAMPBELL MEDICINE COM-
PANY, No. 190 Genesee St., Utica, N. Y., a chan
yr holl Gyfferwyr.

RECOMMENDATION
UTICA, N. Y., June 15, 1888.
GENTLEMEN! It is my pleasure to provide evidence
Of the effectiveness of your popular and
fiduciary Medicines. I have suffered greatly
from a variety of ailments for years, and last
year I suffered from a great pain in one of my
limbs. After taking two bottles of your
medicine, I have undergone a complete recovery. I do not
feel anything from my old malaise
since I took your medicine
                                    LEWIS R. EVANS
On sale from the CAMPBELL MEDICINE COM-
PANY. No 190 Genesse St., Utica, N.Y., and from
all the suppliers.

Figure 9.1 Advertisement from *Y Drych*, August 1888. Adjacent English translation by Bishop, Coupland and Garrett (2005a).

The two languages in the advertisements were found to be generally employed in two separate functional categories according to different indexical values, which themselves shifted over time. In the initial period, Welsh could be seen as the unmarked communicative tool for an ingroup of Welsh readers seeking goods and services within their community localities. Figure 9.1 exemplifies this. English, here, expresses the widest referential functions to reach potential customers (e.g. name of product, company and address). In some advertisements, Welsh also functions as a marker of trustworthiness and intimacy. Figure 9.2 exemplifies this.

The language shift in the advertisements spearheaded the broad shift from Welsh to English in the rest of *Y Drych*. Advertisements that were Welsh-only or Welsh-matrix (i.e. where Welsh provided the textual infrastructure) declined steadily from the 1890s to the 1930s. But as English became the matrix language for the advertisements, Welsh took on different functions from those fulfilled by English in the earlier advertisements. Welsh tended to be displayed iconically and with a strong cultural character. For example, Welsh was used for names of cultural events and celebrations, names of institutions, greetings, sayings and language courses. Sometimes this occurs in conjunction with forms of Celtic iconography or Welsh symbols such as (at least something resembling) the Welsh dragon on the Welsh flag (see Figure 9.3, advertising Welsh

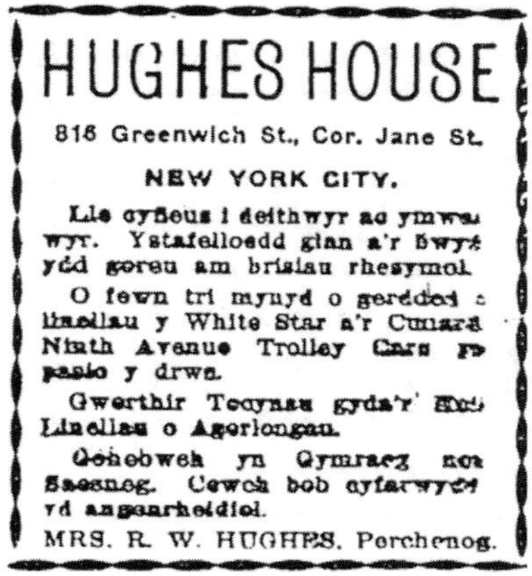

HUGHES HOUSE

816 Greenwich St., Cor. Jane St.

NEW YORK CITY.

Lle cyfleus i deithwyr ac ymwelwyr. Ystafelloedd glan a'r bwyd yd goreu am brisiau rhesymol.

O fewn tri mynyd o gerdded o lineliau y White Star a'r Cunard Ninth Avenue Trolley Cars yn pasio y drws.

Gwerthir Teganau gyda'r Enw Lineliau o Agerlongau.

Gohebwch yn Gymraeg neu Saesneg. Cewch bob cyfarwyddyd angenrheidiol.

MRS. R. W. HUGHES. Perchenog.

Convenient place for travellers and visitors. Clean rooms and the best food at reasonable prices.
Within three minutes walk from the White Star and Cunard Lines and the Ninth Avenue Trolley cars pass by the door.
Contact us in either Welsh or English. You will receive all necessary directions.
Owner MRS. R. W. HUGHES

Figure 9.2 Advertisement from *Y Drych*, January 1908. Adjacent English translation by Bishop, Coupland and Garrett (2005a).

Cyfarchion Dydd Gwyl Dewi

o

SIOp OJ

YOUR SOURCE IN WALES FOR WELSH GOODS.

14 West St., Fishguard/Agergwaun,
Pembrokeshire, SA65 9AE, Wales
Ffôn/ffacs (011+44) 1348 874630
E-bost: siopdj@AOL.COM

St David's Day greetings from Shop DJ
E-mail

Figure 9.3 Advertisement from *Y Drych*, March 1998. Adjacent English translation by Bishop, Coupland and Garrett (2005a).

goods, and Figure 9.4, advertising a Welsh language course). One might view these as evocative of tradition and ways of exoticising the products or companies for North American readers. Welsh, here, has become a display resource for marketing tradition and 'old Wales'. It is noticeable in some of these advertisements, too, that, although encompassed within the unmarked code of English, and

The Board of Cymdeithas Madog is pleased to
announce the fees and to open registration for

Cwrs Cymraeg 2001—Y Cwrs Arian
22–29 July 2001
at Emory University, Atlanta

Adult Resident (sharing)	$595.00
Student Resident (sharing)	$545.00
Commuter	$430.00
Tag-along	$495.00
Upgrade to single room	$55.00

There will be a limit of 80 places on the XXV Cwrs Cymraeg
and reservations will be accepted on a first come, first
served basis. A deposit of $100.00, which is refundable in
full until 1 March 2001, reserves your place.

Please send your deposit of $100.00 US cheque payable
to Cwrs Cymraeg to: Jenny Hubbard Young
                         1085 Fleming Street
                         Smyrna, GA 30080
        Tel. (770) 333-1964 or e-mail cwrs2001@madog.org

Figure 9.4 Advertisement from *Y Drych*, March 2001. Adjacent English
translation by Bishop, Coupland and Garrett (2005a).

restricted in function and reference, the Welsh components are
visually dominating.

Bishop *et al.* point to three types of market value for the two languages in these advertisements. One is the value of reaching markets
and making them responsive. This is partly a matter of encoding
the advertisement in a language that will achieve adequate intelligi-
bility, but also of employing the language that readers will find the
most apposite. The shift towards English doubtless reflected such
changing competences and attitudes. A second type of value concerns
the economics of the language itself, access to which can be purchased,
through language courses, or through travelling to places where
people can be heard speaking it. A third type of value relates to the
ideologising of English and Welsh. The Welsh language can be seen
as the ingroup language for readers, editors, advertisers, etc., for the
whole 150 years. But the ingroup itself changes in the way that it is
ideologically composed. In the recent period characterised by

contemporary globalisation, the ingroup economy, for advertisers, is no longer limited to a specific geographically local community, defined by its history and cultural continuity, but is far more open and fluid, to the point where the purchase of Welsh goods is an acceptable credential to be in the ingroup.

These three studies, then, allow us to see how languages of very different statuses in three quite different cultural contexts can be imbued with quite different values and symbolic meanings. Societal treatment studies of this kind can give us insights into broadly based language attitudes. Bishop *et al.*'s study demonstrates how societal treatment data can offer additional advantages. To begin with, documentation or other sources that are available from earlier historical periods can provide us with a window into earlier attitudes on particular issues. But secondly, as in this study, some such sources span a considerable or critical period of time, and having access to historically continuous data allows insights into changes in ideological stances, and changing attitudes to languages and their users over time. (See also Lieberson's 1981 study of the Francophone and Anglophone communities in Montreal, drawing upon various business and employment entries in *Yellow Pages* and in two Montreal newspapers for the period 1939–64.)

LINGUISTIC LANDSCAPES

Landry and Bourhis (1997: 25) define linguistic landscape as:
'The language of public road signs, advertising billboards, street names, place names, commercial shop signs, and public signs on government buildings combines to form the linguistic landscape of a given territory, region, or urban agglomeration.'

Perhaps inevitably, the scope of the term has varied a little in research. Others have included mobile texts, such as newspapers and visiting cards. Coupland (2010) has suggested that the scope can be usefully extended to other carriers of language in the public environment, such as bumper stickers, body tattoos and more.

Landry and Bourhis (1997) distinguish between private signs (e.g. commercial signs, advertising signs on private or public transport vehicles) and public signs (e.g. signs used by governmental bodies, including road signs, street and place names, inscriptions on town halls, schools, hospitals, etc.). Greater language diversity is found in private signs. Subsequently, many other studies have used this distinction in their studies, or comparable distinctions such as 'top-down' and 'bottom-up' (e.g. Ben-Rafael, Shohamy, Amara and Trumper-Hecht 2006), although Coupland (2010) questions the validity of this distinction.

Landry and Bourhis see the linguistic landscape as having two over-arching functions: informational and symbolic. At the informational level, it can serve to show boundaries of language groups, showing ingroup and outgroup members the linguistic characteristics and limits of the region they are in. It may guide them in their expectations of which language can be used to communication and obtain services. Where territories are not linguistically homogeneous, the landscape can give information on the sociolinguistic composition of the language groups in the territory, and also on the relative statuses of the languages and their speakers. One language might predominate, for example, while another might be excluded from some types of signs.

For Landry and Bourhis, the symbolic function is most likely to be salient in places where language is the most important dimension of ethnic identity, and can be related to objective and subjective ethno-linguistic vitality. The prevalence of one language might signify the strength of that language group on the institutional and demographic dimensions, and also in terms of status. Exclusion of a language might weaken supportive attitudes and the motivation to pass on the lan-guage to the next generation. Alternatively, for example, psychological reactance can set in (e.g. Brehm and Brehm 1981), where people feel their freedom is threatened, leading to political lobbying, for example, or public demonstrations, graffiti campaigns etc., in defence of their language.

Since Landry and Bourhis' (1997) paper, there has been a flurry of research activity into linguistic landscapes (see, for example, Gorter 2006). Gorter notes that this has doubtless been stimulated in part by the advent of digital photography, making it possible to take large numbers of good quality photographs very cheaply, and with very portable small cameras. Gorter also suggests globalisation has been another reason, with the growing and widespread impact of global lan-guages along with greater mobility amongst people. Coupland (2010) says that linguistic landscaping can be plausibly seen as part of our experience of global change. The value of studying linguistic landscapes, according to Backhaus (2007: 11), is in the insights they can provide into a range of issues that include official language policies, prevalent language attitudes and power relations between linguistic groups.

Backhaus (2007) refers to two studies in Brussels. One early study, before Landry and Bourhis gave a name to the concept of linguistic landscape, was carried out by Tulp (1978). She examined large commercial billboards in and around Brussels and found that about two thirds of them were monolingual French billboards, and the remainder mainly monolingual Dutch, albeit with about a tenth of the total using both languages. More Dutch billboards were evident as one moved north from the city into the areas where the majority of the Flemish population lived. French billboards, on the other hand, dominated the south of Brussels, even in territory that was officially Flemish, and also around the major railway and metro stations in Brussels itself. Tulp argued that the linguistic landscape of Brussels was primarily monolingual French, and that visitors to Brussels would see it as a French-speaking city (thus also leading to additional Frenchification). Over the past two centuries, Brussels has changed from an almost entirely Dutch-speaking city into a predominantly French-speaking one.

Fifteen years later, Wenzel (1996) carried out a similar study in Brussels. She found a similar geographic distribution to Tulp. Changes in the law meant that there was a more equal presence of French and Dutch in public facilities such as railway stations. And she also found a greater presence of English in the city centre, perhaps motivated by a desire to give the city a more international appearance, or perhaps in response to the linguistic pressures of globalisation (given its presence in many linguistic landscape studies around the world). Significantly, though, Wenzel also found that, even on bilingual billboards, French dominated through the order in which the languages appeared. There are many different ways in which one language might dominate another in the landscape, and we return to this below.

In a very different context from Brussels, Reh (2004) investigated the use of English and Lwo in the linguistic landscape of Lira Town in Uganda, a municipality of about 27,000. All signs on official buildings and many other types of signs in Lira were dominated by English. Signs containing Lwo were rare, only occurring in non-governmental contexts, and usually in combination with English, and included in smaller letter size. There was also a functional division. In signs relating to governmental institutions and non-governmental organisations, English monolingual signs were used exclusively. Other contexts where English signs dominated included computer services, the health sector and bookshops. Domains where Lwo was used more than English included the agricultural sector, warning notices, shops selling everyday goods and water kiosks. In other words, there was a relatively clear social dichotomy between Lwo, as the local language, and English, as the official language. Reh (2004: 39) comments that this dichotomy means that English is associated with the modern economic sector and social and economic advancement, while Lwo is associated with daily routine, and this results in relatively negative attitudes to Lwo and a view that it is not suitable for purposes of the modern economy, education and administration. Interestingly, Reh also sees indications of a change in attitudes. Bilingual signs are now appearing in political campaigns, and some national and international companies are beginning to advertise in local languages. It may be that democratisation and marketisation are factors weakening this status dichotomy. Capturing new (or indeed understanding earlier) developments in linguistic landscapes showing political and ideological forces at work are an important component of linguistic landscape research.

A different kind of division was found in the Japanese capital. Backhaus (2006; 2007) found that, although 80 per cent of the signs in the centre of Tokyo were monolingual Japanese, there were two types of multilingual signs. Official agents have provided signs that include English and, to a lesser extent, Chinese and Korean. This is regarded as a 'noteworthy concession to linguistic minorities in Tokyo' (Backhaus, 2006: 64). In these multilingual signs, Japanese, English, Chinese and Korean can be associated with power. The second type are non-official multilingual signs, and these encompass a broader range of foreign languages, including French, Portuguese, Spanish, Italian, Thai, Tagalog, Arabic, Russian and more. The use of foreign languages in these signs seeks to create an overseas atmosphere. This second type then reflects the solidarity dimension rather than the power dimension. The use of Korean is a display of solidarity with a local community through indexing a significant group of Korean language speakers in Tokyo. The use of English projects solidarity through its symbolising a desire to join the international community of English users and the values generally associated with that community. This kind of division across power and solidarity dimensions has also been found elsewhere (e.g. in Israel, by Spolsky and Cooper 1991). A further difference that Backhaus found was that, apart from the overall differences in frequencies that differentiated the languages in official signs, size and order of the languages also played a role. 99 per cent displayed Japanese more prominently than the other languages, emphasising a power hierarchy. In contrast, in the non-official signs, the prominence was more balanced. 40 per cent gave more prominence to other languages than to Japanese, and in this way enhanced their symbolic value as an expression of solidarity with another culture.

Scollon and Wong Scollon (2003) have set out some important theoretical contributions to the linguistic landscape field. These include the ways in which one language can be given preference or dominance over another language in a sign, generally signifying more status or power within that context. They draw upon work by Kress and van Leeuwen (1996; 1998), who argue that the preferred code is to be found on the left, or at the top, or in the centre of a sign. A code found on the right, or at the bottom, or in the margins can be seen as the marginalised code. Positioning, then, can produce a hierarchy. But this can be overridden through making one language appear in a larger script. Scollon and Wong Scollon (2003) provide an example if this in the form of a road signpost in Ireland, where the Gaelic place name appears above, but in a smaller font than, the English version. Scollon and Wong Scollon also point to other ways in which one language can be given more weight over another in a sign. One is where one sign is positioned so that it will be read before another one. They give an example of signs along the edge of a road in Ontario, where motorists driving along the road will first encounter the English sign, and then the French one a short distance further along the road. Other variables that could signify language preferences are the materials employed for the signs, or for parts of the signs. Materials differ in their quality and durability. More durable or expensive materials can suggest greater authority.

Apart from variables that can signify language preference, though, Scollon and Wong Scollon (2003) also point to font types. They mention that until a two or three decades ago, to send a personal note to a friend in typewritten form would have seemed rather formal and distant, if not insulting. Attitudes have changed, but the underlying importance of social conventions remains. 'We feel we are seeing something about the meaning through the resources by which the language was inscribed' (p. 130). In their own analysis, Scollon and Wong Scollon examine the use of simplified and non-simplified Chinese characters in texts. In mainland China, the new, simplified characters are associated with the old socialist state. In Hong Kong, the older, non-simplified characters are associated with opening up to the outside world. These kinds of variables, then, seem to offer more than just an index of positioning in a status hierarchy.

Coupland (2008; 2010) is critical of the linguistic landscape research field for its tendency to focus its attention on the distribution of languages, and on the multilingual landscapes of different urban settings. Drawing an analogy with natural landscapes and quoting from the work of Adam (1998), Coupland (2010) argues that the visible phenomena that make up linguistic landscapes have 'invisible constitutive activities inescapably embedded in them' (Adam 1998: 54), and that a critical approach to linguistic landscape is needed in order to reveal the forces and processes that have conspired to give landscapes their particular forms. There are likely to be important genre distinctions too, with even what appear to be single genres such as 'shop signs' being influenced by, for example, a variety of histories and technologies, and design-inputs (Coupland 2008). In Wales, for example, the linguistic landscape can only be understood in relation to the decades of decline for the Welsh language, a long history of language stigmatisation, leading to the language revitalisation movements beginning in the 1960s and 1970s, direct action campaigns and concerted policy initiatives. Place names in particular, and their presence on road signs, maps and guides, etc., soon became an important target for ideological work on the linguistic landscape, to generate and extend a symbolic and ceremonial Welshness that could also be indexed very economically in this way (Coupland 2010). The extension to other areas of signage and documentation of parallel text bilingualism, and so to what Backhaus (2007: 91) refers to as 'homophonic signs', in which two or more languages constitute complete translations or transliterations of each other, has stemmed from a principle of sociolinguistic equivalence embodied in the subsequent 1993 Welsh Language Act with the objective of creating a 'truly bilingual Wales'. In Wales now there is a *Guide to bilingual design* published by Bwrdd Yr Iaith/The Welsh Language Board in 2001, advising on typefaces, typography, spacial alignment of the two languages. The document itself responds to two main ideological fields. One is the use of Welsh as a requirement of government, and the other concerns gaining commercial advantages in the marketplace. Indeed, the *Guide* refers to a survey undertaken by Bwrdd Yr Iaith which found that '75 per cent believe bilingual signs to be important for organisations offering a bilingual service' (2001: 4). It also says that 'it would appear that attitudes in favour of the language have never been more favourable. It is against this background that we have produced this guide' (p. 4), suggesting then that the presence of Welsh in signage in the linguistic landscape can be taken as reflecting widespread favourable attitudes.

Coupland also points to other aspects of the linguistic landscape in Wales, driven by a different ideology from the 'guided' parallel texts referred to above, and unconfined by the standard language ideologies that underpin such texts. One example he includes is a company ('Cowbois') producing t-shirts. Figure 9.5 shows an example. The t-shirt text refers to 'Merched Beca', written in a culturally challenging form with the omission of some letters and their replacement by numbers, one reversed. It is monolingual Welsh, effectively resisting standardisation, and it refers to the Rebecca Riots of 1839–43, when tenant farmers resisted the introduction of road-tolls by dressing as women

Figure 9.5 Cowbois t-shirt: Merched Beca.

and attacking the tollgates. They were an instance of opposition to English law and to English-speaking landlords. Coupland argues that landscape texts such as these show cultural vitality. 'They engage, ironically and obliquely, with the ideological contest that has defined Wales, rather than flooding the linguistic landscape of Wales with formalist parallelism'.

Linguistic landscapes have been capturing a great deal of sociolinguistic attention. The more distributional studies of linguistic landscapes provide us with a good picture of which languages are evident, and to what extent and in what contexts, and give us insights into their relative values in terms of power and solidarity, and what they index and symbolise. From a language attitudes perspective, the development, too, of the kind of critical stylistics that Coupland (2008) proposes can give us a much fuller picture of the social and cultural meanings of specific linguistic landscapes and how language attitudes can influence them. A combination of the more quantitatively focused work searching for the broader patterns in the landscapes with more qualitative approaches, giving us a deeper understanding of the competing ideological stances involved, would link with a view of language attitudes research that will be argued in chapter 12.

CONCLUSION

In language attitudes reviews, studies mentioned under the societal treatment heading are quite diverse (e.g. see Giles, Hewstone, Ryan and Johnson 1987; Garrett 2005). However, the focus in this chapter on two areas of work has been an attempt to show more clearly the insights such material can provide into social attitudes towards language, along with some of the ideological struggles accompanying them. Earlier in this book, it was mentioned that one common view of studies such as these is that they are too subjective and best regarded as preliminaries to more rigorous social psychological studies. This chapter has hopefully shown that this view is open to challenge.

FURTHER READING ON CHAPTER 9

Readers interested in reading more on the use of foreign languages in advertising might look at one of the studies mentioned in this chapter; for example, the one by Piller:

Piller, I., 2003, Advertising as a site of language contact. *Annual review of applied linguistics* 23, 170–83.

For more on linguistic landscapes, see:

Jaworski, A. and Thurlow, C. (eds.), 2010, *Semiotic landscapes: text, image, space*. London: Continuum.

Scollon, R. and Wong Scollon, S., 2003, *Discourses in place: language in the material world*. London: Routledge.

Shohamy, E. and Gorter, D. (eds.), 2009, *Linguistic landscape: expanding the scenery*. London: Routledge.

QUESTIONS FOR CHAPTER 9

1. Is there more than one language used in some advertisements in your country? Perhaps foreign languages feature in some advertisements, or, if you live in a bilingual or multilingual context, more than one of those languages might appear in a single advertisement. Are you able to assign different social meanings to these languages in the ways that you have seen in this chapter?

2. Do you see more than one language in your linguistic landscape? If so, drawing on the coverage in this chapter, are you able to 'read' the distribution of these languages? Do you see any ideological stances in them?

10   Direct approach

Despite the productiveness of the matched and verbal guise techniques, it is fair to say that the direct approach has probably been the most dominant paradigm if one looks across the broader spectrum of language attitudes research. In the language education field, for example, a great deal of work has been carried out into teachers' and learners' attitudes. Some of this has focused on attitudes and motivation in second and foreign language learning, for example, where direct approach questionnaires have featured a great deal. Questionnaire and interview surveys have also played an important role in minority language environments and language planning and policy fields. In Wales, for example, a significant body of survey work informed Welsh language policy, including the research by Jones in the 1940s and 1950s, by Sharp and colleagues in the 1960s and 1970s, and Baker in the 1980s and 1990s (see the review of some of this work in Garrett *et al.* 2003). The work carried out by such researchers has spawned programmes of research in other parts of the world, using similar methodologies, and indeed often applying or adapting the same research instruments. Huguet (2006), for example, drew upon Sharp *et al.*'s (1973) questionnaire in a study of attitudes and motivation amongst secondary school students in two bilingual contexts in Spain: Asturias and Eastern Aragon. And other work has adapted Baker's (1992) questionnaire to investigate attitudes towards, for example, the Basque language in the Basque Country (Lasagabaster and Huguet 2007), and amongst the Basque diasporic community in the USA (Lasagabaster 2003; 2006; 2008).

THE THREE FOCUSES IN THIS CHAPTER

Given the overwhelming scope of direct approach language attitudes research over the decades, in this chapter I focus on three studies of interest that draw upon very different research methodologies. The first of these (Hyrkestedt and Kalaja 1998) exemplifies the discursive

159

social constructionist approach to language attitudes, which I referred to in chapter 2. This kind of work has not featured much at all in the main body of language attitudes literature, yet the study embodies a significantly different approach and the social constructionist approach has stimulated a great deal of interest and debate. As more social constructivist work on language attitudes evolves, it may well require more detailed treatment under a heading of its own, but for present purposes this study is included in this chapter on the justification that, as it is reported, its data is generated from the elicitation by researchers of consciously formulated attitudinal responses on language issues.

The second study revisits issues of globalisation and people on the move, and reflects a growing recent interest in diaspora. It investigates and compares language attitudes, ethnic identities and ethnolinguistic vitality in two diasporic communities, as well as the language 'homeland'. The third study was a large-scale BBC study conducted over the internet, which, despite differences in research methodology and design, allows some possibility of comparing contemporary attitudes in the UK with those found thirty-five years earlier in the study by Giles (1970), part of which was reviewed in chapters 3 and 4.

ATTITUDES TO ENGLISH IN FINLAND: A SOCIAL CONSTRUCTIONIST STUDY

In Hyrkestedt and Kalaja's (1998) study of attitudes to English in Finland, a 'letter to the editor' was constructed for use in their study. This constructed letter was based on some authentic ones from the Finnish national press, and it was entitled 'Is English our second mother tongue?' It contained three negative arguments: (a) Finnish is losing its vitality to English; (b) it is a good idea to take legislative action to protect the purity of languages, including Finnish, from the assault of English; (c) competence in English is not strong enough amongst Finns, with too much code-mixing, and this could lead to British teachers coming to Finland to get them to learn it properly. Student participants then formulated responses expressing their own opinions for the purpose of the study. The arguments they expressed were then interpreted according to whether they were in agreement or disagreement with each of the three arguments in the original letter. If a response contained arguments agreeing with the negative argument in the original letter, those arguments were regarded as expressing a negative attitude to English, while those disagreeing with the negative argument in the letter were regarded as constituting a positive attitude to English.

They found the positive attitude to English was more prevalent in the data than the negative attitude, but Hyrkestedt and Kalaja explain this as likely to result from disagreeing being a dispreferred turn, and so requiring more detailed justification, thus giving it more prevalence, and so it is not possible to conclude from such prevalence whether overall attitudes were generally positive or negative in nature. Instead, Hyrkestedt and Kalaja's focus was to look at the form and contents of the attitudes that were expressed. This they did by identifying the 'interpretive repertoires' in the responses, by which is meant the recurring systems of terms, or 'building blocks' that characterise the arguments presented in the responses. They identified three that characterised the positive attitude and four that characterised the negative attitude. Briefly summarised under the labels used by the authors, these were as follows:

The three positive repertoires

1) *The empiricist repertoire.* This takes on the role of language expert to argue that language change is universal. These ideas are expressed through generalisations about language change and languages influencing each other, historical facts about language and personal observations about language use.
2) *The nationalist repertoire.* This bolsters the status of Finnish, Finnish identity and the image of Finland through making denigrating comparisons with other countries, such as claiming that Finns speak foreign languages better than people in some other countries. Derogatory colloquialisms are employed in this process.
3) *The utilitarian repertoire.* This emphasises the practical advantages – for Finnish and for international communication – of taking words from English and knowing English.

The four negative repertoires

1) *The segregating repertoire.* This distinguishes those who use 'pure' Finnish from those who code-mix, and condemns the latter, regarding those who code-mix or allow it to happen as inferior. Finland and its people are referred to negatively in relation to other cultures, and as having a negative image abroad.
2) *The national-romanticist repertoire.* This agitates for more respect to be shown to Finnish and the national characteristics of the Finns. Non-Finnish things are derogated in colloquial forms, while Finnish things are argued for in emotional and poetic forms.
3) *The fatalist repertoire.* This constructs a division or conflict between ordinary Finns and those who define the correctness of language.

     Finnish speakers are seen as victims of social institutions such as
the educational system and the media. English is linked with
fashion and superficiality.
4) *The realist repertoire.* This suggests that the impact of English in
Finnish and Finnish speakers is harmful and works against democ-
racy and equality.

Hyrkestedt and Kalaja also found that the repertoires fell into opposing
pairs. The fatalist and the empiricist repertoires both saw the relationship between Finnish and English being affected by the media and cultural exchange. But they had different views of their importance and
functions. The realist and utilitarian repertoires identified consequences
for the Finns from code-mixing, but the realists saw these negatively, and
the utilitarians saw them positively. The segregating and nationalist
perspectives drew on concepts such as national identity through making
justifying comparisons with other countries, but they did this to quite
different ends. Thus it was possible in argumentation to draw upon the
same elements as the other position but to deny the existence or validity
of the other account.

    In addition to repertoires, 'common places' were also identified in the
responses. These were instances where an opposing view was mentioned
but not criticised. They drew upon the same elements as the other
position, but suggested that a different position was possible.

    Hyrkestedt and Kalaja examined how the students argued in their
responses, how they drew upon these repertoires and common places in
that process. They found that the students made use of more than one
interpretive repertoire to justify the arguments in their responses. They
did this in such a way that Hyrkestedt and Kalaja concluded that their
study provided support for the view that attitudes are not stable; even
within a text of 400 words or less in their study, attitudes showed
variability.

    A common pattern in language attitudes studies has been to identify
recurring themes in qualitative data and then follow up with a quantitative stage, for example by devising sets of statements around those
themes and asking respondent samples to indicate how far they agree or
disagree with them on sets of Likert scales. From such data, they might
examine, for example, how responses vary across different subgroups
of respondents, such as socio-economic groups, age groups, different
proficiencies in foreign languages, different levels of ethnocentrism.
Throughout this book, we have seen how language attitude studies
examine variation across different groups or different contexts, according to particular research questions.

However, as we have noted, Hyrkestedt and Kalaja's approach is situated in a different paradigm, that of social constructionism, to which we referred in chapter 2. The social constructionist view is that, traditionally, language attitudes studies separate attitude objects from their evaluation. Rather, attitudes can be seen as stances on issues in public debates, and so as only existing within argumentative contexts. They are not only about issues; they are also ways of arguing about issues. Hence, this approach works with the notion of 'heterogeneous evaluative practices which are used in different settings for different purposes' rather than the idea that people carry around 'the mental equivalent of ready filled-in Likert scales for the attitude objects in their lives' (Potter 1998: 259). It is claimed that, traditionally, language attitudes research looks for homogeneity in judgements, ignoring or suppressing variability, whereas, in contrast, social constructionist research argues that variability can be 'theoretically consequential' (p. 244) and so an important focus of study as people perform a variety of actions in their talk. The same person may provide different evaluations at different times, or even at different stages of the same conversation. Hence to follow up the identification of interpretive repertoires with Likert scales would be theoretically unsound within this paradigm. The main focus is the analysis of how attitudes or views are constructed in their discourse. They are constructed out of the linguistic resources available to individuals, and the identification of interpretive repertoires is itself an analytical route to understanding how they are constructed.

This approach to attitudes research (not limited to language attitudes) was briefly appraised in chapter 2. Here, it is useful to reiterate the value of studying variation of social evaluations according to, and within, social situations, but also to argue that the notion of durability in attitudes need not exclude the notion of variability. In addition, within what social constructivist researchers tend to refer to as the traditional paradigm of language attitudes research, the examination of how social evaluations are constructed through linguistic resources and repertoires can open richer interpretations of traditional data.

NORTH AMERICA, PATAGONIA AND WALES: A SURVEY OF ETHNOLINGUISTIC IDENTIFICATION

This study (Garrett, Bishop and Coupland 2009) compares Welsh ethnolinguistic identification, including attitudes to the Welsh language, in three communities: Wales itself, and the diasporic Welsh-identifying communities in North America and in Patagonia. The survey employed a questionnaire that had been used as a basis for several studies exploring Welsh identity and the Welsh language (e.g. Coupland, Bishop, Williams, Evans and Garrett 2005; Coupland, Bishop, Evans and Garrett 2006; Coupland, Bishop and Garrett 2006). The questionnaire was designed on the basis of a particular model of social identity that comprised three overlapping dimensions: knowledge, affiliation and practice (i.e. knowing, feeling and doing, a reflection of the tripartite model of language attitudes).

An important theoretical issue in this study is, once again, globalisation and the cultural arrangements it brings. Having a 'Welsh identity' is not limited to 'Welsh people' residing in Wales. Other groups elsewhere (e.g. Patagonia and North America) may claim Welshness, and from a variety of experiences. New values for the 'local' (Giddens 1999) can be established through globalisation, through interests in cultural heritage and genealogy from a wider number of Welsh-identifying groups globally. Globalisation is generally a market-driven complex of social changes, and minority languages can benefit from new 'market opportunities', as we saw in the advertisements of Y Drych described in chapter 9. But globalisation can also be threat to cultural continuity, as it fractures previously established social group arrangements, and there is, for example, much more population mobility. Even when a minority language or culture can benefit from globalisation, as might be the case with Welsh and Wales, it can find itself repositioned, reinterpreted and destabilised by global forces. In this study, then, there is an analysis of how Welsh-identifying people in these three geographical and cultural contexts constitute themselves as 'Welsh', and how they view the Welsh language. Using the three dimensions of social identity in the questionnaire provides a way of identifying and understanding some of the differences and similarities.

Background to the three communities

Welsh migration to North America began in the late seventeenth century. Migration was predominantly agricultural until the nineteenth century, when rapid industrial expansion in the USA attracted large numbers of Welsh labourers with valuable skills from railway labouring, ironworks, mining and quarrying. They tended to maintain their Welshness and language by concentrating in their own cultural groups in places such as Scranton in Pennsylvania. Over time, this cultural concentration disappeared, and new Welsh immigration dwindled after about 1900. The use of Welsh declined, and English began to become the predominant language of Welsh America (Jones and Jones 2001). However, Welsh identities and interests and investments in the Welsh language still flourish in North America. There are many Welsh societies and regular meetings and festivals.

It did not go unnoticed in Wales that Welsh migration to North America tended to lead to loss of the Welsh language and attenuation of Welsh cultural and religious values, and the idea emerged of founding a Welsh colony far from other communities, free of any need to integrate, where the Welsh language and Welsh culture could flourish. Through agreements with the Argentinian government, about 160 Welsh colonists founded such a colony in Patagonia in 1865. After considerable initial hardship and some crucial help from the Tehuelche people in the region, the colony established itself and grew, and more colonists arrived from Wales. At the local level, it was fairly independent at first, but Argentinian state control grew at the end of the century. As industrial development drew in more Spanish speakers, and as Argentinian government policy promoted a monolingual country, the Welsh community lost much of its political and economic influence, and the Welsh language suffered (see Williams 1991). However, the centenary celebrations in 1965 gave new salience to the Welsh role as founders of the region, and renewed interest in their culture and language. Currently, the Welsh Assembly Government in Wales sends three Welsh teachers annually to teach adults and school students and support Welsh festivals.

In Wales itself, the twentieth century was largely a period of steady decline for the Welsh language. The 1901 Census indicated that about half the population could speak Welsh. The figure had dropped to 19 per cent in the 1981 Census. But the position stabilised in the 1990s, and Wales is now reaping the benefits of politically driven support for Welsh that arguably began as early as the 1960s, and that has turned it into the most resilient of the Celtic languages. Welsh-speaking 'heartland' communities in rural and coastal north and west Wales are afforded some protection, and, as we saw in chapter 9, the Welsh Assembly Government is committed to establishing a 'truly bilingual' Wales. Amongst the many initiatives, the learning of Welsh is now compulsory in schools in Wales till the age of sixteen.

The study itself

The questionnaire grouped items (some open-ended and others using seven-point scales) under four headings as follows.

A What you think about the Welsh language?

The overall focus of this section was on the respondents' subjective perceptions of the ethnolinguistic vitality of the Welsh language.

It asked whether they felt Welsh was widely used in Wales nowadays, about its status in Wales and the level of support for it in Welsh institutions, and how far they thought that the Welsh language would be stronger in ten years' time. It also asked respondents to comment on the different social domains in which they felt the Welsh language should be used (rather than where it is used). The domains included for comment were: in place and personal names, traditional songs and literature, the family and the workplace.

B   *What do you know about Wales?*

This included an item asking informants to jot down up to five words or phrases that first came to mind when they first thought of Wales.

C   *What do you feel about Wales?*

This section asked about extents of feeling Welsh, feeling that 'Wales is my real home', 'letting others know that I am Welsh', wanting to identify more closely with Wales.

D   *Welsh things that you do*

This asked about their strength of involvement with such things as Welsh history or heritage and with Welsh language issues.

Respondents were given the choice of completing questionnaires in Welsh or English in Wales and North America, and in Welsh or Spanish in Patagonia.

While reaching a reasonable and sizeable convenience sample of respondents in Wales was unproblematic, the very different distributions and social circumstances of Welsh-linked people in the other two environments meant that the data had to be collected in rather different ways, involving the tracking of cultural events, for example, and, in Patagonia, as opportunities arose during fieldwork there (e.g. through shops and offices and contacts).

Table 10.1 sets out the main quantitative findings of this study, showing the results for each of the three groups (North America, Patagonia, Wales) in relation to the items gathered under four broad themes as 'felt affiliation to Wales', 'perceived vitality of Welsh', 'domain priorities for Welsh' and 'engagement with Welsh activities'. The statistical analysis grouped some questionnaire items into factors (e.g. perceived vitality of Welsh), but those that did not group into any factors but which were still of importance in their own right are also included in the table (e.g. personal commitment to supporting the Welsh language). Our primary focus here, of course, is on language issues, but we will discuss each of the four themes in turn. In interpreting

Table 10.1. *How the three regional groups (Wales, Patagonia and North America)*
compared in their Welsh identities and perceptions of the Welsh language

Themes	Factors and items	p values	Means for each Regional Group
Felt affiliation to Wales	Personal affiliation to Wales (factor)	0.001**	Inside Wales = 6.16 Patagonia = 4.24 North America = 4.90
Perceived Welsh language vitality	Perceived vitality of Welsh (factor)	0.001**	Inside Wales = 4.02 Patagonia = 4.42 North America = 3.78
	Welsh language stronger in 10 years	0.001**	Inside Wales = 4.09 Patagonia = 5.36 North America = 4.99
	Personally committed to supporting Welsh	0.001**	Inside Wales = 4.96 Patagonia = 5.26 North America = 5.18
Domain priorities for Welsh	Ceremonial importance of Welsh (factor)	0.001**	Inside Wales = 5.80 Patagonia = 6.26 North America = 6.40
	Important to use Welsh in family	0.001**	Inside Wales = 5.38 Patagonia = 6.73 North America = 6.07
	Important to use Welsh in the workplace	0.001**	Inside Wales = 4.73 Patagonia = 6.22 North America = 4.77
	Important to use Welsh in communities outside Wales	0.001**	Inside Wales = 3.60 Patagonia = 5.11 North America = 4.13
Engagement in Welsh activities	Engaged in history and heritage	0.001**	Inside Wales = 4.14 Patagonia = 3.65 North America = 4.98
	Engaged with people and family	0.001**	Inside Wales = 5.12 Patagonia = 4.78 North America = 5.32
	Engaged in Welsh language	0.001**	Inside Wales = 4.19 Patagonia = 4.21 North America = 3.52
	Engaged in sport	0.001**	Inside Wales = 5.08 Patagonia = 1.83 North America = 2.45
	Engaged in politics	0.001**	Inside Wales = 3.28 Patagonia = 1.57 North America = 2.41

Note: Significance levels for univariate main effects set at 0.005.
** = significant at $p < 0.001$.

the means in the table (in the right hand column), it is important to remember that seven-point scales were used, most of them Likert scales labelled with strongly disagree and strongly agree, and that a mean of four therefore represents the mid-point.

1.   Felt affiliation to Wales

This theme contained all the items listed under heading *C* above. All three regional groups showed positive affiliation, but nevertheless differed significantly from one another; the Wales group reporting the highest level of affiliation (6.16), followed by the North American group (4.90), followed by the Patagonian group (4.24). One of the questionnaire items in this theme focused particularly on Wales: 'I feel Wales is my real home', and the differences in means for this item were particularly large, with the Patagonians showing the lowest of all the means. So it is reasonable to see the affiliation felt by the Patagonian group as different in character from the others, showing affiliation to Welshness and Welsh life in Patagonia, but not to Wales itself, hence not disaffiliating but asserting a level of independence in their Welshness.

2.   Perceptions of Welsh language vitality

This theme contained all the items listed under heading *A* above, except those concerning the domains in which they felt that Welsh should be used. The 'perceived vitality of Welsh' factor, containing the three items about perceptions of how widely used Welsh is in Wales at the present time, along with its status and degree of institutional support, was not high or low for any of the groups, but the Patagonians did nevertheless perceive significantly more vitality for the language than the North American and Wales groups. In terms of how things might look ten years ahead, the two diasporic groups gave significantly higher estimates than the Wales respondents, who were close to the middle of the scale. From the point of view of language planners in Wales, taking heart from the results of the 2001 Census, the lack of subjective positivity can be seen as disappointing (though across different parts of Wales, some differentiation can be found – see Coupland *et al.* 2005). In the case of the two diasporic groups, the Patagonians were significantly more positive about the future of Welsh, perhaps reflecting the recent revitalisation of Welsh in Patagonia, with increased interest in Welsh and some limited provision at primary and secondary school levels, along with visitors from Wales to their own annual Welsh festival (*eisteddfod*).

Despite the general lack of positivity in the perceptions of the Wales group regarding the present and future vitality of Welsh, all three groups reported a positive personal commitment to the Welsh language. Even here, though, despite the positivity across all groups, the two diasporic groups express a greater personal commitment to the language than the Wales group. It is striking to find commitment to a minority language to be stronger overseas than 'at home', and it suggests a particular lens through which language and cultural distinctiveness is viewed 'from afar'. Interestingly, a similar phenomenon has been found amongst respondents of Basque origin in the USA compared to those in the Basque Country in Spain (Lasagabaster 2008).

3. Domain priorities for the use of Welsh

The factor 'ceremonial importance of Welsh' in Table 10.1 comprised judgements regarding whether it is important for Welsh to be used in traditional songs and literature, in place names and people's names, and in ceremonies and cultural events. All three groups attached high importance to the use of Welsh in this ceremonial domain, with the North Americans showing significantly more support than the Patagonians, who in turn showed significantly more support than the Wales group. One could say that this is the easiest domain in which to argue the importance of Welsh, since such ceremonial use (especially people's names, place names, greetings, etc.) is largely formulaic and does not require sustained close engagement with the language in terms of, say, developing an ability to manipulate its grammar.

In the other domains, the Patagonians stood out in the significantly greater importance that they attached to the use of the Welsh language, but it is also notable they also held a different set of priorities from the other two groups. Statistical analysis showed a clear shared hierarchy of importance for the North American and Wales groups. The use of Welsh was seen as important in the four domains in the following order:

> Ceremonial
> Family
> Workplace
> Communities outside Wales

For the Patagonians, in contrast, it was the family domain that was attributed most importance, and in fact statistical analysis showed that they prioritised Welsh-language use in the family significantly higher than all the other domains. Also of interest is the fact that both diasporic groups rated Welsh-language use in this domain higher than the Wales respondents did. There could well be special reasons in diasporic communities why such a high level of importance is given to the family for Welsh-language use, in terms of language continuity and survival.

The Wales and North American respondents attached less importance to the use of Welsh in the workplace, compared to ceremonial and family domains (although their ratings were nevertheless positive). Again, the Patagonians stood out, attributing considerable importance to the use of Welsh in the workplace, and in fact not significantly differentiating between the importance of the ceremonial and workplace use of Welsh. But for the others, ceremonial use was given far more importance than use in the workplace. In the North American context, we noted in chapter 9 how there has been a shift to the ceremonial use of Welsh in the advertisements of *Y Drych* (and in fact in the main body of the newspaper too – see Coupland *et al.* 2003). Within Wales, there is much ceremonial use in the various Welsh cultural festivals (*eisteddfodau*, agricultural fairs, open-air music festivals), and there have been proliferations of Welsh naming practices, as we also saw in chapter 9. And the question remains as to whether such ceremonial language activity will transfer into a greater proportion of proficient Welsh-language speakers. The hierarchy of domains above could signify that Welsh is being naturalised more as a ceremonial resource in Wales than as a language of the workplace.

Finally, as regards the importance of Welsh-language use outside Wales, all three groups were significantly differentiated from each other. The Wales group was negative, and the North Americans relatively neutral overall. The Patagonians gave this domain significantly more importance than the other two groups. From their own experience, the Patagonians are more likely to be aware of how Welsh can achieve or lose continuity in communities outside Wales. In contrast, amongst the Wales respondents, there may be a low level of awareness about, or low interest in, the Welsh language as a phenomenon outside Wales.

4.   *Engagement with Welsh activities*

In Welsh sport and Welsh politics, the Wales group reported more involvement than the two diasporic groups. Political issues in North America and Argentina will anyway have more immediacy to the everyday concerns and aspirations of those groups. Furthermore, it is reasonable to say that sport in Wales primarily means rugby, which receives little attention in North America. And in interviews during fieldwork in Patagonia, when asked which side they supported when Wales played Argentina at rugby, all respondents unhesitatingly answered 'Argentina'.

The highest levels of engagement with the Welsh language were reported by the Wales group and the Patagonians, and both these groups were significantly differentiated from the North Americans. Seen in terms of motivation and opportunity, the opportunities for sustained engagement with the Welsh language are inevitably far less available in the North American context than they are in Wales and Patagonia. Hence there is a situation where the North Americans are generally quite committed to supporting the Welsh language and quite optimistic about its future vitality, but are not very engaged with it. It may be that the largely ceremonial frame through which Welsh is encountered in the North American diaspora and to which we referred above and in chapter 9, does not permit the North Americans generally to claim that they are engaged with the Welsh language. Their involvement with Wales takes other forms, in terms of relatively high involvement with Welsh people or family, and with Welsh history and heritage, while the Patagonians' involvement in those areas is fulfilled within Patagonia itself, where they have their own community and their own unique Welsh history and status as the original founders of the colony.

The three regional communities in this study display quite distinctive profiles, linked to their separate cultural experiences and trajectories over time. All show positive affiliation to Wales, commitment to supporting the Welsh language and positivity about its future. All groups attach some importance to the use of Welsh across a number of domains, and all report some involvement in various activities to stay in touch with Welsh culture, in some cases through involvement with the Welsh language. The Welsh diaspora can be seen as a valuable resource for Welsh culture and the Welsh language. Within this shared positivity, there is variability. The two diasporic groups show more optimistic and enthusiastic attitudes towards the Welsh language than the respondents in Wales, and this is reflected in the lower levels of importance that the Wales group attaches to using Welsh in various domains, compared to the North Americans and Patagonians. The two diasporic communities have also revealed distinctive Welsh social identification processes and values. Despite their optimistic attitude to the language, the North American respondents are marked out by their lower level of engagement with Welsh, and by their looking back at Wales with a nostalgic lens focused more on heritage, history and ancestry. One might argue, though, that the vitality of the Welsh language is underpinned not only by the attitudes of people in Wales, but also by the attitudes of Welsh-identifying people living outside Wales, even in environments where Welsh is not spoken.

THE BBC VOICES STUDY: AN ONLINE SURVEY
OF LANGUAGE ATTITUDES IN THE UK

The BBC Voices project was an interactive exploration of language variation in the United Kingdom, linked to a series of radio and television broadcasts (www.bbc.co.uk/voices/). A preliminary to the project was an online language attitudes survey. Respondents rated thirty-four accents of English, presented conceptually. These included most major indigenous British accents and some accents associated with other countries that have a clear presence and relevance in the UK. A total of 5,010 respondents, all over fifteen years of age, completed the questionnaire by clicking on numerical values of seven-point scales online. They also had to leave information on which region of the UK they lived in, their age and sex, and a response to the 'diversity' statement 'I like hearing a range of accents', as a rough index of their ideological stances towards sociolinguistic diversity. The nature of the online design meant that the respondents were a self-selecting group. This inevitably carries some disadvantages, in that they might have some particular social or attitudinal characteristics. For example, they may be a group defined partly by their interest in completing surveys and who may have had some specific predispositions towards language related to this. As with any attitudes study, one needs to bear in mind the limitations of the respondent sample.

Here, we first compare BBC findings with those of Giles (1970), and then look for indications of any significant general ideological and sociolinguistic-evaluative changes over the decades between these two UK studies. Globalisation processes, for example, might lead to an expectation of a waning of deference towards standard varieties, and some loosening of negative attitudes towards non-standards (see, for example, Coupland 2003; Fabricius 2006). Alongside the matched guise study, Giles (1970) conducted a conceptual study (with a list of accents broadly the same for both, though with small differences), and this latter is therefore the basis of comparison here with the BBC study. As mentioned though in chapter 3, results from Giles' (1970) conceptual and matched guise studies were generally comparable.

The BBC study differed, of course, with its online design, in its demographically more diverse and geographically distributed respondent sample. Giles (1970) and the BBC study also differed in the precise list of accents and labels used. Those that featured in both studies were: 'an accent identical to your own', French, German, North American, Scottish, Liverpool and Birmingham. For those that differed,

Table 10.2. *Comparison of prestige findings from Giles (1970) and the BBC (2005) Voices study*

Giles 1970 (conceptual)			BBC Voices		
Rank	Accent	Mean	Accent	Mean	Rank
1	RP	6.1	Std. English	5.3	1
			Queen's English	5.8	
2	Identical	4.7	Identical	4.1	2
2	French	4.7	French	3.8	6
4	North American	4.2	North American	3.8	5
4	Scottish	4.2	Scottish	4.0	4
6	German	4.1	German	3.3	11
7	Irish	3.8	Northern Irish	3.6	7
			Southern Irish	3.7	
8	South Welsh	3.7	Cardiff	3.3	10
			Swansea	3.2	
8	Northern England	3.7	Lancashire	3.5	8
8	Somerset	3.7	West Country	3.3	12
11	Italian	3.3	Spanish	3.4	9
12	West Indies	3.0	Afro-Caribbean	3.0	13
12	Liverpool	3.0	Liverpool	2.8	16
14	Indian	2.9	Asian	2.8	15
14	Cockney	2.9	London	4.0	3
16	Birmingham	2.8	Birmingham	2.8	14

Giles' are here listed in brackets: 'Standard English' and 'Queen's English' (RP), Northern Irish and Southern Irish (Irish), Cardiff and Swansea (South Welsh), Lancashire (North England), West Country (Somerset), Spanish (Italian), Afro-Caribbean (West Indies), Asian (Indian) and London (Cockney). Overall, though, the studies provide a very reasonable basis on which to compare. The BBC study in fact included a greater range of accents than this list, and some others will be referred to in the discussion below.

Tables 10.2 and 10.3 set out the main findings for both studies for the accent ratings regarding prestige and social attractiveness dimensions. The means are in terms of scales where 1 is negative and 7 is positive. Table 10.2 shows a striking similarity between the findings for prestige in Giles' study and the BBC results. Standard British varieties retain their 1970 position as the most prestigious accent of English, with 'Queen's English' clearly favoured over the label 'Standard English'. This is then followed by 'an accent identical to your own', a clear suggestion of ingroup loyalty effects. The Scottish and North American accents maintain their favoured prestige ratings. The Birmingham accent still holds its *bête noire* status at the bottom of the rank order for prestige,

Table 10.3. *Comparison of social attractiveness findings from Giles (1970) and the BBC (2005) Voices study*

Giles 1970 (conceptual)			BBC Voices		
Rank	Accent	Mean	Accent	Mean	Rank
1	RP	5.5 ′	Std. English •	4.96	2
			Queen's English •	4.28	
2	Identical	5.1	Identical	4.87	1
3	French	5.0	French	4.09	6
4	Scottish	4.6	Scottish	4.53	3
5	Irish	4.3	Northern Irish	4.05	4
			Southern Irish	4.68	
6	Northern English	4.0	Lancashire	3.90	7
6	Somerset	4.0	West Country	4.16	5
8	Italian	3.9	Spanish	3.88	9
8	German	3.9	German	3.20	15
10	South Welsh	3.8	Cardiff	3.67	12
			Swansea	3.64	
11	West Indies	3.7	Afro-Caribbean	3.72	10
12	North America	3.5	North America	3.90	7
13	Indian	3.4	Asian	3.21	14
14	Birmingham	3.3	Birmingham	2.92	16
14	Liverpool	3.3	Liverpool	3.40	13
16	Cockney	3.2	London	3.70	11

with Liverpool also rated very low. Asian and Afro-Caribbean accents of English also receive low prestige ratings. The results for prestige are especially discouraging in view of the fact that the majority of the Voices informants reported that they were positive about the sociolinguistic diversity around them.

Amongst differences, it is notable that mean scores for most accents falls below 4.0 (the scalar mid-point), and almost all are below those from Giles' study, and this finding also applies to the younger (and so more comparable in age) of the respondents in the BBC study. However, it is difficult on this basis of these two studies alone to be certain that this reflects any kind of move to a more grudging attitude to accent prestige. It is also notable that the prestige profiles of some non-native English accents, such as French and German, are less favourable in the BBC data. A further difference concerns the label 'London', which receives a quite different ranking from Giles' 'Cockney', and this is doubtless because 'London' fuses stereotypes of working-class speech with those of a dynamic and overall prosperous metropolis.

Social attractiveness results (Table 10.3) again show a great similarity with Giles' study regarding 'an accent identical to your own' and the labels 'RP' and 'Standard English'. However, 'Queen's English', despite its prestige ratings, indexes a more sullied social attractiveness (and even more so for the younger BBC respondents, for whom the mean was 3.84). The Birmingham and Liverpool accents are once again disfavoured, as well as the Asian accent. The Afro-Caribbean accent ⟵ is less disfavoured, particularly by younger informants (mean = 4.04), who perhaps associate it with influences in popular culture. German-accented English is downgraded in the BBC data from its mid-ranking position in Giles' study. The moderate prestige rating of London is matched by moderate ratings for social attractiveness. But Southern Irish and Scottish-accented English are seen as the most attractive accents apart from the RP-type accents, and in fact the younger BBC respondents see Southern Irish as the most attractive of all the accents, including RP-type varieties and 'an accent identical to your own'.

Some interesting patterns emerged in the BBC Voices data regarding the sex, age and regional location of the respondents, as well as their orientation towards sociolinguistic diversity. Regarding sex, there was a reliable tendency for women to afford more prestige to accents; men were significantly more positive to only two of the accents: an accent identical to your own, and West Country English. A great deal of sociolinguistic research has shown that women tend to use more standard speech than men do for a given social class and speaking context. The Voices finding shows women nevertheless awarding more prestige to most regional varieties, but not to their own speech. For social attractiveness, again, there was a general pattern for women to afford more of this to accents than men did. Also, as with prestige, more men than women judged 'an accent identical to your own' as attractive. While, compared to women, then, males tended to withhold favourable evaluations of other people's speech, they made more favourable judgements of their own speech.

For the age variable, it was the oldest respondents who attributed the most prestige to 'Standard English', with a progressive decline in positivity to the youngest age group (still positive nonetheless). A similar pattern occurred with the judgements of social attractiveness of 'Standard English' and 'Queen's English'. It would seem that younger people were less influenced by the conservative ideology of valuing standard accents. Alongside this, compared to the older age groups, they also judged Afro-Caribbean, Belfast and Glasgow English as more attractive.

The regional locations of the respondents were also significant, in that, in a number of cases, findings show ingroup loyalties. This was especially the case with the Scottish respondents. For two of the Scotland accents – 'Scottish English' and 'Edinburgh English' – Scottish respondents provided more positive prestige judgements than respondents from all other regions. Also, respondents living in Wales were significantly more positive regarding the prestige of Welsh English than were all other groups except Northern Ireland respondents. Northern Ireland respondents were significantly more positive about the prestige of Northern Irish English than all others except Scottish respondents. Similar patterns emerge for social attractiveness, but with some interesting differences regarding the respective capital cities. The Belfast and Cardiff accents are not favoured by the Northern Irish and Welsh respectively. But the Scots are more favourable about the social attractiveness of Edinburgh (and Glasgow) English than all other groups except the Northern Irish.

Respondents who said they were more open to linguistic diversity penalised accents less heavily. Generally, they gave accents higher prestige and social attractiveness. This general criterion of whether and to what extent people value sociolinguistic diversity is clearly a particularly powerful one and it cuts across sociodemographic variation. It has not received attention in language attitudes research previously, but seemingly deserves more attention.

There are a number of points to sum up. To begin with, it is noteworthy in the prestige ratings in both studies that there is a great gap between, on the one hand, RP, Standard English and Queen's English, and, on the other hand, all other varieties in Table 10.2, including even 'an accent identical to your own'. At this level of the data, there seems little shift in deference towards standard varieties over the past thirty-five years. However, this view needs to be seen in the context of other findings in the study. That younger respondents were found to be less negative about the stigmatised varieties (even if still negative) provides some signs at least of liberal sentiment and perhaps a suggestion at least of ideological shift over time. For social attractiveness, it is interesting that respondents placed their own accents, plus Southern Irish English, Scottish English and Edinburgh English ahead of Queen's English. There are perhaps some signs of a 'rise of the regional' (Mugglestone 2003), even if this process still has a long way to go.

Secondly, the Celtic varieties show interesting patterns of ingroup loyalty, and they also fare quite well overall. In addition, looking at the overall findings for age, sex, regional location and diversity, it is clear that the sociolinguistic ideology found in the BBC study is not homo-geneous across the UK.

Thirdly, as so often needs to be said in language attitudes work, some approaches are more decontextualised than others, and the judgement patterns in the BBC study would appear to reflect broad language ideological structures that constitute a backdrop to accent encounters in the UK today, and constitute familiar discourses about language within that environment. Within particular contexts, as argued elsewhere in this book, they are likely to play themselves out in a variety of ways and shapes, and other research approaches will be needed in order to investigate them.

CONCLUSION

In this chapter, we have looked at three very different direct approach studies, employing their own research methods to investigate quite different kinds of research questions. Chapter 11 extends this direct approach focus to some recent developments in folklinguistic methods of accessing language attitudes.

FURTHER READING ON CHAPTER 10

For more background on the discourse analytic approaches to the study of attitudes:

Potter, J. and Wetherell, M., 1987, *Discourse and social psychology: beyond attitudes and behaviour*. London: Sage.

For a further example of, as well as more background on, the discourse-based study of language attitudes, this time looking at how individuals construct attitudes in their conversational interaction:

Liebscher, G. and Dailey-O'Cain, J., 2009, Language attitudes in interaction. *Journal of sociolinguistics* 13, 195–222.

For more detailed accounts of the BBC Voices study and findings:

Bishop, H., Coupland, N. and Garrett, P., 2005b, Conceptual accent evaluation: thirty years of accent prejudice in the UK. *Acta linguistica hafniensia* 37, 131–54.

Coupland, N. and Bishop, H., 2007, Ideologised values for British accents. *Journal of sociolinguistics* 11, 74–93.

The following book contains reviews of language attitudes research in a range of European contexts, and reports the results from a direct approach project in which a questionnaire was used to gather comparable data in these same contexts: the Basque Country, Catalonia, Galicia, the Valencian Community, Brussels, Friesland, Ireland, Malta and Wales:

Lasagabaster, D. and Huguet, Á., 2007, *Multilingualism in European bilingual contexts. language use and attitudes*. Clevedon: Multilingual Matters.

QUESTIONS FOR CHAPTER 10

1. Give your view on the advantages and limitations of the social constructionist approach to studying language attitudes, compared to other approaches you have read about in this book.
2. What is your own view of the importance of the 'ceremonial domain' for minority languages?
3. Do you feel that web-based surveys of the BBC Voices type offer a fruitful new option for language attitudes research?

11 Folklinguistics

Folklinguistics underlies another direct approach to language attitudes research. The term is not used here to suggest that the data in such studies is impoverished, although, as Niedzielski and Preston (2000: 3) have noted, it has certainly received such criticism. Rather, the term is used simply to refer to the views and perceptions of those who are not formally trained experts in the area being investigated – here, perhaps, 'non-linguists'. The approach attracted increasing attention through the 1990s and is particularly identified with Dennis Preston (e.g. 1989; 1993; 1996; 1999). Referring to the limitations of traditional dialectology in particular, Preston (1999) points to Hoenigswald's (1966: 20) claim that 'we should be interested not only in what goes on (in language) but also in how people react to what goes on, and in what people say goes on (talk about language)'. Apart from re-stating the view of Labov that the evaluative side of language is pivotal to the understanding of language variation and change, it also underlines the importance of language attitudes in metalanguage generally (Jaworski, Coupland and Galasiński 2004).

One could argue, of course, that most language attitudes work tries to access the attitudes of 'ordinary people', or the 'folk'. Against that, Preston argues that, despite the contribution that language attitudes work has made to our understanding of a speech community's set of beliefs about language and language use, much of it has nevertheless been too limited in scope, making it hard to interpret at times. He argues, as others have done, that a far more contextualised view is needed, and that this is better provided in people's representations of language variation, and their articulation of their beliefs about language, its use and its users. Relatively structured interviews and questionnaires which are generally characteristic of direct approach studies, and the equally highly focused nature of, say, the matched guise technique, work against such contextualisation, and focus on relatively limited aspects of people's attitudes. Preston's view is that to study adequately the attitudinal component of the communication competence of ordinary speakers, some attention needs to be given to beliefs about the geographical distribution of speech, beliefs about standard and affectively preferred language varieties, the degree of difference perceived in relation to surrounding varieties, imitations of other varieties, and anecdotal accounts of how such beliefs and strategies develop and persist (Preston 1989: 4). This additional component, he argues, will help to broaden the scope of language attitudes work.

FOLKLINGUISTIC PROCEDURES

There is quite a range of folklinguistic procedures developed by Preston and his colleagues (see especially Preston 1989; 1999; Niedzielski and Preston 2000; Long and Preston 2002). A large proportion of studies have focused on folk perceptions of dialects (perceptual dialectology), using various kinds of map tasks. Other studies have focused more on discourse. In order to give a very brief illustration of the sorts of tasks used in such perceptual dialectological studies, set out below are examples of Preston's work carried out in the USA.

DRAW A 'DIALECT MAP' OF THE USA

Respondents are given a blank map of a country – here, the USA – and are asked to outline (by drawing lines on the map) and label what they believe are the main speech regions of the USA. Figures 11.1 to 11.4 show four such maps from individual respondents, taken from Niedzielski and Preston (2000). The first is from a Michigan respondent (i.e. from the North), the second from a North Carolina respondent and the last two from South Carolina respondents (i.e. three from the South). In the studies from which these maps were taken, the state boundaries were included on the 'blank' maps given to respondents.

It is notable in these maps that the labels placed on the regions are not always purely descriptive, but often strongly attitudinal. The reference to southern talk as 'hillbilly' in figure 11.1 is a typical characterisation of the speech of that region by northerners. Niedzielski and Preston (2000: 59) refer to other labels used, such as 'hicks' and 'the worst English in America', again reflecting the low esteem which northerners often hold for southern speakers. Despite the differences amongst these individual maps as regards where the respondents drew their lines, Niedzielski and Preston (2000: 60) note that the general outlines drawn by southern and northern respondents in their study

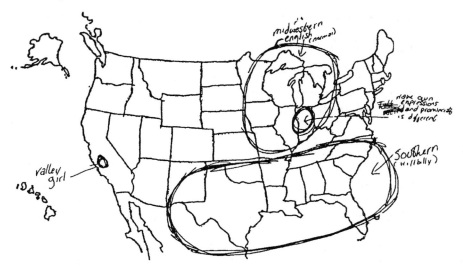

Figure 11.1 Hand-drawn dialect map by Michigan respondent.

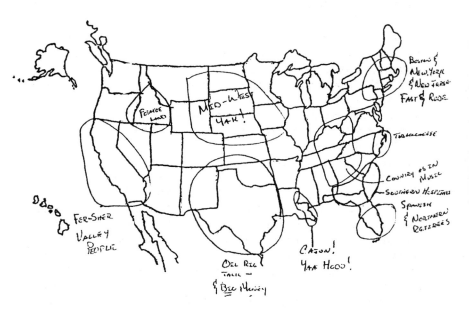

Figure 11.2 Hand-drawn dialect map by North Carolina respondent.

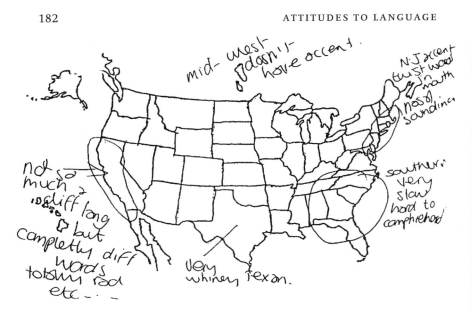

Figure 11.3 Hand-drawn dialect map by South Carolina respondent.

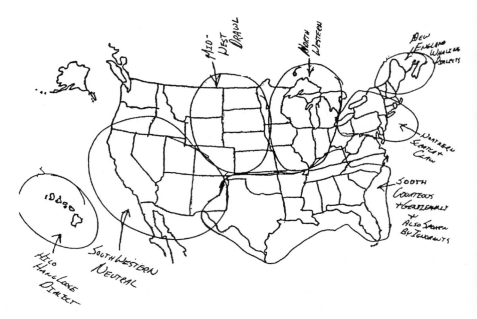

Figure 11.4 Hand-drawn map by South Carolina respondent.

were the same. Indeed, some of the labelling is also largely shared. For example, they note how there is a perception amongst both northern and southern respondents that 'Midwestern' speech is accent-free (e.g. see the 'normal' in figure 11.1 and the 'doesn't have accent' in figure 11.3). But for the South, the labels differed. Amongst the southerners' own labels for the South are items such as 'southern hospitality', 'country as in music', in contrast to the 'hicks' and 'hillbilly' labels used by the northern respondents. Niedzielski and Preston conclude that southerners show awareness of how their speech is commented on by northerners, and some even incorporate these views into their own folk linguistic accounts. They note that these instances of linguistic insecurity are tempered by signs of regional pride: e.g. 'courteous and gentlemanly', 'southern hospitality'. This pride appears to protect them from the intense type of linguistic insecurity that Labov (1966) found in his seminal sociolinguistic work in New York City.

The usefulness of this kind of perceptual dialectological study is at least twofold. Firstly, it provides some insight into what and where dialect regions actually exist in people's minds (where they draw their lines). Without this, argues Preston (1993: 193), it is difficult to study people's attitudes to such language variation. We need to know what it is they think they are judging, where it is located regionally, and how concentrated or extensive that region is. It is also useful to see how and how far these perceptions approximate or differ from the maps of dialectologists. Secondly, the task generates attitudinal comment alongside more descriptive data.

Perceptions of correct English in the USA

In this study, also reported in Niedzielski and Preston (2000), one group of respondents from Michigan and another from Alabama and South Carolina were asked to rate all the states of the USA for language correctness, using a ten-point scale (1 = least correct and 10 = most correct). Figures 11.5 and 11.6 are shaded maps representing the mean scores for each group for each state. The differences between them are immediately striking. For the Michigan respondents, the least correct English is spoken in the South and New York City. These are the only areas with mean scores below 5.00. Areas bordering these locations are rated next lowest for correctness, between 5.00 and 5.99, perhaps because of their closeness to these lowest-rated areas. Hawaii may share this same rating on account of its association with non-native speakers of English. At the other end, the Michigan respondents appear to have a great deal of linguistic confidence. Their highest rating for correctness goes to themselves, and only to themselves – in

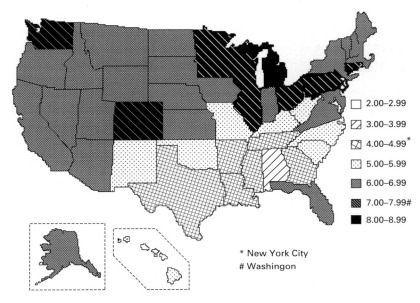

Figure 11.5 Michigan 'correctness' ratings and map.

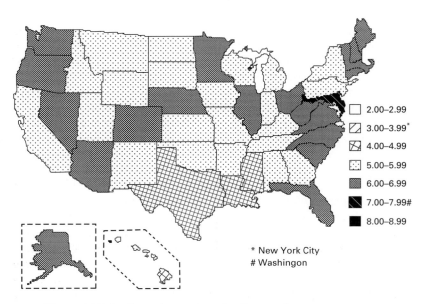

Figure 11.6 Southern 'correctness' ratings and map.

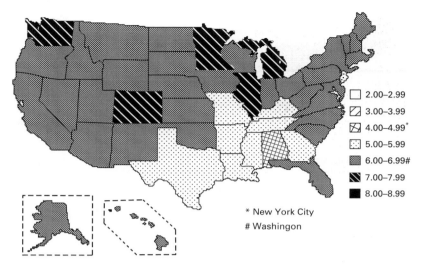

Figure 11.7 Michigan 'pleasantness' ratings and map.

the 8.00 to 8.99 range – seemingly attributing to themselves the position of Standard American English speakers.

As with the hand-drawn maps we considered above, the Southerners' map of correctness certainly does not suggest a trough of linguistic insecurity. The Carolinas, Virginia and West Virginia all achieve mean ratings of 6.00–6.99, well above the middle of the scale. Other parts of the South are in the 5.00–5.99 range, which is on a par with their ratings for much of the rest of the USA. Apart from New York City and New Jersey, the lowest ratings for correctness (4.00–4.99) are given to the 'western' South (Texas, Louisiana and Mississippi), the first two of which are generally not counted as the 'true' South (Niedzielski and Preston 2000: 67).

Perceptions of pleasant English in the USA

The same rating task was also given for 'pleasantness'. The differences, shown in Figures 11.7 and 11.8, are again marked between the Michigan and South respondents. The Michigan respondents rate themselves highest (7.00–7.99) and share this high rating with Washington, Colorado and Minnesota. Overall they do not rate the South highly (about the mid-point of the scale, at 5.00–5.99), with Alabama taking the lowest rating of 4.00–4.99, which it shares only with New York City (Niedzielski and Preston 2000: 70).

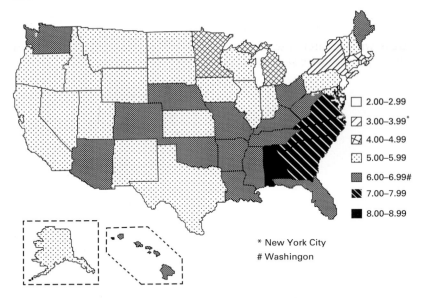

Figure 11.8 Southern 'pleasantness' ratings and map.

The ratings made by the Southerners are tougher. New Jersey achieves the only 2.00–2.99 rating in the study. New York City and New York State are rated 3.00–3.99, while Massachusetts, Michigan and Minnesota (these last two rated so highly by the Michigan respondents) are rated below the mid-point at 4.00–4.99, which is in fact the lowest rating that the Michigan respondents themselves awarded any of the states. Finally, the Southerners rate the whole of the south-east (Virginia, the Carolinas and Georgia) in the high category of 7.00–7.99, with only their own state – Alabama – rated in the top category of 8.00–8.99. Niedzielski and Preston (2000: 70) note that this high self-rating for pleasantness is matched only by Michigan's assessment of its own correctness, and it perhaps shows a strong preference for local affective norms in instances of linguistic insecurity.

Summing up this and other folklinguistic work on language attitudes in the USA, Preston (1996: 54) writes about correctness: 'I personally believe it is no exaggeration to say that it may be the most powerful contributor to awareness in American English.' While, for linguists, 'good' and 'bad' language appears to achieve such status from links with particular groups in society, for non-linguists 'good' language is primarily good because it is logical, authentic etc., and they can even define what a language may or may not contain: e.g. 'Ain't ain't a word, is it?' (p. 54). The significance of the pleasantness ratings, according to Niedzielski and Preston (2000: 76), is bound up in linguistic insecurity. Areas with greater insecurity focus on pleasantness to project local identity; those with security do not do so, since status already satisfies their need for uniqueness.

We have introduced folklinguistic approaches to the study of language attitudes by reviewing some perceptual dialectology studies. Perceptual dialectology, by its very dialect-linked nature, has regional dialects as its focus. But there is other work carried out in the folklinguistic field, focusing on folk-comment about ethnicity, style, gender, language in education, first language acquisition, for example. (See, for example, Niedzielski and Preston 2000 for more on these and other areas.) But having provided an introduction to folklinguistic perspectives, we now move on to a study for the remainder of this chapter that does not employ perceptual map tasks, but in which respondents simply throw down their first associations with language varieties, producing what we might call a 'shorthand for evaluative discourse' (Garrett, Coupland and Williams 2003; 2004).

ATTITUDES TO 'INNER CIRCLE' ENGLISHES: A FOLKLINGUISTIC VIEW

Chapter 4 reviewed Bayard *et al.*'s (2001) study of attitudes towards New Zealand, Australian, US and English Englishes, employing a verbal guise design and semantic differential scales, and drawing data from three of those countries: New Zealand, Australia and the USA. We now turn to a folklinguistic study of these same Englishes. Data was collected in New Zealand, Australia, China, Japan, New Zealand, the UK, the USA (Garrett 2009). This chapter will just consider the data from New Zealand, Australia, the UK and the USA (reported more fully in Garrett, Williams and Evans 2005a) to facilitate comparisons with Bayard *et al.*'s (2001) findings. The Chinese and Japanese attitudes to Englishes are reported in Garrett (2009).

In a simple open-ended questionnaire, the respondents were asked to name the countries around the world, apart from their own, where they knew that English was spoken as a native language, and to jot down some words to say 'how the English spoken there strikes you when you hear it spoken'. The responses, referred to here as 'keywords' (see also Garrett, Williams and Evans 2005b), were analysed to establish the general patterning of their contents and the social evaluations of the Englishes they included. The keywords were grouped into the following categories.

1. *Linguistic features.* These were keywords that could reasonably be taken as non-technical descriptions of some linguistic qualities of the Englishes, with no overt or clear evaluative meaning. In line with Preston's (1996) view of folklinguistic description as extending along a 'detailed' to 'global' continuum, some comments were very focused, such as 'clipped' and 'six = sux', while others were more global and general, such as 'different pronunciation', 'words have a different meaning'.

2. *Affective.* These keywords implied a variety of emotional consequences. They were subdivided into two broad types.

   a) Affective positive: expressing liking at a comfort level (e.g. 'pleasant to listen to', 'friendly', 'softer sounds') and also at a level of higher arousal (e.g. 'fun', 'enthusiastic', 'I love it').

   b) Affective negative: expressing discomfort (e.g. 'ugly', 'harsh', 'snobbish') and also higher arousal (e.g. 'annoying', 'irritating', 'twang that hurts your ear').

3. *Status and social norms.* These were about correctness, level of education and social status associated with the varieties, and are divided into two subgroups.

   a) Cultured: e.g. 'intelligent', 'refined', 'posh', 'well-spoken'.

   b) Uncultured: e.g. 'sounds slangy', 'incorrect', 'perverted English', 'tacky'.

4. *Cultural associations.* These suggested some iconic relationship to the culture (e.g. 'McDonalds'), generally not clearly or unambiguously evaluative in themselves. Some were media-focused, again ranging from specific (e.g. 'Jerry Springer') to more global (e.g. 'sit-coms').

These four categories were discrete in that each keyword could be placed in only one of them. But once this was done, there were other interesting patterns discernible that cut across the four categories. So as not to allow the categories to hide these from view and prevent the keywords from 'telling their story', a few new (non-discrete) groupings were formed of such items, sometimes only relating to one variety. The two largest additional groupings were:

5. *Diversity.* Some keyword responses concerned language diversity (e.g. 'many regional accents'). Such an item, then, would be included in the headings *Linguistic features* and *Diversity*.

6. *Comparison.* Some comments were grounded in comparisons with other varieties (e.g. 'similar to New Zealand', 'like us but with a little difference', 'Australian, but not!').

Table 11.1 gives an overall picture of the salience of each of the thematic categories. The percentages in the table are worked out as

Table 11.1. *Percentages of comments in each category as a proportion of total comments made by each group of respondents about each variety of English*

Varieties of English				
	USA	England	New Zealand	Australia
USA judges (n = 192)		*Items: n = 298*	*Items: n = 122*	*Items: n = 245*
Ling features		11%	6%	20%
Affective +		5%	16%	29%
Affective −		15%	4%	3%
Cultured +		56%	9%	4%
Cultured −		1%	7%	11%
Associations		6% media 4%	2% media 1%	28% media 8%
		Compare 3%	*Compare 41%*	*Compare 5%*
			D/know 20%	*Tough 8%*
UK judges (n = 152)	*Items: n = 216*		*Items: n = 128*	*Items: n = 185*
Ling features	21%		13%	17%
Affective +	12%		20%	38%
Affective −	46%		7%	4%
Cultured +	4%		2%	0%
Cultured −	10%		3%	10%
Associations	7% media 6%		11% media 2%	25% media12%
	Compare 2%		*Compare 46%*	*Compare 5%*
	Diverse 3%		*Blank 11%*	
	Excess 8%			
NZ judges (n = 70)	*Items: n = 119*	*Items: n = 106*		*Items: n = 98*
Ling features	23%	23%		24%
Affective +	10%	10%		4%
Affective −	33%	13%		24%
Cultured +	2%	40%		0%
Cultured −	17%	2%		12%
Associations	13% media 4%	3% media 1%		12% media 0%
	Compare 3%	*Compare 0%*		*Compare 13%*
	Diverse 13%	*Diverse 30%*		*Labels 8%*
	Excess 8%			
AUS judges (n = 103)	*Items: n = 158*	*Items: n = 133*	*Items: n = 94*	
Ling features	16%	12%	14%	
Affective +	10%	13%	18%	
Affective −	50%	15%	15%	
Cultured +	2%	50%	1%	
Cultured −	11%	3%	12%	
Associations	8% media 7%	2% media 0%	7% media 0%	
	Compare 1%	*Compare 1%*	*Compare 27%*	
	Diverse 4%	*Diverse 10%*		
	Excess 11%			

follows. The total number of keywords written by each group of judges was calculated for each of the varieties in turn. The number of words appearing in each of the categories was then worked out as a percentage of that total. So, for example, of the total of 298 keywords written by the USA respondents about English in England, 11 per cent referred to linguistic features. In the cultural associations category, there is also a separate percentage given for media-focused keywords, So, for example, 28 per cent of the USA respondents' keywords on Australian English referred to cultural associations generally, including the media keywords, and these media keywords accounted for 11 per cent of their total keywords on Australian English. Below, each variety is considered in turn before making comparisons with Bayard *et al.*'s (2001) findings. To give more focus to attitudes, the relatively neutral linguistic features category is not considered in depth in this chapter.

Australian English

Of the three groups of respondents, there was much similarity between the US and UK views of Australian English. Their keywords suggest considerable liking (i.e. positive affect) for the connotations of Australian English (more so, those of the UK sample), while at the same time viewing it as relatively uncultured ('sloppier', 'less educated – spends all the time at the beach'). Cultural associations were 'strong' for Australia, it seems (in terms of high proportions). Apart from the comments referring specifically to the media, there were many others. (And these others may, of course, have been transmitted *through* the media in various ways.) These others contained subthemes. Keywords such as 'sand', 'sun', 'beaches', 'coastal', 'surfer' clearly form one of these. Items such as 'beer drinking', 'the barbie', 'food and lager' are another. 'Koalas', 'kangaroos', 'dingos' are another. And there were a number of expressions that seem to be almost iconic representations of Australian English – 'down under', 'outback', 'Sheila', 'g'day mate'.

Cutting across one or two categories in the keywords from the US respondents, there was a subgroup of items concerning 'toughness' (listed as 'tough' in Table 11.1). No other variety of English in this study attracted such associations. They included items such as 'rugged', 'rough', 'macho', 'rustic', 'outdoors person', 'male features', 'messy, tough English'. There were also fifteen mentions of Crocodile Dundee in the US respondents' keywords and this is presumably a prime source of these 'tough' comments. The UK respondents mentioned him only twice, and the New Zealanders made no media references at all in relation to Australian English. One interpretation of this 'tough' grouping is that the US respondents may have been relying on more limited media representations for their stereotype than the other respondents. Crocodile Dundee was the only Australian individual mentioned in these media comments, and then, of course, only by the character name. The actor himself was never named, and nor were any other media people who are Australian and active in the US film industry, such as Nicole Kidman, Cate Blanchett and Russell Crowe. Perhaps this can be attributed in part to their playing a variety of non-Australian roles with non-Australian accents. Crocodile Dundee, in contrast, is most unambiguously an Australian character played with an Australian accent. The UK respondents, who made a greater proportion of media comments than the US judges, made more mention of TV soaps, where a greater range of Australian characters featured. Although these different types of media reference possibly accounted for the 'toughness' grouping appearing in the US but not the UK comments, the overall balance of judgements about affect and culturedness were nevertheless still comparable for these two groups of respondents.

More can be added regarding the salience of the Crocodile Dundee association in the US keywords. Bredella (1991) has argued, from a relativist perspective in cultural analysis, for the importance of focusing attention on the *observer* of foreign cultures. It is after all worth noting that the 1986 film was 'the most popular imported film in US history' (Miller, Govil, McMurria and Maxwell 2001: 173). Looking at the US respondents themselves, then, arguably the tough male individual who knows how to survive alone in tough frontier terrain, has some understanding of the animal and human life that already inhabits it, makes sure, even when he is greatly outnumbered, that any opposition always comes off worse in fights, and also displays some sense of justice even if stepping outside the law himself already features large in the media folklore of the USA (see, for example, Pumphrey 1993: 181). With the addition of modern urban scenes and a disarming ignorance of urban etiquette (Moore 1991), Crocodile Dundee's toughness (and perhaps dress-style) might represent a salient and more recent Australian variant of this famously valued and respected character-type of the US frontier.

Like the UK and US respondents, the New Zealanders viewed Australian English as uncultured. But there were some marked differences. Their affective view of Australian English was very negative – e.g. 'yuk', 'terrible accent', 'annoying', 'being a NZer makes me cringe at their accent sometimes'. Added to this category was a further grouping of items that were labels (referred to as 'labels' in Table 11.1) relating more explicitly to the people: e.g. 'Bastards', 'Bloody Aussie', 'Unfair'.

While one or two of these pointed to an amicable exchange of insults (e.g. 'Damn Aussies – friendly rivalry') most seem to be more parsimoniously interpretable as negative in orientation, particularly given the high proportion of comments in their negative affect category. Also, compared to the US and UK respondents, the New Zealanders drew less on cultural associations, and not at all (explicitly at least) on the media. It may be that relative geographical proximity and a greater degree of contact reduced the salience of these in their stereotype, compared to people in the USA and UK, where perhaps the media representations of Australia and its English have helped create a positive view in affective terms. On the other hand, the New Zealand negative judgements may also be attributable to their being neighbours to a much larger, more influential culture that in turn reduces their own visibility to outsiders. One could speculate that such irritation with a 'larger tiresome neighbour', to the point where outsiders will often assume you are from or part of the neighbouring culture rather than your own, is not uncommon for people in comparable contexts (e.g. Canadian attitudes to the USA, Welsh and Scottish attitudes to England).

New Zealand English

The negativity in the New Zealanders' view of Australian English was much less marked in the Australians' judgements of New Zealand English. They did evaluate it as uncultured, certainly more so than the US and UK respondents. But although their affective judgements accounted for about a third of their comments, these were quite balanced between positive and negative, suggesting some disagreement or lack of certainty about this dimension. The affective comments certainly did not carry the overwhelming tone of negativity that their own variety carried for the New Zealanders.

For the UK and US judges, New Zealand English was regarded with positive rather than negative affect, though not to the same degree as Australian English. Comments in the cultured category in Table 11.1 were quite balanced between positive and negative, again differentiating New Zealand from the Australian variety. The cultural association category was much emptier for New Zealand English, with next to no media reference. The cultural association keywords suggested a New Zealand stereotype that differed somewhat in its salient features from the Australian one – e.g. 'sheep', 'too many sheep, it's just not natural', 'British countryside with a better climate'.

All three groups of judges, especially the UK and US ones, relied a great deal on comparison in their comments about New Zealand English, much more so than judges did even for Australian English – e.g. 'in between UK and Australian English', 'kind of mix of Australian, Irish and English'. To some extent, this might be explained by a lack of clarity or certainty in the judges about what New Zealand English is in its own distinctive terms (the lack of visibility again, perhaps). This is also suggested by the large proportions of the comment 'don't know' amongst the US respondents, and their very low number of comments about linguistic features, for example, plus the noticeable proportion of spaces for comment that were left blank by UK judges. The Australians' comments were, perhaps understandably, less oriented to comparison than the others, but the proportion was nevertheless still high compared to those for the other varieties. The majority were simple comments linking New Zealand English to Australian – e.g. 'like Australian', 'similar to Australia', 'practically Aussies'.

English English

The keywords about English English largely aligned with the evaluative profile of RP in earlier studies. The overall weight of comment was to be found in the very high proportions of positive remarks in the cultured category. Mainly, these large groupings contained comments of three broad types. One type evaluated English English as 'correct', 'standard', 'proper' etc. The second focused more on tokens of high social status (e.g. 'wealthy', 'rich', 'high society'). The third referred to authenticity and heritage (e.g. 'original', 'traditional').

In the US keywords for English English, the strong salience of the cultured category was accompanied by the commonly found bias towards negativity in the affective comments – e.g. 'stuffy', 'they feel they are better than you', 'conceited and full-of-yourself attitude'. The New Zealanders and Australians, however, expressed a more balanced affective category. Apart from the traditional negative comments, there were, against expectations from earlier studies, positive ones too – e.g. 'I love it', 'nice to listen to', 'sexy accent', 'I love English people and when I hear the accent I want to go over there then I wish I sounded like that.' The New Zealanders in particular, as well as the Australians, showed awareness of diversity in their comments, as if other varieties of English in England also held some salience for them. Such comment was absent in the US keywords.

The cultural association category was small for all groups, though the proportion in the US keywords was slightly more – e.g. 'Royal family', 'Ancient times with a king and queen', 'play polo', 'don't like Americans'. Few media references occurred, with people presumably associated with very English or British roles or qualities – 'Hugh Grant', 'Elizabeth Hurley', 'James Bond'. 'Music' and 'The Beatles' also feature.

These contrasted with the relatively few made by the Australians and New Zealanders, which were also arguably more everyday – e.g. 'cups of tea', 'hot guys', 'makes me associate people with London. I think they must have pale skin and wear trench coats a lot', 'likes to follow the USA'. Both Australians and New Zealanders also recorded just a small quantity of outgrouping labels – 'Poms', 'British Poms', 'Pommies' – whose value is harder to interpret in terms of negativity or neutrality, given the balance in the affective category.

US English

All three groups showed considerable agreement in their comments on US English. The cultured category attracted less comment than it did in the case of English English, but the proportions were broadly comparable with Australian and New Zealand English. For US English, the comment in this category was clearly negative in balance for all groups. There was some salience afforded to diversity, but this was primarily from the New Zealand respondents again.

The affective category attracted by far the most comment, and while there were both positive and negative items, the overall balance was overwhelmingly negative. Positive affective keywords typically included comments such as 'friendly', 'casual', 'confident', 'energetic' and 'enthusiastic'. The negative keywords, though, differentiated the attitudes to US English from those towards the other varieties. Apart from the usual sorts of negative affect items such as 'harsh', 'ugly', 'not a very nice accent to listen to', three distinctive subthemes emerged across all three groups of respondents. These accounted for 10 per cent of the pooled comments of all the three groups about US English. One referred to arrogance and power – e.g. 'arrogant', 'they think they are better than everyone else', 'overpowering', accounting for about 6 per cent out of the 10 per cent. The remaining 4 per cent was fairly evenly split amongst the other two subthemes. One of these referred to exaggeration – e.g. 'over the top', 'overemphasised', 'melodramatic'. And the third subtheme referred to insincerity – e.g. 'false', 'phoney', 'artificial'. Cutting across these three subthemes, a further grouping was identifiable, referred to as 'excess' in Table 11.1. This contained items that explicitly referred to perceivedly unacceptable excesses, such as 'overpowering', 'overstated', 'overly confident', 'overrepresented everywhere', 'overexaggerated', 'don't like Americans – too outspoken'. Arguably, of course, other items here also suggest, implicitly rather than explicitly, unacceptable excess, for example overstepping norms of the use of power (e.g. 'imperialistic', 'belligerent'), norms of modesty and freedom of thought and expression (e.g. 'opinionated', 'arrogant', 'abrasive') and norms of truthfulness (e.g. 'falsifying what is said', 'fake').

Multiple standards and ideologies

This keywords study, as we concluded in Garrett *et al.* 2005a, shows a mosaic of overlapping and differentiating values, of certainty and uncertainty. Chapter 4 introduced Edwards and Jacobsen's (1987) notion of 'regional standard', and we might consider this in the global context of English, and alongside the idea that there can be different standard varieties for different domains. (Kristiansen 2001 claims that there is now one standard variety of Danish for the educational domain and another for the media). While 'American English has become the world's primary transnational language in culture and the arts as well as science, technology and commerce' (Barber 1996), the evaluative profile of this 'Global Standard English' seemed fairly uniform across all groups in this keywords study, associated in particular with power and dominance, and with respondents orienting to this in a conspicuously negative way, and all groups pointing to excesses of various kinds. The view of English English was a little more varied, displaying an unexpected balance of negativity and positivity in affective judgements by the Australians and New Zealanders, not shared by the US respondents. Its cultural associations across all three groups echoed an image of heritage that many argue the UK actively strives to produce of itself (e.g. Urry 2002: 94), and which Pegrum (2004) indeed has identified as a key marketing strategy for courses in British English as a foreign language. There is a suggestion in the keywords data, then, of a Standard English of heritage, tradition, history and authenticity, supporting and extending the speculation of Edwards and Jacobsen (1987) of a lingering loyalty to what is now a foreign variety but with valued historical links.

From the many 'don't knows' and response lines left blank, it was clear that the New Zealand stereotype was not well defined. Alongside images of sheep, there were references to New Zealand English being 'strange', and to how it was 'hard to get a clear picture'. Many resorted to defining it as being like some other variety. Apart from the rivalry in the Australians' comments, it was seen favourably on solidarity. But its definition as a kind of standard amongst these other three Englishes was not yet clear. The stereotypes linked to Australian English seemed clearer, further differentiated than the US and English Englishes, and winning a strong fondness from the US and the UK. But the visual representation for the North Americans was strongly influenced by the, for them, respected laid-back toughness of Crocodile Dundee, whereas for the UK the central image was of people with a valued down-to-earth, trustworthy nature. In contrast, the New Zealand picture seemed to be of a thoroughly irritating neighbour. If the profile from the US and UK respondents was projecting (albeit as outsiders and from a considerable distance) Australian English as a Regional or National Standard for Australia, the New Zealanders were seemingly resisting recognition of it as their own region.

Findings compared

When comparing with Bayard *et al*.'s (2001) earlier results, it needs to be borne in mind that the two studies differ in design and type of data. In the study reported here, the data did not include respondents' attitudes towards their own varieties, whereas in Bayard *et al*. (2001), UK English was not judged by its own speakers. Also, the conceptual design of the present study suggested judgements of the speech communities as single entities, merging potential differences relating to age, sex, etc. Judgements of the paired (male and female) speakers of each variety in Bayard *et al*. sometimes split the pairs, perhaps because of gender effects, or perhaps because of other features of the speech performance that over-rules speech variety alone as a basis for judgement (see Garrett, Coupland and Williams 1999 for examples of the same phenomenon with pairs of speakers). Readers might wish to refer back occasionally to Table 4.2 in chapter 4 during this comparison of findings.

As a whole, the evaluative profile of Australian English in Bayard *et al*. (2001) is very favourable, with the two speakers often closely paired in judgements. The Australian pair is always within the top-five rated speakers, with judgements never falling below 3.0 on the six-point scale. New Zealand English contrasts with this, however. There is close pairing again, but with both speakers always in the bottom three positions, except for solidarity, where the speakers divide. The female New Zealand speaker is viewed more favourably than the English pair on solidarity by both the US and Australian respondents. In the key-words study, the saliences of the positive affective categories appear broadly to reflect the relative position of both these varieties in terms of the Australian pair and the New Zealand female rather than the male. As regards the power dimension in Bayard *et al*. (2001), the keywords do not refer much to issues of power for Australian and New Zealand Englishes. (Another instance of this, where keywords do not include items that respondents were prepared to fill in scales for, is found in Garrett, Coupland and Williams 1995.) One interpretation is that, although respondents are prepared to give an answer to a question when asked (i.e. given a pre-labelled scale), it may not be about an issue that is particularly salient or important to them for that particular language variety, and so not surface in their open-ended comment about it. One reason for its absence in the open-ended coments may be simply that they associate little of that particular quality with that particular language variety but do not feel that this denotes an unacceptable deficiency that makes it noteworthy. (In the discussion of Lambert *et al.* 1960 in chapter 5, mention was made that the issue of importance to respondents of the ratings they are asked to make on scales is often not given sufficient attention in language attitudes research.)

It is notable how much the English pair in the Bayard *et al.* study are split apart. The English female is usually ranked seventh or eighth and never rises above sixth place, and never achieves a mean score exceeding 3.4. Again, one cannot be sure whether this splitting is due to individual (e.g. performance) factors, or whether it represents an interaction between language variety and gender, with very different stereotypes for the men and women for power, status and competence, but not solidarity, where they pair closely. In any event, the low ratings for the pair on the solidarity dimension do resemble the affective findings in the keywords from the US respondents in particular (as well as in other studies reviewed in chapter 4). But this aside, the keywords findings on the 'cultured' dimension are more suggestive of the English male in Bayard *et al.*'s study than the English female. As in the case of Australian and New Zealand Englishes, respondents seem to have little to say about the power dimension in their keywords.

The US speakers' profile in Bayard *et al.* differs the most dramatically from the keywords data. While there is a slight division of the two US speakers on the power and competence dimensions of the Australian and New Zealand respondents, they pair closely on the solidarity dimension, where they achieve the highest ratings of all speakers. But the same degree of positive solidarity is not found in the affective keywords. In this case, though, comments about power are incorporated into the affective category, since, as mentioned above, they carry a strongly negative flavour, with some respondents clearly hostile.

There are a number of possible interpretations for these differences. Firstly, there is the methodological issue of how the respondents record their evaluations. It has been mentioned earlier in this book that attitude rating scales have high utility, not least in their lending themselves to valuable and rigorous statistical analysis to discover overall patterns of association and difference in the data, and in the ease and speed with which they can usually be completed and analysed. The keywords approach is lacking in that regard. Nevertheless, a genuine methodological difficulty arises when one considers how respondents would approach a scale labelled, for example, 'not at all assertive' at one end, and 'very assertive' at the other, if their view was that the speakers sounded *over*assertive. If they completed the scale, they would (arguably) be likely to record 'very assertive' on the scale. Problems occur if a researcher then interprets this positive scale rating as a positive attitude, where the directionality of the semantic differential is confused with that of the attitudinal differential, a point referred to in chapter 5. While the keywords approach has, like any method, limitations of its own, it can nevertheless allow such orientations to surface more clearly at times. So one possible explanation for the differences in results regarding the US in particular is that respondents' orientations to high degrees of power ('overpowering'), for example, would not normally show securely on conventional attitude rating scales. To some extent, this problem occurs with keywords too, since they, like scale labels, are also a reduced discourse. If a respondent simply writes down 'power', for example, the same difficulty exists, but the opportunities to write more freely than scales allow permit other forms to surface alongside.

There are other (and not mutually exclusive) explanations too for the differences in findings between the two studies. The keywords data was collected in late 2002/early 2003, and it is possible that world events, political, economic and military, since the time of Bayard *et al.*'s data collection had changed attitudes in these communities. Bayard *et al.* speculate (albeit stressing the need for caution) on the possible impact of the media in influencing attitudes to US English, given its high profile in the global media. Certainly media coverage of events around controversial military conflicts involving the US featured large in the media during the period between the studies. Respondents' comments do not flag up specific conflicts, but a smattering of general comments such as 'war', 'belligerent', 'imperialistic', 'powerful dominating country' suggest that this is not an explanation to be quickly ruled out.

In contrast, there are no such comments about any of the other Englishes, at a time when their speakers, too, were playing visible and controversial roles in the same conflicts. This is harder to explain, but may relate to media coverage giving the US a much higher profile in these affairs, and the powerful links to the destruction of the World Trade Centre in New York. But if US English is dominating the media more and more, then perhaps this can be at a cost – both in terms of solidarity and orientations to the use of power associated with the language – when relevant media content generates hostility. Though speculative, it is a suggestion that merits further investigation over time, to see if attitudes to a global standard variety operate differently from those towards national and regional (and other?) standards.

CONCLUSION

In this chapter, then, we have examined folklinguistic approaches to the study of language attitudes, and with particular focus on keywords. The gathering of this kind of open-ended data has sometimes been seen as a preliminary stage of research to help decide what labels to put on scales (an issue considered in chapter 4, and illustrated in the study by Paltridge and Giles 1984 in chapter 5). The keywords study showed the value of this kind of data as main data. It has been noted that the approach does not allow a rigorous statistical investigation of differences, associations or interactions. Used alongside accompanying data from rating scales, however, keywords can fill out a more highly structured narrative. Nevertheless, here, even without such accompanying data from within the same study, they have afforded a degree of patterning that has facilitated illuminating and, at times, colourful insights into the stereotypes associated with these Englishes. Chapter 1 referred to Lippmann's (1922) idea of stereotypes being 'pictures in the head', simplified images of what groups look like and what they do. Certainly, through the cultural associations, other thematic groupings and labels used in the keywords – from 'dingos' to 'cups of tea' to 'sheep' to 'McDonalds', a more vividly pictorial image is gained of the social and cultural connotations attached to these language varieties, as well as some measure of the way in which respondents orientate to their judgements of how much power, status, enthusiasm or confidence a variety projects to them, how they measure against norms, and the relative importances the respondents attach to them.

Through close comparison of studies with a similar focus, it has been possible, to some extent at least, to show how methods can bring different contributions to the study of this complex field of language attitudes. Chapter 12 exemplifies this further with a larger scale study.

FURTHER READING ON CHAPTER 11

Key further reading for folklinguistic approaches to language attitudes includes:

Jaworski, A., Coupland, N. and Galasiński, D. (eds.), 2004, *Metalanguage: social and ideological perspectives*. The Hague: Mouton.

Long, D. and Preston, D. (eds.), 2002, *Handbook of perceptual dialectology* (vol. II). Amsterdam: Benjamins.

Niedzielski, N. and Preston, D., 2000, *Folk linguistics*. New York: Mouton.

Preston, D. (ed.), 1999, *Handbook of perceptual dialectology* (vol. I). Amsterdam: Benjamins.

QUESTIONS FOR CHAPTER 11

1. In this chapter, we have referred to notions of 'regional standards' and different standard varieties for different domains, such as education and the media. How do you see the 'standard language' situation in your own language context?

2. We have referred to the presence of 'cultural associations' (e.g. cups of tea, Crocodile Dundee, sheep) in the social meanings linked to language varieties in this chapter. What sorts of cultural associations linked to language varieties in your country are you aware of? What media influence, if any, do you think there might be in these? What, if anything, do you think they tell you about people's language attitudes?

12   An integrated programme of language attitudes research

Earlier in this book, it was mentioned that many language attitudes studies are relatively small-scale 'one-off' studies. Cumulatively, by gradually exploring more aspects of language attitudes, they provide the bedrock of what we know and understand about language attitudes, and, also as mentioned and elaborated earlier, we have to acknowledge that particular research methods have their own advantages and limitations. In this chapter we will consider an instance where a range of methods were integrated into the same language attitudes project. Often such work is not feasible, since it requires considerable resources devoted to one area of language attitudes. Usually studies have to be carried out on a smaller scale. But consideration of this multiple-method programme of research offers an opportunity to show how methods can complement each other.

In terms of content, the study provides insights into attitudes towards varieties of English spoken in different parts of Wales, the setting of this research. It is a common feature that findings from one study throw up questions or new issues to be investigated in future research, and in earlier studies of attitudes towards Welsh English there had been some diversity in findings that were worth exploring. For example, while Welsh English had been found to be more favourably evaluated than RP, and on a par with the Welsh language itself (Bourhis *et al.* 1973), it had elsewhere been downgraded in relation to both Welsh and RP (Price *et al.* 1983). In addition, as we saw in Bourhis and Giles (1976) in chapter 5, Welsh English has also been found to be downgraded alongside RP in relation to Welsh. With such diverse findings, Price *et al.* (1983) called for an investigation over the whole region, and the study summarised here responded to this. It consisted of two parts. One was a questionnaire study of teachers all over Wales, conceptual in approach, involving the completion of scales and maps. The other was a verbal guise study, involving scales and keywords. Each is reported in turn below. More details of these studies can be found in

Coupland, Williams and Garrett 1994; 1999; Williams, Garrett and
Coupland 1996; 1999; Garrett, *et al.* 1995; 1999; 2003; 2004).

AN OVERVIEW OF DIALECT REGIONS IN WALES

Since this is a study across all of Wales, brief preliminary sketches are
given here of the main socio-cultural characteristics of the six dialect
regions included in the study. Figure 12.1 shows the six dialect regions
studied.

1. The south-east urban area. This contains the Cardiff conurbation.
   Cardiff, the capital of Wales, established itself as an industrial
   urban centre during the nineteenth century. Historically, it is

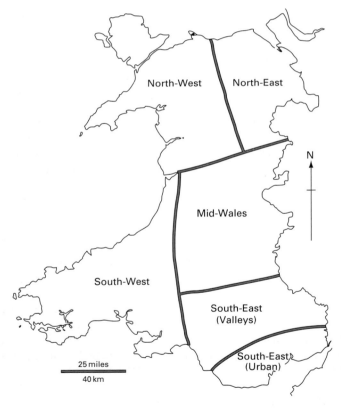

Figure 12.1 Map of Wales, showing each of the six dialect regions.

very anglicised. Cardiff is economically more buoyant than the other Welsh regions.

2. The south-east Wales Valleys. Until the 1980s, this was a heavy industrial zone producing coal and steel, but the closure of these industries led to high levels of unemployment and social deprivation.

3. The south-west: a rural, agricultural, and traditionally Welsh-speaking 'heartland', now somewhat fragmenting in terms of its Welsh language speakers (Aitchison and Carter 1994; 2004). The Welsh language has had more influence on English in this region than in the previous two (see Parry 1990).

4. Mid-Wales: a predominantly agricultural zone occupying the centre of Wales, but excluding western coastal areas. Compared to the 'heartlands' of the north-west and south-west, it is largely non-Welsh-speaking. The eastern mid-Wales English dialect is characteristically rhotic, in some respects aligning with the features of the 'Upper South West' dialect area of England (see Trudgill 1990).

5. The north-east: a comparatively urban industrial zone, relatively anglicised in contrast to the north-west and south-west regions. The nearby Liverpool conurbation has had an influence on English in this region.

6. The north-west: a predominantly rural and agricultural zone, associated with slate quarrying (which has declined over recent decades) and sheep-farming. The region is a key part of the Welsh-language heartland, with strong Welsh-language influence on its English.

THE QUESTIONNAIRE STUDY: RATING SCALES

Secondary school teachers all over Wales completed a questionnaire. In one task, they were given a blank map of Wales and asked to draw in what they felt were the main dialect regions of Wales, to give each one a label and write a brief characterisation of the English spoken there. Another task – considered first, below – asked them to rate on scales the dialects spoken in the six regions described above, along with RP.

Factor analysis of the attitude scales identified four dimensions: prestige, dynamism, pleasantness and Welshness. Multivariate and univariate statistical analysis showed that the dialects were judged differently from each other on all these dimensions. Table 12.1 shows how each of these varieties has its own evaluative profile.

Table 12.1. *Means and **standard deviations** of teachers' judgements of the accent/ dialect communities (1 = very, 7 = not at all)*

	Prestigious	Pleasant	Dynamic	Truly Welsh
North-west	4.47	4.25	4.42	2.52
	1.2	1.3	1.6	1.2
Cardiff	4.72	4.75	3.97	4.87
	1.2	1.4	1.3	1.7
South-west	3.77	2.63	3.68	2.10
	1.1	1.1	1.2	1.4
South-east/Valleys	5.03	3.25	3.63	2.43
	1.2	1.6	1.4	1.6
Mid-Wales	3.92	3.33	4.25	4.41
	1.2	1.2	1.2	1.7
North-east	4.82	4.78	4.58	4.86
	1.1	1.3	1.3	1.9
RP	2.32	4.08	4.09	6.66
	1.2	1.1	1.3	1.2

Cardiff and (also urbanised) north-east Wales are both seen as lacking in Welshness, prestige, and pleasantness. RP is viewed as carrying the most prestige, but the teachers award it little else on the scales used in the study. South-west Wales, on the other hand, has the 'fullest' profile, with its positive ratings across all four dimensions, and if a standard variety needs subjective definition as such (Haugen 1966), then south-west Wales English emerges as a strong contender for the title of standard Welsh English in Wales, with positive ratings for prestige and Welshness. Welshness, in fact, turns out to be a strong discriminator of these Welsh English dialects, quite independently of the other dimensions. For example, Welshness and prestige are distinguished. In contrast with the pattern for south-west Wales English, the south-east/Valleys variety associated with the Welsh coal-mining communities has high Welshness but low prestige, and this is also the case with north-west Wales. Welshness and pleasantness are also separated. While both south-west and north-west Wales Englishes are seen as very Welsh, the south-west variety is seen as very pleasant and the north-west variety is viewed as unpleasant.

Statistical analysis showed some differences in the attitudes of the North Wales teachers and the South Wales teachers. The southern teachers saw the Cardiff and south-east/Valleys varieties as significantly less prestigious than the northerners did, as well as less 'truly Welsh-sounding'. They also saw the south-east Valleys variety as sounding less pleasant than northerners did. These differences may be due to familiarity effects. The southern teachers obviously included teachers from the Cardiff, south-east/Valleys areas and nearby, and teachers may be a group less affected by sentiments of language loyalty found in some other language attitudes studies. Southern teachers may be more familiar, then, with the sociolinguistic stigma associated with Cardiff English, and the northerners' remoteness might lead them to be more influenced by some 'rosy picture' representations of the south-east/Valleys region in traditional films.

Differences were also found between the Welsh-speaking teachers and the non-Welsh-speaking teachers. Non-Welsh speakers down-graded the Cardiff and north-east Wales varieties on prestige. They also judged RP as more dynamic than did the Welsh speakers, who in turn judged south-west Wales and south-east/Valleys as more dynamic than RP. Several possible explanations are offered for this in Coupland *et al.* (1994). One is that the two groups of teachers could be operating with different notions of the territorial scope of prestige, with the non-Welsh speakers making their social comparisons with a wider range of varieties of English. Prestige might be seen as high if comparisons are restricted to Wales, but lower if extended to a larger sociolinguistic (e.g. national, international) context. The explanation for the differences in dynamism ratings could be similar: i.e. that the Welsh speakers are more comfortable anchoring their perceptions of dynamism in the ingroup bilingual situation. In any event, these results suggest that the diverse findings in the earlier studies are in part due to there being a number of Welsh English varieties having distinct profiles, and so Welsh English cannot be seen as one single variety, and also in part due to different social groups in Wales holding different attitudes.

THE QUESTIONNAIRE STUDY: DIALECT REGION LABELS AND CHARACTERISATIONS

The dialect regions identified by the teachers as they drew their maps were comparable with but more differentiated than the descriptive dialectological map of Wales that formed the basis of the six regions given to them to judge in the scales task above. They echoed the division of North Wales English to distinguish a zone under the influ-ence of the Liverpool conurbation (hence the separate 'North Wales' and 'Liverpool' columns in Table 12.2). And within the South West, they also distinguished the area of Pembrokeshire from the rest of the

Table 12.2. *Frequencies of categorised comments for the labelled areas (numbers of instances mentioned, with rounded percentages in bold below)*

	Valleys	Cardiff	North Wales	Mid-Wales	South-west Wales	Liverpool	Pembrokeshire
Linguistic form	14 **18**	26 **34**	22 **34**	4 **7**	3 **6**	6 **13**	2 **4**
Affective positive	22 **29**	4 **5**	3 **5**	12 **21**	15 **32**	3 **7**	4 **9**
Affective negative	9 **12**	33 **43**	19 **30**	7 **13**	3 **6**	5 **11**	5 **11**
Welsh	24 **31**	1 **1**	15 **23**	7 **13**	14 **29**	1 **2**	1 **2**
Not Welsh	3 **4**	5 **7**	8 **13**	14 **25**	4 **8**	35 **76**	31 **69**
Cultured	0	2 **3**	0	3 **5**	1 **2**	0	2 **4**
Uncultured	4 **5**	2 **5**	0	0	0	1 **2**	0
Rural	0	0	1 **2**	3 **5**	2 **4**	0	5 **11**
Urban	0	4 **5**	0	0	0	0	0
Total	76	77	64	56	48	46	45

South West. Pembrokeshire is the most south-westerly region of Wales, associated primarily with tourism through the beauty of its country-side and beaches. It has a popular image of being an 'un-Welsh' enclave due to its historical popularity with the English.

Our primary focus here is on the sorts of labels that the teachers used and the dominant traits attributed to the dialect communities through the labels and characterisations. These findings, set out in Table 12.2, again showed dialect regions having quite separate evalu-ative profiles, this time expressed in the teachers' own words rather than as the researchers' labels given to them on seven-point scales. We will consider the dialect regions shown in Table 12.2 (the column headings), and the categories of comments they made in their charac-terisations (the row headings). The categories are similar to those in Garrett *et al.* (2005a) in chapter 11 (linguistic forms, positive and negative affect, cultured/uncultured, etc.), but with the additions of comments about Welshness, and rural/urban associations of the dia-lects. We will look briefly at the profile of each region in turn and give examples of items in the categories in the process.

Valleys

Given its crucial place in the political history and popular cultural mythology of Wales, it is not surprising that the Valleys was the most frequently identified and labelled English dialect region of Wales. About 18 per cent of the respondents identifying this region com-mented on linguistic forms, but there was no predominating linguis-tic stereotype discernible in these comments. Examples include 'stressed', and 'closed' or 'elongated' vowel forms. It was typically described in terms of positive affect (29 per cent, second only to south-west Wales), commonly attracting comments such as 'friendly', 'warm' and 'soft', as well as 'lively' and 'strong'. Echoing the findings in the scales reported above, Welshness was frequently mentioned (more than other varieties, though similar once again to south-west Wales). There were few comments in the cultured/uncultured category, but a few comments associated Valleys English with being uncultured: e.g. 'common', 'working class without higher education', 'uneducated'.

Cardiff

Cardiff was the second most commonly identified region. Along with North Wales, it attracted the highest proportion of comments about linguistic form. A large majority focused on vowel features: e.g. 'stretched', 'flattened', with some respondents using the labels

'Caerdiff', 'Carediff', 'Ceydiff', suggesting the raised and fronted long /aː/ variable in Cardiff English. This dialect attracted the highest proportion of negative affective comments: e.g. 'ugly', 'harsh', 'hard', 'irritating', 'annoying'. Once again, findings matched the scales findings, and Cardiff English was not associated with Welshness.

North Wales

This was a somewhat diffuse region, since some teachers were clearly referring to north-west Wales, and others to north-east. Those focusing on the north-west had more to say about Welshness (e.g. 'strongly influenced by Welsh', 'Welsh order to words'), while those focusing on the north-east part made more mention of Liverpool, and the dialect being 'not Welsh'. The proportion of linguistic form characterisations was as high as for Cardiff, with many comments referring to the variety as 'nasal' and 'guttural'. Like Cardiff again, North Wales attracted a clear preponderance of negative over positive affect: e.g. 'unpleasant', 'annoying', 'harsh', 'painful', 'sound as if they have a bad cold'.

Mid-Wales

This dialect area of Wales is very diverse and diffuse, and this appears to be reflected in the characterisations. There were few references to linguistic form, and comments about affect and Welshness are divided. 21 per cent made positive affective evaluations (e.g. 'soft', 'gentle', 'pleasant') and 13 per cent made ones coded as negative (e.g. 'bland', 'plain'). Welshness comments included 'very Welsh', 'pleasant Welsh' as well as 'English feel and can be more English than Welsh'. Comments made about parts closer to the border with England tended more towards 'not Welsh', and there were some references to the influence of the English regions. The area's rural character was also reflected: e.g. 'country', 'rustic', 'rich farmer', 'yokel'.

South-west Wales

Similar to the Valleys, this region attracted the most positive affective evaluations (e.g. 'soft', 'pleasant', 'melodious'), as well as high Welshness. The Welshness comments, though, revealed a different Welshness from the Valleys, in that there were frequent comments for south-west Wales about authenticity (e.g. 'the true accent of Wales', 'heartland accent', 'inherent', 'acute Welsh') and the influence of the Welsh language (e.g. 'high percentage of Welsh speakers', 'English spoken with difficulty').

Liverpool

The strongest feature in these characterisations is that this variety is highly un-Welsh, and few other characteristics are recorded. There are one or two references to 'nasal' qualities, and its being 'unattractive', 'ugly' and 'grating'. But otherwise, the dialect region is strongly associated with the very large English urban centre of Liverpool, with comments such as 'Scouse', 'Liverpudlian', 'back end of Liverpool, and 'Liverpool softened with Welsh'.

Pembrokeshire

Like the Liverpool region, Pembrokeshire was most strongly associated with non-Welshness. Affective comments are evenly split between positive (e.g. 'soft', 'delightful', 'relaxing') and negative, which have no real pattern (e.g. 'shrill', 'husky', 'bland' and 'odd'). There are frequent comments about Englishness, including 'does not sound as if the people live in Wales' and 'send them back to England'. A few comments refer to this dialect region's rurality, and to rural areas of England ('Somerset' and 'Cornish'), perhaps also reflecting the rhoticity of the Pembrokeshire dialect.

DISCUSSION OF THE QUESTIONNAIRE STUDY FINDINGS

An unexpected finding in the characterisations was that the teachers made very little use of the cultured/uncultured category. Status is one of the most firmly established evaluative dimensions in language attitudes research generally, and the teachers did differentiate Welsh-English varieties along this dimension in the phase of the questionnaire in which they were given labelled scales to complete. The infrequency of status comments in the open-ended characterisations might mean that they were subscribing to a professional norm which tabooed claims that social status can be associated with language use, and that this was more visible when the task required more time for cognitive processing and elaboration.

When the teachers were asked to produce their own characterisations, rather than simply complete scales given to them, the Welsh dimension was confirmed as salient, and a very strong discriminator of the Welsh English dialects. And the characterisations also confirm the independence of the Welshness dimension from affect, as we saw in the scales findings. Attributed Welshness, then, appears as a productive resource for sociolinguistic stereotyping. It is highly salient for characterising as un-Welsh the urban north-east of Wales and Pembrokeshire in the extreme south-west. In contrast, the Valleys, south-west and north-west Wales are all identified as 'Welsh', 'true' or 'deep Wales'. In addition to these different degrees of Welshness associated with the Welsh English varieties both in the maps data and in the scales results, the labels and characterisations provided in the maps data also appear to distinguish qualitatively between different kinds of Welshness. For example, although south-west Wales and the Valleys are attributed high levels of Welshness, the Welshness of south-west Wales English seems to carry associations with authenticity, as well as Welsh-language influence (as does north-west Wales English). This richness in the characterisations also provides more detail than the attitude scales alone can give. The scales findings, on the other hand, in which statistical analysis reveals significant patterns in the data, provide a framework around which the open-ended data can elaborate.

THE VERBAL GUISE STUDY

In each of the six dialect regions that were the basis of the scales study above, secondary school students were asked to listen to audio-recorded narratives told by similar-aged male students from other locations within the same six dialect regions. There were two speakers from each region, plus two RP-speaking students, so fourteen in all. The student respondents, and a group of teachers, completed two tasks. The first was a keywords task, such as we saw in chapter 11, in which they jotted down their first reactions as they listened. The second task involved completing attitude rating scales. The questions and labels for the scales had been arrived at through discussions with other students of the same age (15) at the design stage of the study. They were:

> How interesting does this story sound?
> Do you think the speaker is a good laugh?
> Do you think this speaker does well at school?
> How much like you do you think this speaker is?
> Overall, do you like this speaker?
> Do you think you could make friends with this speaker?
> How Welsh do you think this speaker sounds?

The narratives were the 15-year-old teenagers' own stories about something funny, frightening or embarrassing that had happened to them or someone they knew. The study employed self-contained episodes from their stories, to keep them about the same length. They differed considerably in content. They were coded to represent their dialect (Cardiff, NE, NW, SW, Mid, Valleys) plus a randomly allocated number. Here, each is listed with its code label, and very briefly summarised.

> *Cardiff 1*: He and his cousin are staying in Spain, selling cigarette lighters to bars. On the way home, he feels sick from being in the sun all day.
>
> *NE2*: He goes into a nightclub, under-age. A media company and music band arrive. By fighting off many much bigger people, he manages to get a good haul of albums, autographs and t-shirts.
>
> *RP3*: He has an accident with a belt-sander at school when his hand slips and he scrapes his fingers. He feels ill and tells the teacher, who says it is 'quite nasty' and sends him to sit outside.
>
> *SW4*: A vivid description of a friend trying to get into an under-size rugby shirt. The teenagers often call his friend 'Michelin man' because they think he is overweight and unfit.
>
> *Valleys5*: His father has a car accident, trying to avoid sheep in the rain. His father hits three lamp-posts and, not wearing a seat-belt, is thrown through the windscreen and loses his foot. The car engine lands in the front seat where he had been sitting.
>
> *Mid6*: He is driving a tractor, helping his father on his farm. The tractor tips up, and sways around. He manages to jump off. His father comes and stops the tractor.
>
> *NW7*: Someone he knows buys a new helmet. To test it, he throws a brick in the air so that it will land on the helmet. He puts his hands on top of his head and the brick breaks his fingers.
>
> *Valleys8*: Out with a friend, they find a sewage pump. His friend turns it on and sewage squirts everywhere.
>
> *NE9*: He is out at a restaurant with his family. Something is tickling their feet under the table. They look, and see cock-roaches everywhere.
>
> *NW10*: Someone he knows gets into trouble for stealing a gate from the fire brigade, and making a motorbike with it. Later, he builds another motorbike. A fault causes him to collide with and somersault over a car, and he then hits a police car, badly injuring his knee.
>
> *Cardiff 11*: A humorous story. Trying to steal a free game from a pool table, he gets his hand stuck in it. Eventually the care-taker arrives and says the only solution is to saw the pool table in half, so goes off and comes back with a chainsaw.

RP 12: He sees a chair fall off the big-wheel at a fairground. The people in it get up, stunned, and walk off. The operator puts the chair back on and continues as normal. RP12 is 'flabbergasted'.

SW 13: His father told him and his brother to take the motorbike and trailer to do a job on their farm. Afterwards, they were racing around the field when they realised the trailer had come loose. It had landed in a hedge.

Mid14: He hears bats while in bed. He turns the light on but sees nothing. Later, he turns it on again, sees one on the landing, and calls for his dad. He wakes later again when he hears more.

THE SCALES RESULTS

The statistical analysis in this part of the study took a different form from those more commonly used in language attitudes studies. It comprised a combination of cluster analysis and multidimensional scaling (MDS). Cluster analysis made it possible to see how the narratives/dialects fell into groups, or clusters on the basis of attitudinal ratings. The motivation for using MDS was to identify a set of cognitive maps relating to Welsh English varieties around Wales (see also similar work by Preston and his colleagues in Preston 1999). The end result is a 'map' of clusters spread out along two dimensions, represented by a vertical and a horizontal axis, as in Figures 12.2–12.7 below. There is some subjectivity in interpreting why narratives/dialects cluster together, and why they are spread around the two axes as they are. Reference to the narratives and dialects themselves can help in this interpretation. Below, we consider the results for three of the scales listed above, comparing the teachers' and teenagers' responses.

How Welsh do you think this speaker sounds?

The teenagers' assessments in Figure 12.2 generate four clusters for this question. In relation to the horizontal axis, they are interpretable in terms of Welshness on the left, moving towards increased un-Welshness or Englishness on the right, and this reflects the Welshness judgements in the questionnaire study summarised earlier. It is notable that each regional pair of speakers is located within the same cluster, indicating the regionality in the speech is very salient when the respondents judge qualities of Welshness in the voices. The 'English' cluster on the right shows that north-east and mid-Wales speakers are perceived to be as English as the RP speakers here.

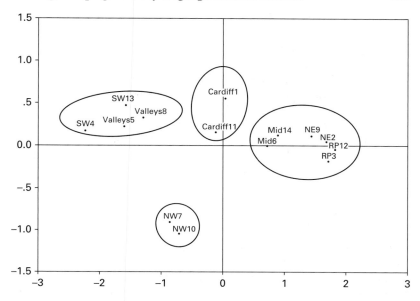

Figure 12.2 Teenagers: 'How Welsh do you think this speaker sounds?'

The south-west Wales and Valleys, in contrast, are seen as conjoined heartlands of Welsh identity, and Cardiff finds its location in the middle, not Welsh enough to be in the Welsh cluster, but not anglicised enough to be in the English cluster.

The clusters are spread along the vertical axis too, however. While, horizontally, the north-west Wales speakers are in the 'Welsh half', they are vertically at some distance from the others, suggesting that Welshness occupies other perceptual spaces. North-west Wales English dialects are strongly influenced by the Welsh language, and the north-west is geographically more remote from large urban centres than the south-west and the Valleys. In fact, if the lower and upper halves of Figure 12.2 are inverted (and this would be perfectly acceptable with MDS as long as the spatial relationships remain unchanged, since MDS simply produces a spatial representation of quantitative distance data), the result bears a close resemblance to the geographical map of Wales, but with the Valleys joining south-west Wales in a composite Welsh heartland. So the vertical axis seems almost to be a perceptual north–south axis.

The teachers follow a similar pattern in Figure 12.3, but this time the north-west speakers are included into just one Welsh heartland

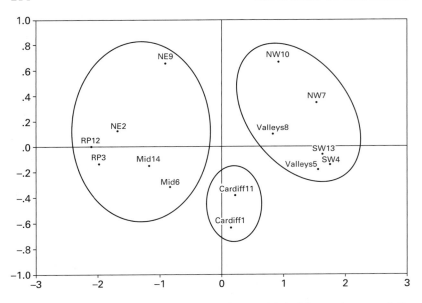

Figure 12.3 Teachers: 'How Welsh do you think this speaker sounds?'

with south-west Wales and the Valleys. Again, each regional pair is located in the same cluster, never split into different clusters, once more indicating a salience for regionality to the question of Welshness, regardless of other variables, such as the differences in the stories themselves and the individual differences in the voice and performance qualities between the individual speakers.

Do you think this speaker is a good laugh?

The 'good laugh' scale correlates quite highly with the other affiliative/ social attractiveness scales ('make friends', 'like you' and 'you like'), so it suffices to report on this one here, and just refer to the others where of value.

In Figures 12.4 and 12.5, the horizontal axis is an overall reflection of the positivity of ratings on this scale, with a tendency towards more positivity as you move from left to right along the axis. For the teenagers, nine of the less favourable stories cluster at one end of the axis, and the other five form two clusters at the other, with NE2 forming its own 'cluster' away from the others on the vertical axis. For the teachers, there are two clusters, one with twelve speakers with less

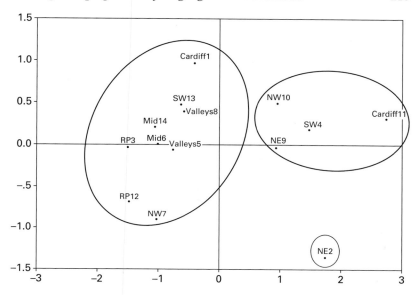

Figure 12.4 Teenagers: 'Do you think this speaker is a good laugh?'

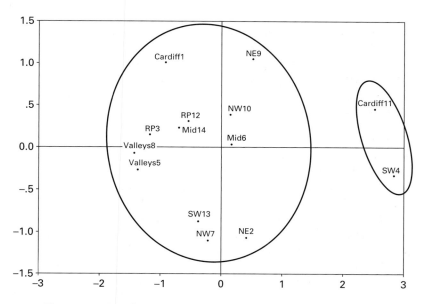

Figure 12.5 Teachers: 'Do you think this speaker is a good laugh?'

favourable, mid-range ratings, and the other with Cardiff and SW4 at the other end.

On this social attaractiveness dimension, then, is some splitting of speaker-pairs. In the teachers' results, the Cardiff speakers are distinguished from each other, as are the two south-west Wales speakers, while Cardiff11 and SW4 share their own cluster. There is even more splitting in the teenagers' findings. This suggests, then, that, unlike the 'Welshness' scale, judgements of the speakers' social attractiveness are less influenced by regional dialect on this dimension, but that there are story/performance factors at work. It is notable, for example, that the teenagers' large low-scoring cluster contains a group of stories that can be regarded as relatively 'harmless': e.g. Cardiff1 felt sick, but wasn't, and Mid6's tractor did not actually tip over. Also in this cluster are NW7 and Valleys5, who, respectively, have the slowest speech rate and the highest degree of hesitation, which, as we have seen in earlier chapters, can affect evaluations negatively.

Amongst the other affiliative scales ('make friends', 'like you' and 'you like'), there is one aspect of the patterning in the data that is not captured in Figure 12.5. That is the fact that, while the two RP speakers always fall into the teachers' higher rated clusters, the teenagers always have them in their lowest rated cluster. There is a big difference in attitudes here. In addition, the two Valleys speakers always appear in the teachers' lowest rated cluster. A further differentiation concerns NE2. In the teenagers' data, he has his own perceptual space, far out from the others on the vertical axis. His distinctiveness seemingly relates to his excursion into the glitz of nightclubs, with alcohol and music bands, making his story more remote from the teenagers' world. But the teachers do not share this view, and he is part of their large cluster.

It is interesting that some of the storytellers project powerful confirmations of their regional stereotypes in their stories. NE2's encounter with rock groups could be said to reflect the image of youth in the Liverpool-influenced north-east. SW4's rugby shirt story is very congruent with the sporting image of the rural south-west. Cardiff11's story has urban associations with streetwise kids hanging out in pool halls. In contrast to these well-performed embodiments of regional stereotypes, Cardiff1's story is set in Spain and has no Cardiff connections, and it may be this that causes the Cardiff dialect pair to be split by the attitudinal judgements, similarly with NW7 and NW10. This kind of analysis, then, helps us to see the operation of different attitudinal forces – dialect and non-dialect features – often pulling in different directions, and leading to different evaluations for two speakers of

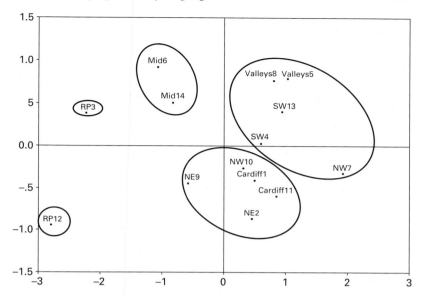

Figure 12.6 Teenagers: 'Do you think this speaker does well at school?'

what would be seen as the same regional variety in many of the kinds of studies reviewed earlier in this book.

Do you think this speaker does well at school? ▬▬▬▬▬▬▬

The horizontal axes in Figures 12.6 and 12.7 move from 'not well' on the right to 'well' on the left, and in the teachers' results there is clear RP (well) versus Valleys (not well) opposition, as the pairs form their own unique clusters. It seems that, for the teachers, the social background of the RP speakers provides educational advantages that the Valleys do not have. All other speakers cluster together between these two pairs. The teenagers have a different view. The RP speakers are both 'loners', separated from each other and clustering with no one else. Moving across to the right, Mid6 and Mid 14 are seen as a pair. The contents and ordering of the two larger clusters shows that, for the teenagers, the horizontal axis of school success is seen pretty much in terms of an English–Welsh dimension. The anglicised varieties gather in one of the larger clusters, and then come the Welsh varieties (NW10 excepted) at the right end of the axis.

The vertical axes reveal another influence on the attitudes towards these speakers of both the teachers and, more so, the teenagers, since it

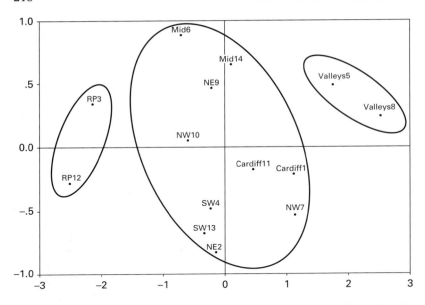

Figure 12.7 Teachers: 'Do you think this speaker does well at school?'

affects the distribution of their clusters. The speakers below the horizontal axis tell stories happening in leisure activities (NE2 nightclubbing; Cardiff11 in a pool hall, RP12 at a fairground, etc.). None of these project a staid home life where parents might be ensuring that these fifteen year olds do their schoolwork. This, then appears to be a force at work on attitudes regarding this question of likely success at school. It is notable, though, that the teenagers single out RP12 from the others below the horizontal axis, and they do not seem to doubt his likely success at school. Again, then, we see how this combination of cluster analysis and MDS helps us to identify the different factors at work and to tease out the combined variables – dialectal and non-dialectal – when voice samples consist of people not only producing their regional varieties, but also telling their own stories in a non-controlled manner, and so doing things with language in a specific context.

THE KEYWORDS RESULTS

This section examines the keyword responses of the teenagers to the teenage storytellers. There are two overall properties of these to mention to begin with. One is the *negativity* in these evaluations and the other is the *range* of evaluative content. This is probably connected with the fact that fifteen is an age at which teenagers are exploring a range of available identities, and so this may require an equivalent range of discriminating evaluative descriptors. Positioning themselves in this process may involve rejecting a large proportion of identities that they find unsatisfying, and so lead to more negative than favourable evaluations. (The teenagers' scale ratings in this storytelling part of the study were also lower than those of the teachers.)

Taboo/pejorative

Analysis of the keywords from the teenage respondents from all of the six dialect communities in Wales generated a number of main themes. The largest of these was a category of taboo or pejorative items. This is arguably to be expected in teenagers, since their functions include the reinforcement of group membership and the signalling of shared knowledge and interests (de Klerk 1997: 147). The category accounted for over 10 per cent of all keywords, and this figure needs to be understood in the light of many taboo words not being included because they referred to another group of items (e.g. 'sheepshagger' and 'shitshoveller' are instead grouped under farming activity below).

It is not straightforward to interpret the ways these items are aimed at individual speakers. One cannot claim, for example, that higher proportions of such items necessarily mean more negativity. Indeed, the second largest proportion of them is awarded to Cardiff11, and he is the most popular and least negatively rated speaker overall in the scales results just reported. It seems that some items are almost invariably meant negatively (e.g. 'arsehole'), whereas others have a more frequently variable force (e.g. 'prat'). Both RP3 and Cardiff11 are labelled 'prat' numerous times, but Cardiff11 appears to be seen as an entertaining prat, while it seems more likely that RP3 is being condemned by these fifteen year olds as an upper-class prat who needs teacher's help. For the most part, taking the 'establishment' view, this group of labels can be regarded as offensive. An important characteristic of them is their strong tendency to be categorial nominals. Hence, labelling someone as an 'arsehole' relegates and outgroups them to a social category of 'arseholes'. These evaluative items, then, not only hang attributes on individuals, but also place them in a social space, as well as indicating where the evaluator stands in relation to that space, and this is an important function of social evaluation.

Boring

This group of items accounted for just under 10 per cent of all keywords. It seems mainly to convey a general sense of lack of engagement by the listener, and may well serve an outgrouping function in this sense, rather than through relegating the speaker to a named group. It is something of an umbrella response, relating to a range of possible factors. It thus has high utility, since it can relate to an aspect of performance (tempo, monotone, dialect) or content (not interesting, not exciting, lacking humour), or both, or some perception of the speaker's personality. The negativity of this grouping can be more securely claimed than was the case with the taboo items. It is noticeable that Cardiff11, who attracted the second highest proportion of taboo items, receives almost no mention at all of 'boring'. Cardiff1, in contrast, received the second highest proportion of 'boring' comments, once again implying that more than regional dialect was influencing evaluations. The others that attracted the lowest proportion of 'boring' comments were NE2, SW4 and NW10, and others receiving higher proportions were Mid14 and Mid6, RP3 and RP12, Valleys8 and SW13.

Interestingly, too, the distribution of 'boring' comments varied according to the respondents' communities. The respondents in the more rural communities employed fewer 'boring' keywords when they commented on the speakers. This might suggest higher thresholds of boredom in those communities, or less willingness to downgrade speakers of their own age for not engaging them.

Welshness/Englishness

As in the other parts of the study, this showed itself to be a meaningful and active dimension of language attitudes. Overall, the distribution of these keywords reflected the results from the other parts of the study. As in the scales section above, the pairs of speakers tended to be seen similarly, in most cases. Overall, ethnicity comments were about Welshness far more than about Englishness, but there were some interesting differences amongst the respondents in different regions.

Most comments directed at RP12 and RP3 about Englishness came from the respondents in south-west Wales, often alongside keywords such as 'snob' or 'posh', as if English itself were a pejorative item. Sometimes English was expressed with conspicuous hostility, for example, together with a swastika or skull and crossbones. This again exemplifies the richer picture that can be gained from keywords data than from filling in a scale for 'How English do you think this person sounds?'

The south-west and the north-west are the communities that have the most to say about ethnicity on both sides, in fact: i.e. Welshness and Englishness. Indeed, it is between these two Welsh heartlands where the greatest exchange about Welshness takes place, as if this is an important dimension for these two groups of respondents in particular. The south-west comments about the north-west speakers seem to be more exclusionary. There are many references to 'gog' (from the Welsh 'gogledd' meaning 'north'), and to 'North Wales' and 'North Wales accent'. In contrast, the north-westerners tend to refer to the south-west Wales speakers as 'Welsh', as if ingrouping their south-west neighbours. Hence, although in other parts of this study there have been signs of different types of Welshness rather than just a unidimensional scale showing degree of Welshness, it would seem that this might not be a universal view in Wales, and that it is the south-west that plays a strong role in that dynamic rather than the north-west.

Farming and other activities

There was also a group of keywords exemplified by 'farmer', 'country type', 'sheepshagger', etc. These comments were indeed made largely about the speakers who told stories that were rural in content, and suggested a link between the speaker and living on a farm. More significant is the fact that most of these comments were made by the three communities of judges in the most rural regions (south-west and north-west Wales and mid-Wales). Hence, the connotations of farming and rural life can be attributed to the rurality of the respondents themselves as much as to the stories. This salience probably stems from the contact, especially in market towns, contrasting agricultural life with the lure of urban lifestyles, perhaps especially for young teenagers. The fact that the scale ratings of these particular stories were negative can reasonably be interpreted as a rejection of farming and country life by these teenagers.

The patterns of keywords referring to activities in the stories themselves are also of interest. There is no reference to pool, for example, in the keywords about Cardiff11, or to fairgrounds in keywords about RP12, but SW4 attracts lots of comments about rugby, an activity that goes right to the heart of Welsh cultural traditions and stereotypes. And given the positive scale ratings of SW4, it is reasonable to see these comments in favourable terms. Also interesting, though, is that most of these comments come from the Cardiff respondents (where the national rugby stadium is situated). But the north-west respondents give little attention to this aspect of SW4. These patterns, then, illustrate how evaluations are made in terms of the categories and qualities available in the culture (farming, rugby), and how the loadings of such evaluations can vary on that basis. We saw something of this in the 'toughness' comments made by the US respondents about Australian English in chapter 11.

Summing up

The several strands and methods in this study have collaborated in a number of ways, then, to provide a more secure and richer picture of language attitudes in Wales. In some ways, data from the different parts of the project have reinforced each other by throwing up similar patterns. In other ways, they have elaborated on each other, as we have seen more vivid detail emerging from the open-ended data to fill out the view obtained from the rating scales. The combination of MDS and cluster analysis has also allowed us to see how component factors can pull in different directions and contribute in different ways to people's attitudes. And this has allowed us to explore attitudes to verbal presentations that are often avoided in more traditional designs, and to explore more contextualised attitudes. Keywords, which have their own limitations, allow more insight into the cultural worlds of the respondents themselves and their contrasting ideologies than studies based on applying a set of dimensions universally to a whole host of separate communities. This integrated approach is of course certainly not any kind of ultimate solution to the difficulties involved in researching attitudes, but it has been a demonstration of how gains can come, resources permitting, from employing a combination of methods to suit a particular attitudinal research task.

FURTHER READING ON CHAPTER 12

The Wales studies are reported in more depth in:

Garrett, P., Coupland, N. and Williams, A., 2003, *Investigating language attitudes: social meanings of dialect, ethnicity and performance*. Cardiff: University of Wales Press.

QUESTIONS FOR CHAPTER 12

1. Could you envisage an integrated study of this kind being conducted in, or within a region of, your own country? What would such a study look like? What sorts of respondents would you

include? What sorts of findings might you anticipate based on your current knowledge and familiarity?

2. What do you yourself see as the main advantages and disadvantages of integrated studies such as this one? Would you yourself prefer to use the resources differently, to carry out different kinds of language attitudes work?

13 Conclusion

No book of this size can do justice to the huge amount of work in the field of language attitudes. However, the chapters of this book have at least provided introductory coverage to the scope, importance and pervasiveness in social life of attitudes towards language, covering some of the main areas of research as the field has evolved, along with methodological and theoretical approaches, developments and debates.

We have seen how language attitudes may be created or reinforced by the ways in which realities are represented through language ideologies, stereotypes, and also the many myths about language. We have also seen how we might see clues to language attitudes from our physical communication environments, such as in advertisements, street signs, and our linguistic landscapes, as well as in our everyday social interactions. We have seen how attitudes may be evidenced in angry complaints relating to what is correct and incorrect, appropriate or inappropriate, acceptable and unacceptable in language use, in political action to save endangered languages or to introduce more socially sensitive, politically correct forms, in lack of co-operation or even violent reactions, and in prejudices that can intrude into many areas of social life, including professional environments. Language attitudes can drive change, both in the way that languages themselves may change over time, and also at the individual level when people are prepared to direct considerable dedication and sums of money to modify their own language behaviours through such processes as accent reduction programmes. Similarly, large amounts of money can be invested in the anticipation of attitudinal reactions towards language and communication choices, when companies are selecting brand names, for example, or when political candidates are running election campaigns, when politicians and educationists are engaged in language-planning initiatives, or when health professionals are designing public health or public safety campaigns.

Such applied or professional contexts seem particularly important to investigate when language attitudes can affect people's wellbeing and social freedom, and working lives, in terms of career opportunities. We have looked at studies into how attitudes to language might affect how people fare in legal contexts, in healthcare, in their employment and careers, and in terms of educational performance and success. It is important to investigate such phenomena more thoroughly, in an effort to gain a good understanding of the nature of such effects. As we have noted too, each such area is extremely broad, comprising many different sorts of settings, goals and practices. We have mentioned that the legal area comprises many very different contexts, for example, from police interviews to courtroom examinations and verdicts, to parole board decisions. Language attitudes could play very different roles and have varying shapes and effects across these contexts, and overall, one can easily be left with an impression that, despite all the research that has so far been conducted, we have barely scratched the surface. Mindful of ethical constraints, research needs to be extended into more of these areas.

It was noted that the evaluative profiles of language varieties found in more general language attitudes studies appeared sometimes to work differently in professional contexts: for example, the RP speakers in Fielding and Evered's (1980) medical study and in Seggie's (1983) legal study. And we interpreted this as an example of one of the ways in which language attitudes can be multidimensional. In other ways, too, this book has drawn attention to the multidimensional qualities of language attitudes. Most obviously, of course, there are the three main evaluative dimensions identified by Zahn and Hopper (1985): prestige, social attractiveness and dynamism, and it has been argued in this book that we should not assume that only these three are of interest to language attitudes scholars. We saw the significance, for example, of the independent 'Welshness' dimension in the studies in Wales and the Welsh-identifying communities in North America and Argentina. However, it was also noted, particularly when discussing the qualitative (e.g. keywords) data that these dimensions themselves contained their own dimensions. There were quite different sorts of Welshness, for example, rather than simply varying degrees of it. There were rural and urban, northern and southern, dimensions within Wales, quite different Argentinian and North American perspectives, also with some respondents distancing themselves from other Welshnesses. It was also noted that the teachers and teenagers in chapter 12 both identified RP with school success, but at another level took quite different standpoints towards RP speakers and their school success connotations. Similarly, the social attractiveness dimension also seemed too superficial in some data if looked at only in terms of degrees. Amongst some teenagers in Wales, lack of social attractiveness was clarified in terms of 'sheepshaggers', for example, giving a deeper picture of what this lack of social attractiveness comprised. Language attitudes are not only about whether language users are regarded as being more or less intelligent or honest, but also how people interpret and orient towards these qualities and position themselves regarding these speakers, for example. We have seen how these interpretations and orientations can vary across context. Capturing and understanding this variation is one the challenges for language attitudes scholars, as this book has highlighted (see also Preston's (in press) recent work on the notion of an 'attitudinal cognitorium').

Apart from the importance of attending to multidimensionality in researching more settings and contexts, the opening up of multidimensionality is also related to the methodological developments in the field, as researchers have tended to gather more open-ended data either alongside or instead of using attitude rating scales. This book has of course been largely structured around methodological approaches to investigating language attitudes and has given much focus throughout to the strengths and weaknesses of various methods that any researcher needs to take into account as they design and conduct studies around their particular research questions, and that any language attitudes scholar needs to understand as they read and evaluate published studies. Through these chapters, we have trodden a path through the recurrent issues that arise as we choose amongst methods to address research questions, relating, at bottom, to the fact that attitudes are constructs: social desirability (and other) biases, distinctions between ideologised values, public and private attitudes, interpretations of the research task by respondents, interpretations of the data by researchers.

Research in the traditions of matched and verbal guise and direct approach have built up a considerable body of knowledge over the years, and facilitated significant theoretical development within the language attitudes field. This itself is an important indicator of the strengths of these methods and their immense usefulness for addressing significant research questions. As in all research fields and disciplines, there has always been, and is now too, a debate about the relative strengths and limitations of different methods of researching language attitudes. As in all such debates, they go on as much between researchers, with some strongly committed to a particular approach and negative towards others, as they do *within* the thoughts of individual researchers, perhaps leading to their moving more freely, albeit still critically, amongst the methodological alternatives.

In the past decade or so, though, there has been a significant re-appraisal of ways of researching language attitudes, and a growing vibrant forum of debate about research methods. This has included calls for more research employing discourse analytic approaches, which are arguably underrepresented in mainstream accounts of the language attitudes field. There has also been some extension of attention to new phenomena, such as the impacts of globalisation. We have looked at this most notably in the increased attention to the consequences of the increases in quantity and extensivity of flows of populations, information and ideas. Traditional categories have tended to become more fractionalised, for example, and communities have not needed to be so territorially defined or bounded. More and more languages have come under threat. The notion of ethnolinguistic vitality, too, is receiving some reconsideration. Multilingual cities are developing new linguistic landscapes. Diasporas may be touched by processes of retraditionalisation and heritage to re-appraise and redefine their identities in terms of the nature of their beliefs, practices and affiliations. This book has included some of these recent focuses of interest, as well as considering some of these developing methods, used both singly and also in integrated designs.

The potential scope of language attitudes work is both vast and worthwhile, and the coming period is likely to be very productive and illuminating. Language attitudes research can build a better understanding of the complex worlds in which sociolinguistic varieties exist and language users negotiate their way through their everyday lives. Hopefully, readers of this book not already researching language attitudes will be attracted to join this venture.

Glossary

Accommodation theory – the theory that people, for various motivations, tend to modify their communication with each other to reduce differences (convergence) or accentuate differences (divergence). Also known as speech, or communication, accommodation theory.

Codeswitching – the use of more than one language or variety in a conversation.

Contact hypothesis – the theory that types of direct contact between members of groups will diminish prejudice between them.

Direct approach attitude studies – studies of attitudes of human informants in which they are aware of what is being investigated.

Elaboration likelihood model – a theory about the processes and variables involved in influencing attitudes, and the strength of resulting judgements. It postulates that two basic routes (central and peripheral) operate in tandem.

Ethnocentrism – the tendency to see the world mainly from the viewpoint of one's own culture.

Ethnolinguistic vitality – the degree of life in a language in a society in relation to ethnic groupings. Vitality is generally seen in terms of status, demographic factors and institutional support.

Folklinguistics – the study of the language beliefs of non-linguists.

Imposed norm hypothesis – the theory that attitudes to language reflect social connotations, which are imposed by the listener.

Indirect approach studies – studies of human informants in which they are unaware of what is being investigated.

Inherent value hypothesis – the theory that attitudes to language are triggered by qualities that are intrinsic in language.

Language expectancy theory – the theory that people hold expectations about how language and message strategies are used in attempts to influence attitudes or behaviours.

Language intensity – the degree to which language deviates positively or negatively from neutrality.

Lexical diversity – the range of vocabulary used.

Linguistic landscape – the language presence in the physical environment: e.g. road signs, street names, posters, signs in shops. The term is extended by some to include multimodal aspects, such as culturally salient symbols and images.

Matched guise technique – a technique of eliciting attitudinal responses from informants by presenting them with a number of speech varieties, all of which are spoken by the same person.

Minority language – a language spoken by a numerical minority within a region, having less status than the language of the dominant wider community.

Non-attitude – opinion that does not express a pre-existing view, but which is created on the spot on the basis of little or no information.

Perceptual dialectology – the study of ordinary people's (as opposed to linguists') beliefs about the distribution of language varieties in their own and neighbouring speech communities, and of the origins and implementation of such beliefs.

Phonoaesthetics – the study of inherent pleasantness or unpleasantness in the sound of some linguistic utterances.

Script – an expected sequence of behaviours for a specific situation.

Social categorisation – the identification of individuals as members of groups because they share features that are typical of those groups.

Social identity theory – the theory that a driving force behind ingroup bias is people's motivation to gain positive self-esteem from membership of their groups.

Societal treatment studies – studies of attitudes to language as they are evident in sources available in public social domains, such as the media, policy documentation, literature, etc.

Speech rate – speaking rate, often measured in words per minute.

Standard language ideology – a pervasive set of beliefs about the superiority of an idealised language variety imposed by dominant social groups who are its speakers.

Stereotype – a cognitive representation or impression of a social group that stems from the association of particular characteristics with that group.

Theory of planned behaviour – the theory that a combination of attitudes, perceived social norms and perceived control influences people's behaviour.

Theory of reasoned action – the theory that a person's intention to act in a certain way depends on subjective norms and the person's attitude concerning the behaviour.

Tripartite model – a view of attitudes as consisting of three components: cognitions, affect and behaviours. Sometimes also referred to as the 'triadic model'.

Verbal guise technique – a technique of eliciting attitudinal responses from informants by presenting them with a number of speech varieties, each of which is spoken by someone who is a natural speaker of the variety.

Vivid language – language likely to attract our attention and excite the imagination.

References

Abelson, R., 1982, Three modes of attitude–behaviour consistency, in M. P. Zanna, E. T. Higgins and C. P. Herman (eds.), *Consistency in social behaviour: the Ontario symposium* (vol. II, pp. 131–46). Hillsdale, NJ: Erlbaum.

Aboud, F., Clément, R. and Taylor, D., 1974, Evaluational reactions to discrepancies between social class and language. *Sociometry* 37, 239–50.

Abrams, D. and Hogg, M., 1987, Language attitudes, frames of reference and social identity: a Scottish dimension. *Journal of language and social psychology* 6, 201–14.

Adam, B., 1998, *Timescapes of modernity: the environment and invisible hazards*. London: Routledge.

Adegbija, E., 1994, *Language attitudes in sub-Saharan Africa*. Clevedon: Multilingual Matters.

Adler, R., Rosenfeld, L. and Towne, N., 1995, *Interplay: the process of interpersonal communication*. Fort Worth, TX: Harcourt Brace.

Aitchison, J. and Carter, H., 1994, *A geography of Welsh*. Cardiff: University of Wales Press.

2004, *Spreading the word: the Welsh language 2001*. Talybont: Y Lolfa Cyf.

Ajzen, I., 1985, From intentions to actions: a theory of planned behaviour, in J. Kuhland and J. Beckman (eds.), *Action-control: from cognition to behaviour*. Heidelberg: Springer.

Ajzen, I. and Fishbein, M., 1980, *Understanding attitudes and predicting social behaviour*. Englewood Cliffs, NJ: Prentice Hall.

Akbar, R., 2007, Students' and teachers' attitudes towards Kuwaiti/English code-switching. Unpublished PhD thesis, Centre for Language and Communication Research, Cardiff University.

Alford, J., Funk, C. and Hibbing, J., 2005, Are political orientations genetically transmitted? *American political science review* 99, 153–67.

Algeo, J., 1998, *America is ruining the English language*, in L. Bauer and P. Trudgill (eds.), pp. 176–82.

Allport, G., 1935, Attitudes, in C. Murchison (ed.), *A handbook of social psychology* (vol. II, pp. 798–844). Worcester, MA: Clark University Press.

1954, The historical background of modern social psychology, in G. Lindzey (ed.), *Handbook of social psychology* (vol. 1: *Theory and method*, pp. 3–56). Cambridge, MA: Addison-Wesley.

Andersen, J., Norton, R. and Nussbaum, J., 1981, Three investigations exploring relationships between perceived teacher communication behaviors and student learning. *Communication education* 30, 377–92.

Atkins, C., 1993, Do employment recruiters discriminate on the basis of nonstandard dialect? *Journal of employment counseling* 30, 108–18.

Austin, C., 1989, The English genitive apostrophe. Unpublished MA dissertation, University of Wales, Bangor.

Backhaus, P., 2006, *Multilingualism in Tokyo: a look into the linguistic landscape*, in D. Gorter (ed.), pp. 52–66.

2007, *Linguistic landscapes: a comparative study of urban multilingualism in Tokyo*. Clevedon: Multilingual Matters.

Bailey, K., 1984, The 'foreign TA problem', in K. Bailey, F. Pialorsi and J. Zukowski/Faust (eds.), *Foreign teaching assistants in US universities* (pp. 3–15). Washington, DC: National Association for Foreign Student Affairs.

Baker, C., 1988, *Key issues in bilingualism and bilingual education*. Clevedon: Multilingual Matters.

1992, *Attitudes and language*. Clevedon: Multilingual Matters.

Ball, P., 1983, Stereotypes of Anglo-Saxon and non-Anglo-Saxon accents: some exploratory Australian studies with the matched-guise technique. *Language sciences* 5, 163–84.

Ball, P. and Giles, H., 1982, *Speech style and employment selection: the matched guise technique*, in G. Breakwell, H. Foot and R. Gilmour (eds.), pp. 101–22.

Ball, P., Giles, H., Byrne, J. and Berechree, P., 1984, Situational constraints on the evaluative significance of speech accommodation: some Australian data. *International journal of the sociology of language* 46, 115–29.

Barber, B., 1996, *Jihad vs McWorld*. New York: Ballantine.

Barr, S. and Hitt, M., 1986, A comparison of selection decision models in manager versus student samples. *Personnel psychology* 39, 599–617.

Barry, H. and Harper, A., 1995, Increased choice of female phonetic attributes in first names. *Sex roles* 32 (11/12), 809–19.

Bauer, L. and Trudgill, P. (eds.), 1998, *Language myths*. London: Penguin.

Bauer, W., 1998, *Some languages have no grammar*, in L. Bauer and P. Trudgill (eds.), pp. 77–84.

Bayard, D., 1990, 'God help us if we all sound like this': attitudes to New Zealand and other English accents, in A. Bell and J. Holmes (eds.), *New Zealand ways of speaking English* (pp. 67–96). Clevedon: Multilingual Matters.

Bayard, D., Weatherall, A., Gallois, C. and Pittam, J., 2001, Pax Americana?: Accent attitudinal evaluations in New Zealand, Australia and America. *Journal of sociolinguistics* 5, 22–49.

BBC, 2005, Regional accents 'bad for trade'. 29th December 2005. http://news.bbc.co.uk/1/hi/england/4566028.stm. Accessed 30 March 2006.

Bell, A., 1991, *The language of news media*. Oxford: Blackwell.

Bell, B. and Loftus, A., 1985, Vivid persuasion in the courtroom. *Journal of personality assessment* 49, 659–64.

Bellin, W., Matsuyama, A. and Schott, G., 1999, Teaching a 'dead' language, teaching through a 'dead' language: conflict and consensus during language revitalization in *Eusko Jauralitza/Gobierno Basco Proceedings of the seventh International Minority Languages conference*, Bilbao, Spain.

Ben-Rafael, E., Shohamy, E., Amara, M. and Trumper-Hecht, N., 2006, Linguistic landscape as symbolic construction of the public space: the case of Israel, in D. Gorter (ed.), pp. 7–30.

Berk-Seligson, S., 1984, Subjective reactions to phonological variation in Costa Rican Spanish. *Journal of psycholinguistic research* 13, 415–42.

Bernstein, V., Hakel, M. and Harlan, A., 1975, The college student as interviewer: a threat to generalisability. *Journal of applied psychology* 60, 260–8.

Bettinghaus, E. and Cody, M., 1994, *Persuasive communication*. Fort Worth, TX: Harcourt Brace.

Bilous, F. and Krauss, R., 1988, Dominance and accommodation in the conversational behaviours of same- and mixed-gender dyads. *Language and communication* 8, 183–94.

Bishop, H., Coupland, N. and Garrett, P., 2005a, Globalisation, advertising and language choice: shifting values for Welsh and Welshness. *Multilingua* 24, 343–78.

2005b, Conceptual accent evaluation: thirty years of accent prejudice in the UK. *Acta linguistica hafniensia* 37, 131–54.

Bless, H., Bohner, G., Schwarz, N. and Strack, F., 1990, Mood and persuasion: a cognitive response analysis. *Personality and social psychology bulletin* 16, 331–45.

Blommaert, J. and Verschueren, J., 1998, *Debating diversity: analysing the discourse of tolerance*. London: Routledge.

Boninger, D., Krosnick, J. and Berent, M., 1995, Origins of attitude importance: self interest, social identification, and value relevance. *Journal of personality and social psychology* 68, 61–80.

Bostrom, R., Baseheart, J. and Rossiter, C., 1973, The effects of three types of profane language in persuasive messages. *Journal of communication* 23, 461–75.

Bourhis, R., 1977, Language and social evaluation in Wales. Unpublished PhD thesis, University of Bristol.

1991, Organisational communication and accommodation: toward some conceptual and empirical links, in H. Giles, J. Coupland and N. Coupland (eds.), pp. 270–303.

Bourhis, R. and Giles, H., 1976, The language of co-operation in Wales: a field study. *Language sciences* 42, 13–16.

1977, The language of intergroup distinctiveness, in H. Giles (ed.), *Language, ethnicity and intergroup relations* (pp. 119–35). London: Academic Press.

Bourhis, R., Giles, H. and Lambert, W., 1975, Social consequences of accommodating one's style of speech. *International journal of the sociology of language* 6, 55–72.

Bourhis, R., Giles, H. and Rosenthal, D., 1981, Notes on the construction of a 'subjective vitality questionnaire' for ethnolinguistic groups. *Journal of multilingual and multicultural development* 2, 145–55.

Bourhis, R., Giles, H. and Tajfel, H., 1973, Language as a determinant of Welsh identity. *European journal of social psychology* 3, 447–60.

Bourhis, R., Roth, S. and MacQueen, G., 1989, Communication in the hospital setting: a survey of medical and everyday language use amongst patients, nurses and doctors. *Social science and medicine* 28, 339–46.

Boyd, S., 2003, Foreign-born teachers in the multilingual classroom in Sweden: the role of attitudes to foreign accent. *International journal of bilingual education and bilingualism* 6, 283–95.

Bradac, J., 1990, Language attitudes and impression formation, in H. Giles and P. Robinson (eds.), pp. 387–412.

Bradac, J.J., Bowers, J.W. and Courtright, J.A., 1980, Lexical variations in intensity, immediacy, and diversity: an axiomatic theory and causal model, in R.N. St. Clair and H. Giles (eds.), *The social and psychological contexts of language* (pp. 193–223). Hillsdale, NJ: Lawrence Erlbaum.

Bradac, J., Cargile, A. and Hallett, J., 2001, Language attitudes: retrospect, conspect, and prospect, in W.P. Robinson and H. Giles (eds.), *The new handbook of language and social psychology* (pp. 137–55).

Bradac, J. and Mulac, A., 1984, A molecular view of powerful and powerless speech: attributional consequences of specific language features and communicator intentions. *Communication monographs* 51, 307–19.

Bradac, J., Mulac, A. and House, A., 1988, Lexical diversity and magnitude of convergent versus divergent style shifting: perceptual and evaluative consequences. *Language and communication* 8, 213–28.

Bradac, J. and Wisegarver, R., 1984, Ascribed status, lexical diversity, and accent: determinants of perceived status, solidarity, and control of speech style. *Journal of language and social psychology* 3, 239–53.

Breakwell, G., Foot, H. and Gilmour, R. (eds.), 1982, *Social psychology: a practical manual* (pp. 19–37). Basingstoke: Macmillan.

Breckler, S., 1984, Empirical validation of affect, behaviour, and cognition as distinct components of attitude. *Journal of personality and social psychology* 47, 1191–205.

Bredella, L., 1991, Objectivism and relativism in analysing mediations of a foreign culture, in L. Bredella (ed.), *Mediating a foreign culture: the United States and Germany* (pp. 7–35). Tubingen: Gunter Narr.

Brehm, S. and Brehm, J., 1981, *Psychological reactance: a theory of freedom and control*. New York: Academic Press.

Brennan, E. and Brennan, J., 1981, Accent scaling and language attitudes: reactions to Mexican American English speech. *Language and speech* 24, 207–21.

Brennan, E., Ryan, E. B. and Dawson, W., 1975, Scaling of apparent accentedness by magnitude estimation and sensory modality matching. *Journal of psycholinguistic research* 4, 27–36.

Brown, B., 1980, Effects of speech rate on personality attributions and competency evaluations, in H. Giles, W. P. Robinson and P. Smith (eds.), *Language: social psychological perspectives* (pp. 293–300). New York: Pergamon.

Brown, B., Giles, H. and Thakerar, J., 1985, Speaker evaluations as a function of speech rate, accent and context. *Language and communication* 5, 207–20.

Buller, D. and Aune, R., 1988, The effects of vocalics and nonverbal sensitivity on compliance: a speech accommodation theory explanation. *Human communication research* 14, 310–32.

Burgoon, M., 1995, Language expectancy theory: elaboration, explication, and extension, in C. Berger and M. Burgoon (eds.), *Communication and social influence processes* (pp. 29–51). East Lansing: Michigan State University Press.

Burgoon, M., Denning, V. and Roberts, L., 2002, Language expectancy theory, in J. Dillard and M. Pfau (eds.), pp. 117–136.

Burrell, N. and Koper, R., 1998, The efficacy of powerful/powerless language on attitudes and source credibility, in M. Allen and R. Preiss (eds.), *Persuasion: advances through meta-analysis* (pp. 203–15). Cresskill, NJ: Hampton Press.

Bwrdd Yr Iaith/The Welsh Language Board, 2001, A guide to bilingual design. www.byig-wlb.org.uk/English/publications/Publications/32.pdf.

Cairns, E. and Duriez, B., 1976, The influence of speaker's accent on recall by Catholic and Protestant schoolchildren in Northern Ireland. *Journal of social and clinical psychology* 15, 441–42.

Cargile, A., 1997, Attitudes toward Chinese-accented speech: an investigation in two contexts. *Journal of language and social psychology* 16, 434–43.

2000, Evaluations of employment suitability: does accent always matter? *Journal of employment counseling* 37, 165–77.

Cargile, A. and Giles, H., 1997, Understanding language attitudes: exploring listener affect and identity. *Language and communication* 17, 195–217.

Cargile, A., Giles, H., Ryan, E. B. and Bradac, J., 1994, Language attitudes as a social process: a conceptual model and new directions. *Language and communication* 14, 211–36.

Carranza, M. and Ryan, E. B., 1975, Evaluative reactions of bilingual Anglo- and Mexican American adolescents towards speakers of English and Spanish. *International journal of the sociology of language* 6, 83–104.

Chaiken, S., 1987, The heuristic model of persuasion, in M. Zanna, J. Olson and C. Herman (eds.), *Social influence: the Ontario Symposium* (vol. V, pp. 3–39). Hillsdale, NJ: Erlbaum.

Chandler, P., Robinson, W. P. and Noyes, P., 1988, The level of linguistic knowledge and awareness amongst students training to be primary teachers. *Language and education* 2, 161–73.

Cheshire, J., 1998, Double negatives are illogical, in L. Bauer and P. Trudgill (eds.), pp. 113–22.

Cheshire, J. and Moser, L.-M., 1994, English as a cultural symbol. *Journal of multilingual and multicultural development* 15, 451–69.

Cheyne, W., 1970, Stereotyped reactions to speakers with Scottish and English regional accents. *British journal of social and clinical psychology* 9, 77–9.

Choy, S. and Dodd, D., 1976, Standard English and non-standard Hawaiian English speaking children: comprehension of both dialects and teachers' evaluations. *Journal of educational psychology* 68, 184–93.

Clore, G. and Schnall, S., 2005, The influence of affect on attitude, in D. Albarracín, B. Johnson and M. Zanna (eds.), *The handbook of attitudes* (pp. 437–89). Mahwah, NJ: Erlbaum.

Coates, J., 2004, *Women, men and language*. Harlow: Pearson.

Cook, S. and Sellitz, C., 1964, A multiple-indicator approach to attitude measurement. *Psychological bulletin* 62, 36–55.

Conley, John M. and O'Barr, William M., 1998, *Just words: law, language and power*. Chicago: University of Chicago Press.

Cots, J. and Nussbaum, L., 1999, Schooling, language and teachers: language awareness and the discourse of educational reform in Catalonia. *Language awareness* 8, 174–89.

Coupland, N., 1984, Accommodation at work: some phonological data and their implications. *International journal of the sociology of language* 46, 49–70.

2003, Sociolinguistic authenticities. *Journal of sociolinguistics* 7, 417–31.

2007, *Style: language variation and identity*. Cambridge: Cambridge University Press.

2008, Review of P. Backhaus, 2007, *Linguistic landscapes, a comparative analysis of urban multilingualism in Tokyo*, and D. Gorter (ed.), 2006, *Linguistic landscape: a new approach to multilingualism*. Published by Multilingual Matters. *Journal of sociolinguistics* 12, 250–4.

2009, Dialects, standards and social change, in M. Maegaard, F. Gregersen, P. Quist and J. Normann Jørgensen (eds.), *Language attitudes, standardisation and language change* (pp. 27–49). Oslo, Novus.

2010, Linguistic landscapes from above and below, in A. Jaworski and C. Thurlow (eds.), *Semiotic landscapes: text, image, space*. London: Continuum.

Coupland, N. and Bishop, H., 2007, Ideologised values for British accents. *Journal of sociolinguistics* 11, 74–93.

Coupland, N., Bishop, H. and Garrett, P., 2003, Home truths: globalization and the iconising of Welsh in a Welsh-American newspaper. *Journal of multilingual and multicultural development* 24, 153–77.

2006, One Wales?: reassessing diversity in Welsh ethnolinguistic identification. *Contemporary Wales* 18, 1–27.

Coupland, N., Bishop, H., Williams, A., Evans, B. and Garrett, P., 2005, Affiliation, engagement, language use and vitality: secondary school students' subjective orientations to Welsh and Welshness. *International journal of bilingual education and bilingualism* 8, 1–24.

Coupland, N., Bishop, H., Evans, B. and Garrett, P., 2006, Imagining Wales and the Welsh language: ethnolinguistic subjectivities and demographic flow. *Journal of language and social psychology* 25, 351–76.

Coupland, N. and Jaworski, A. (eds.), 1997, *Sociolinguistics: a reader and coursebook*. Basingstoke: Macmillan.

Coupland, N., Williams, A. and Garrett, P., 1994, The social meanings of Welsh English: teachers' stereotyped judgements. *Journal of multilingual and multicultural development* 15, 471–91.

1999, Welshness and Englishness as attitudinal dimensions of English language varieties in Wales, in D. Preston (ed.), pp. 333–43.

Crystal, D., 1981, Language on the air – has it degenerated? *The listener*, 9 July, 37–39.

1984, *Who cares about English usage?* Harmondsworth: Penguin.

1987, *The Cambridge encyclopedia of language*. Cambridge: Cambridge University Press.

1995, Phonoaesthetically speaking. *English today*, 42, vol. 11 (2), 8–12.

1996, *Rediscover grammar*. London: Longman.

1997, *The Cambridge encyclopedia of language* (second edition). Cambridge: Cambridge University Press.

Curran, J. and Seaton, J., 2003, *Power without responsibility*. London: Routledge.

Daly, N. and Warren, P., 2001, Pitching it differently in New Zealand English: speaker sex and intonation patterns. *Journal of sociolinguistics* 5, 85–96.

Danet, B., 1990, Language and law: an overview of 15 years of research, in H. Giles and W. P. Robinson (eds.), pp. 537–59.

Dawes, R. and Smith, T., 1985, Attitude and opinion measurement, in G. Lindzey and E. Aronson (eds.), *Handbook of social psychology* (pp. 509–66). New York: Random House.

Day, R., 1982, Children's attitudes towards language, in E. B. Ryan and H. Giles (eds.), pp. 116–31.

de Klerk, V., 1997, The role of expletives in the construction of masculinity, in S. Johnson and U. Meinhof (eds.), *Language and masculinity* (pp. 144–58). Oxford: Blackwell.

de la Zerda, N. and Hopper, R., 1979, Employment interviewers' reactions to Mexican American speech. *Communication monographs* 46, 126–34.

Derwing, T., Rossiter, M. and Munro, M., 2002, Teaching native speakers to listen to foreign-accented speech. *Journal of multilingual and multicultural development* 23, 245–59.

Désirat, C. and Hordé, T., 1976, *La langue Française au 20e Siécle.* Paris: Bordas.

Dillard, J. and Meijnders, A., 2002, Persuasion and the structure of affect., in J. Dillard and M. Pfau (eds.), pp. 309–27.

Dillard, J. and Pfau, M. (eds.), 2002, *The persuasion handbook: developments in theory and practice.* Thousand Oaks, CA: Sage.

Dixon, J. and Mahoney, B., 2004, The effect of accent evaluation and evidence on a suspect's perceived guilt and criminality. *The journal of social psychology* 144, 63–73.

Dixon, J., Mahoney, B. and Cocks, R., 2002, Accents of guilt?: effects of regional accent, race and crime type on attributions of guilt. *Journal of language and social psychology* 21, 162–68.

Dixon, J., Tredoux, C., Durrheim, K. and Foster, D., 1994, The role of speech accommodation and crime type in attribution of guilt. *The journal of social psychology* 134, 465–73.

Dörnyei, Z., 2000, Motivation, in M. Byram (ed.), *Routledge encyclopaedia of language teaching and learning* (pp. 425–32). London: Routledge.

Dryden, C. and Giles, H., 1987, Language, social identity and health, in H. Beloff and A. Coleman (eds.), *Psychological survey, no. 6.* Leicester: British Psychological Society Press.

Eastman, C. and Stein, R., 1993, Language display: authenticating claims to social identity. *Journal of multilingual and multicultural development* 14, 187–202.

Edwards, J., 1982, Language attitudes and their implications amongst English speakers, in E. B. Ryan and H. Giles (eds.), pp. 20–33.

1994, *Multilingualism.* London: Routledge.

Edwards, J. and Jacobsen, M., 1987, Standard and regional speech: distinctions and similarities. *Language in society* 16, 369–80.

El-Dash, L. and Tucker, R., 1975, Subjective reactions to various speech styles in Egypt. *International journal of the sociology of language* 6, 33–54.

Elwell, C., Brown, R. and Rutter, D., 1984, Effects of accent and visual information on impression formation. *Journal of language and social psychology* 3, 297–9.

Erwin, P., 2001, *Attitudes and persuasion.* Hove: Psychology Press.

Evans, N., 1998, Aborigines speak a primitive language, in L. Bauer and P. Trudgill (eds.), pp. 159–68.

Fabricius, A., 2006, The 'vivid sociolinguistic profiling' of Received Pronunciation: responses to gendered dialect in discourse. *Journal of sociolinguistics* 10, 111–22.

Fabrigar, L., Krosnik, J. and MacDougall, B., 2005, Attitude measurement: techniques for measuring the unobservable, in T. Brock and M. Green (eds.), *Persuasion: psychological insights and perspectives*, 2nd edition, (pp. 17–40). Thousand Oaks, CA: Sage.

Fairclough, N. 1995, *Critical discourse analysis.* London: Longman.

Ferrara, K., 1991, Accommodation in therapy, in H. Giles, J. Coupland and N. Coupland (eds.), pp. 187–222.

Festinger, L., 1957, *A theory of cognitive dissonance*. Stanford, CA: Stanford University Press.

Fielding, G. and Evered, C., 1980, The influence of patients' speech upon doctors: the diagnostic interview, in R. St. Clair and H. Giles (eds.), *The social and psychological contexts of language* (pp. 51–72). Hillsdale, NJ: Erlbaum.

Fink, E., Kaplowitz, S. and McGreevy Hubbard, S., 2002, Oscillation in beliefs and decisions, in J. Dillard and M. Pfau (eds.), pp. 17–37.

Fitch, K. and Hopper, R., 1983, If you speak Spanish, they'll think you're a German: attitudes toward language choice in multilingual environments. *Journal of multilingual and multicultural development* 4, 115–27.

Forgas, J. and Bower, G., 1987, Mood effects on person-perception judgements. *Journal of personality and social psychology* 53, 53–60.

Gallois, C. and Callan, V., 1991, Interethnic communication: the role of norms, in H. Giles, J. Coupland and N. Coupland (eds.), pp. 245–69.

Gallois, C., Callan, V. and Johnstone, M., 1984, Personality judgements of Australian Aborigine and white speakers: ethnicity, sex and context. *Journal of language and social psychology* 3, 39–58.

Gallois, C., Franklyn-Stokes, A., Giles, H. and Coupland, N., 1988, Communication accommodation theory and intercultural encounters: intergroup and interpersonal considerations, in Y. Kim and W. Gudykunst (eds.), *Theories in intercultural communication* (pp. 157–85). Newbury Park, CA: Sage.

Gardner, R., 1985, *Social psychology and second language learning: the role of attitudes and motivation*. London: Edward Arnold.

Garrett, P., 2005, Attitude measurement, in U. Ammon, N. Dittmar, K. Mattheier and P. Trudgill (eds.), *Sociolinguistics: an international handbook of the science of language and society* (pp. 1251–60). Berlin: Mouton de Gruyter.

2009, Attitudes in Japan and China towards Australian, Canadian, New Zealand, UK and US Englishes, in M. Maegaard, F. Gregersen, P. Quist and J. Normann Jørgensen (eds.), *Language attitudes, standardisation and language change* (pp. 273–95). Oslo: Novus.

Garrett, P. and Austin, C., 1993, The English genitive apostrophe. *Language awareness* 2, 61–75.

Garrett, P., Bishop, H. and Coupland, N., 2009, Diasporic ethnolinguistic subjectivities: Patagonia, North America and Wales. *International journal of the sociology of language* 195, 173–99.

Garrett, P., Coupland, N. and Williams, A., 1995, 'City harsh' and 'the Welsh version of RP': some ways in which teachers view dialects of Welsh English. *Language awareness* 4, 99–107.

1999, Evaluating dialect in discourse: teachers' and teenagers' responses to young English speakers in Wales. *Language in society* 28, 321–54.

2003, *Investigating language attitudes: social meanings of dialect, ethnicity and performance*. Cardiff: University of Wales Press.

2004, Adolescents' lexical repertoires of peer evaluation: 'boring prats' and 'English snobs', in A. Jaworski, N. Coupland and D. Galasiński (eds.), (pp. 193–225).

Garrett, P., Williams, A. and Evans, B., 2005a, Attitudinal data from New Zealand, Australia, the USA and the UK about each other's Englishes: recent changes? Or consequences of methodology? *Multilingua* 24, 211–35.

2005b, Accessing social meanings: values *of* keywords, values *in* keywords. *Acta linguistica hafniensia* 37, 37–54.

Gass, R. and Seiter, J. 1999. *Persuasion, social influence, and compliance gaining.* Boston: Allyn and Bacon.

2003, *Persuasion, social influence and compliance gaining* (second edition). Boston, MA: Allyn and Bacon.

Genesee, F. and Holobrow, N., 1989, Change and stability in intergroup perceptions. *Journal of language and social psychology* 8, 17–38.

Gibbons, J., 1983, Attitudes towards language and code-mixing in Hong Kong. *Journal of multilingual and multicultural development* 4, 129–47.

Giddens, A., 1999, *Runaway world: how globalisation is reshaping our lives.* London: Profile Books.

Giles, H., 1970, Evaluative reactions to accents. *Educational review* 22, 211–27.

1971, Ethnocentrism and the evaluation of accented speech. *British journal of clinical psychology* 10, 187–8.

1973, Accent mobility: a model and some data. *Anthropological linguistics* 15, 87–105.

Giles, H., Bourhis, R. and Taylor, D., 1977, Towards a theory of language in ethnic group relations, in H. Giles (ed.), *Language, ethnicity and intergroup relations* (pp. 307–48). London: Academic Press.

Giles, H. and Coupland, N., 1991, *Language: contexts and consequences.* Buckingham: Open University Press.

Giles, H., Coupland, J. and Coupland, N. (eds.), 1991, *Contexts of accommodation.* Cambridge: Cambridge University Press.

Giles, H., Coupland, N., Henwood, K., Harriman, J. and Coupland, J., 1990, The social meaning of RP: an intergenerational perspective, in S. Ramsaran (ed.), *Studies in the pronunciation of English: a commemorative volume in honour of A. C. Gimson* (pp. 191–211). London: Routledge.

Giles, H. and Farrar, K., 1979, Some behavioural consequences of speech and dress styles. *British journal of social and clinical psychology* 18, 209–10.

Giles, H., Fortman, J., Dailey, R., Hajek, C., Anderson, M. and Rule, N., 2006, Communication accommodation: law enforcement and the public, in R. Dailey and B. LePoire (eds.), *Applied research in interpersonal communication: family communication, health communication and communicating across social boundaries* (pp. 241–69). New York: Peter Lang.

Giles, H., Hajek, C., Barker, V., Anderson, M., Chen-M.-L., Zhang, Y. B. and Hummert, M. L., 2007, Applied communicative dimensions of police–civilian interaction, in A. Weatherall, B. Watson and C. Gallois (eds.), *Language, discourse and social psychology* (pp. 131–59). Basingstoke: Palgrave Macmillan.

Giles, H., Hewstone, M., Ryan, E. B. and Johnson, P., 1987, Research on language attitudes, in U. Ammon, N. Dittmar and K. Mattheier (eds.), *Sociolinguistics: an international handbook of the science of language and society* (pp. 585–97). Berlin: Walter de Gruyter.

Giles, H., Makoni, S. and Dailey, R., 2006, Intergenerational communication beliefs across the lifespan: comparative data from Ghana and South Africa. *Journal of cross-cultural gerontology* 20, 191–211.

Giles, H., Mulac, A., Bradac, J. and Johnson, P., 1987, Speech accommodation theory: the first decade and beyond, in M. McLaughlin (ed.), *Communication yearbook*, 10 (pp. 13–48). Beverley Hills, CA: Sage.

Giles, H. and Powesland, P., 1975, *Speech style and social evaluation*. London: Academic Press.

Giles, H. and Robinson, W. P. (eds.), 1990, *Handbook of language and social psychology*. Chichester: Wiley.

Giles, H. and Sassoon, C., 1983, The effect of speaker's accent, social class background and message style on British listeners' social judgements. *Language and communication* 3, 305–13.

Giles, H. and Smith, P., 1979, Accommodation theory: optimal levels of convergence, in H. Giles and R. St. Clair (eds.), *Language and social psychology* (pp. 45–65). Oxford: Blackwell.

Giles, H., Taylor, D. and Bourhis, R., 1977, Dimensions of Welsh identity. *European journal of social psychology* 7, 29–39.

Giles, H., Williams, A., Mackie, D. and Rosselli, F., 1995, Reactions to Anglo- and Hispanic-American accented speakers: affect, identity, persuasion, and the English-Only controversy. *Language and communication* 15, 107–20.

Giles, H., Wilson, P. and Conway, A., 1981, Accent and lexical diversity as determinants of impression formation and perceived employment suitability. *Language sciences* 3, 91–103.

Gill, M., 1994, Accent and stereotypes: their effect on perceptions of teachers and lecture comprehension. *Journal of applied communication research* 22, 348–61.

Goddard, A., 2002, *The language of advertising*. London: Routledge.

Gordon, E. and Abell, M., 1990, 'This objectionable colonial dialect': historical and contemporary attitudes to New Zealand speech, in A. Bell and J. Holmes (eds.), *New Zealand ways of speaking English* (pp. 21–48). Clevedon: Multilingual Matters.

Gorter, D. (ed.), 2006, *Linguistic landscape: a new approach to multilingualism*. Clevedon: Multilingual Matters.

Gould, O. and Dixon, R., 1997, Recall of medication instructions by young and elderly adult women: is overaccommodative speech helpful? *Journal of language and social psychology* 16, 50–69.

Gould, P., 1977, Changing mental maps: childhood to adulthood. *Ekistics* 255, 100–21.

Graddol, D. and Swann, J., 1988, Trapping linguists. *Language and education*, 2, 95–111.

Granger, R., Mathews, M., Quay, L. and Verner, R., 1977, Teacher judgements of the communication effectiveness of children using different speech patterns. *Journal of educational psychology* 69, 793–6.

Greenbaum, S. (ed.), 1985, *The English language today*. Oxford: Pergamon.

Griffiths, M., 2009, Exploring the forensic audiofit: non-linguist perceptions, conceptions, descriptions and evaluations of unfamiliar voices in a forensic context. Unpublished PhD thesis, Centre for Language and Communication Research, Cardiff University.

Haarmann, H., 1984, The role of ethnocultural stereotypes and foreign languages in Japanese commercials. *International journal of the sociology of language* 50, 101–21.

1989, *Symbolic values of foreign language use: from the Japanese case to a general sociolinguistic perspective*. Berlin: Mouton de Gruyter.

Haleta, L., 1996, Student perceptions of teachers' use of language: the effects of powerful and powerless language on impression formation and uncertainty. *Communication education* 45, 16–28.

Hamilton, H., 1991, Accommodation and mental disability, in H. Giles, J. Coupland and N. Coupland (eds.), pp. 157–86.

Hamilton, M. and Hunter, J., 1998, The effect of language intensity on receiver evaluations of message, source, and topic, in M. Allen and R. Preiss (eds.), *Persuasion: advances through meta-analysis* (pp. 99–138). Cresskill, NJ: Hampton Press.

Hanson, D., 1980, Relationship between methods and findings in attitude–behaviour research. *Psychology* 17, 11–13.

Harari, H. and McDavid, J., 1973, Name stereotypes and teachers' expectations. *Journal of educational psychology* 65, 222–5.

Hargreaves, J., 2004, Wilfred Pickles. *Oxford dictionary of national biography*. Oxford: Oxford University Press.

Harlow, R., 1998, Some languages are just not good enough, in L. Bauer and P. Trudgill (eds.), pp. 9–14.

Harvey, J., 1977, *The Plantagenets*. London: Fontana.

Haugen, E., 1966, Dialect, language, nation, in J. Pride and J. Holmes (eds.), 1972, *Sociolinguistics*. Harmondsworth: Penguin.

Heise, D., 1970, The semantic differential scale in attitude research, in G. F. Summers (ed.), *Attitude measurement*. New York: Rand McNally.

Hernandez, R., 1993, When an accent becomes an issue: immigrants turn to speech classes to reduce sting of bias. *The New York Times*, 2 March.

Hewstone, M., 1989, *Causal attribution*. Oxford: Blackwell.

Hewstone, M., Manstead, A. and Stroebe, W. (eds.), 1997, *The Blackwell social psychology reader*. Oxford: Blackwell.

Hinckley, J., Craig, H. and Anderson, L., 1989, Communication characteristics of provider–patient information exchanges, in H. Giles and W. P. Robinson (eds.), pp. 519–35.

Hoenigswald, H., 1966, A proposal for the study of folklinguistics, in W. Bright (ed.), *Sociolinguistics*, (pp. 16–26). The Hague: Mouton.

Holmes, J., 2001, *An introduction to sociolinguistics*. London: Longman.

Homans, G., 1961, *Social behaviour*. New York: Harcourt, Brace and World.

Hopper, R., 1977, Language attitudes in the job interview. *Communication monographs* 44, 346–51.

Hopper, R. and Williams, F., 1973, Speech characteristics and employability. *Speech monographs* 40, 296–302.

Hosman, L., 1989, The evaluative consequences of hedges, hesitations and intensifiers. *Human communication research* 15, 383–406.

2002, Language and persuasion, in J. Dillard and M. Pfau (eds.), pp. 371–90.

Huguet, Á., 2006, Attitudes and motivation versus language achievement in cross-linguistic settings: what is cause and what effect? *Journal of multilingual and multicultural development* 27, 413–29.

Huygens, I. and Vaughan, G., 1983, Language attitudes, ethnicity, and social class in New Zealand. *Journal of multilingual and multicultural development* 4, 207–23.

Hymes, D., 1971, Competence and performance in linguistic theory, in R. Huxley and E. Ingram (eds.), *Language acquisition: models and methods* (pp. 67–99). London: Academic Press.

Hyrkestedt, I. and Kalaja, P., 1998, Attitudes toward English and its functions in Finland: a discourse-analytic study. *World Englishes* 17, 345–57.

Irvine, J. and Gal, S., 2000, Language ideology and linguistic differentiation, in P. Kroskrity (ed.), *Regimes of language: ideologies, politics and identities* (pp. 85–138). Santa Fe, NM: School for American Research Press.

Isen, A., Horn, N. and Rosenhan, D., 1973, Effects of success and failure on children's generosity. *Journal of personality and social psychology* 27, 239–47.

Isen, A., Shalker, T., Clark, M. and Karp, L., 1978, Affect, accessibility of material in memory and behaviour: a cognitive loop? *Journal of personality and social psychology* 36, 1–12.

Jaworski, A. and Coupland, N., (eds.), 1999, *The discourse reader*. London: Routledge.

Jaworski, A. and Thurlow, C. (eds.), 2010, *Semiotic landscapes: text, image, space*. London: Continuum.

Jaworski, A., Coupland, N. and Galasiński, D. (eds.), 2004, *Metalanguage: social and ideological perspectives*. The Hague: Mouton.

Jones, Aled and Jones, William, 2001, *Welsh reflections: Y Drych and America 1851–2001*. Llandysul: Gomer Press.

Jørgensen, J. and Quist, P., 2001, Native speakers' judgements of second language Danish. *Language awareness* 10, 41–56.

Kachru, B., 1985, Standards, codification and sociolinguistic realism: the English language in the outer circle, in R. Quirk and H. Widdowson (eds.), *English in the world: teaching and learning the language and literatures* (pp. 11–30). Cambridge: Cambridge University Press.

1988, Teaching World Englishes. *ERIC/CLL News Bulletin* 12 (1), 3–4, 7–8.

Kalin, R., 1982, The social significance of speech in medical and occupational settings, in E. B. Ryan and H. Giles (eds.), pp. 148–63.

Kalin, R. and Rayko, D., 1980, The social significance of speech in the job interview, in R. St. Clair and H. Giles (eds.), *The social and psychological contexts of language* (pp. 39–50). Hillsdale, NJ: Erlbaum.

Kalin, R., Rayko, D. and Love, N., 1980, The perception and evaluation of job candidates with four different ethnic accents, in H. Giles, W. P. Robinson and P. Smith (eds.), *Language: social psychological perspectives* (pp. 197–202). Oxford: Pergamon.

Kelly-Holmes, H., 2000, Bier, parfum, kaas: language fetish in European advertising. *European journal of cultural studies* 3, 67–82.

Khan, S., 2003, Number's up for cut-glass accent. *The Observer*, 24 August.

Klingle, R., 2004, Compliance-gaining in medical contexts, in J. Seiter and R. Gass (eds.), *Perspectives in persuasion, social influence and compliance gaining* (pp. 289–315). Boston: Allyn and Bacon.

Knight, I., 2001, Speak proper? Not likely. *The Sunday Times*, 11 November.

Knops, U. and van Hout, R., 1988, Language attitudes in the Dutch language area: an introduction, in R. van Hout and U. Knops (eds.), *Language attitudes in the Dutch language area* (pp. 1–23). Dordrecht: Foris.

Kottke, J. and MacLeod, C., 1989, Use of profanity in the counseling interview. *Psychological Reports* 65, 627–34.

Kramarae, C., 1982, Gender: how she speaks, in E. B. Ryan and H. Giles (eds.), pp. 84–98.

Kramer, C., 1974, Stereotypes of women's speech: the word from cartoons. *Journal of popular culture* 8, 622–38.

Kress, G. and van Leeuwen, T., 1996, *Reading images: the grammar of visual design*. London: Routledge.

1998, Front pages: the (critical) analysis of newspaper layout, in A. Bell and P. Garrett (eds.), *Approaches to media discourse* (pp. 186–219). Oxford: Blackwell.

Kristiansen, T., 1997, Language attitudes in a Danish cinema, in N. Coupland and A. Jaworski (eds.), pp. 291–305.

2001, Two standards: one for the media and one for the school. *Language Awareness* 10, 9–24.

2005, The power of tradition: a study of attitudes towards English in seven Nordic communities. *Acta linguistica hafniensia* 37, 155–69.

2009, The macro-level social meanings of late-modern Danish accents. *Acta linguistica hafniensia* 41.

Kurklen, R. and Kassinove, H., 1991, Effects of profanities, touch, and subject's religiosity on perceptions of a psychologist and behavioral compliance. *The journal of social psychology* 131, 899–901.

Labov, W., 1966, *The social significance of speech in New York City*. Washington DC: Centre for Applied Linguistics.

1972, *Sociolinguistic patterns*. Oxford: Blackwell.

1984, Field methods of the project on linguistic change and variation, in J. Baugh and J. Sherzer (eds.), *Language in use* (pp. 28–53). Englewood Cliffs, NJ: Prentice Hall.

Ladegaard, H.J., 1998, National stereotypes and language attitudes: the perception of British, American and Australian language and culture in Denmark. *Language and communication* 18, 251–74.

Lakoff, R., 1975, *Language and woman's place*. New York: Harper and Row.

Lambert, W., Anisfeld, M. and Yeni-Komshian, G., 1965, Evaluational reactions of Jewish and Arab adolescents to dialect and language variations. *Journal of personality and social psychology* 2, 84–90.

Lambert, W., Hodgson, R. Gardner, R. and Fillenbaum, S., 1960, Evaluational reactions to spoken languages. *Journal of abnormal and social psychology* 60, 44–51.

Landry, R. and Bourhis, R., 1997, Linguistic landscape and ethnolinguistic vitality: an empirical study. *Journal of language and social psychology* 16, 23–49.

La Piere, R., 1934, Attitudes versus actions. *Social forces* 13, 230–7.

Lasagabaster, D., 2003, *Trilingüismo en la enseñanza: actitudes hacia la lengua minoritaria, la mayoritaria y la extranjera*. Lleida: Milenio.

2006, *Las lenguas de la diáspora Vasca en el oueste de los Estados Unidos*. Bilbao: Lete.

2008, Basque diaspora in the USA and language maintenance. *Journal of multilingual and multicultural development* 29, 66–90.

Lasagabaster, D. and Huguet, Á., 2007, *Multilingualism in European bilingual contexts. language use and attitudes*. Clevedon: Multilingual Matters.

Lee, R., 1971, Dialect perception: a critical view and re-evaluation. *Quarterly journal of speech* 57, 410–417.

Leech, G., 1966, *English in advertising*. Harlow: Longman.

Lemann, N., 2000, The Word Lab. *The New Yorker*, 16–23 October, pp. 100–12.

Lerond, A., 1980, *Dictionnaire de la pronunciation*. Paris: Larousse.

Levin, H., Giles, H. and Garrett, P., 1994, The effects of lexical formality on accent and trait attributions. *Language and Communication* 14, 265–74.

Lieberson, S., 1981, *Language diversity and language contact*. Stanford, CA: Stanford University Press.

Liebscher, G. and Dailey-O'Cain, J., 2009, Language attitudes in interaction. *Journal of sociolinguistics* 13, 195–222.

Lind, E. and O'Barr, W., 1979, The social significance of speech in the courtroom, in H. Giles and R. St. Clair (eds.), *Language and social psychology* (pp. 66–87). Oxford: Blackwell.

Linell, P., 1991, Accommodation on trial: processes of communicative accommodation in courtroom interaction, in H. Giles, J. Coupland and N. Coupland (eds.), pp. 103–30.

Lippi-Green, R., 1994, Accent, standard language ideology, and discriminatory pretext in courts. *Language in society* 23, 163–98.

1997, *English with an accent: language, ideology, and discrimination in the United States*. London: Routledge.

Lippmann, W., 1922, *Public opinion*. New York: Harcourt Brace.

Llurda, E. (ed.), 2005, *Non-native language teachers: perceptions, challenges and contributions to the profession*. New York: Springer.

Long, M., 1983, Linguistic and conversational adjustments to non-native speakers. *Studies in second language acquisition* 5, 177–249.

Long, D. and Preston, D. (eds.), 2002, *Handbook of perceptual dialectology*, vol. II. Amsterdam: Benjamins.

MacKinnon, K., 1981, *Scottish opinion on Gaelic*. Hatfield Polytechnic Social Science Research Publications SS14.

Macrae, C., Bodenhausen, G., Milne, A. and Jetten, J., 1994, Out of mind but back in sight: stereotypes on the rebound. *Journal of personality and social psychology* 67, 808–17.

Mandrake, 2007, Prime Minister's words do not ring true for Sir Sean. *The Sunday Telegraph*, 28 October.

Manstead, A. and McCulloch, C., 1981, Sex role stereotyping in British television advertisements. *British journal of social psychology* 20, 171–80.

Matross, R., Paige, R. and Hendricks, G., 1982, American student attitudes toward foreign students before and during an international crisis. *Journal of college student personnel* 23, 58–65.

Mazzella, R. and Feingold, A., 1994, The effects of physical attractiveness, race, socioeconomic status, and gender of defendants and victims on judgements of mock jurors: a meta-analysis. *Journal of applied social psychology* 24, 1315–44.

McCroskey, J. and Young, T., 1981, Ethos and credibility: the construct and its measurement after three decades. *Central states speech journal* 32, 24–34.

McKenzie, R., 2008, The role of variety recognition in Japanese university students' attitudes towards English speech varieties. *Journal of multilingual and multicultural development* 29, 139–53.

McKirnan, D. and Hamayan, E., 1984, Speech norms and attitudes toward outgroup members: a test of a model in a bicultural context. *Journal of language and social psychology* 3, 21–38.

Metcalf, A., 1985, Newspaper stylebooks: strictures teach tolerance, in S. Greenbaum (ed.), pp. 106–15.

Miller, T., Govil, N., McMurria, J. and Maxwell, R., 2001, *Global Hollywood*. London: British Film Institute.

Milroy, J., 2007, The ideology of standard language, in C. Llamas, L. Mullany and P. Stockwell (eds.), *The Routledge companion to sociolinguistics*, (pp. 133–9). London: Routledge.

Milroy, L., 1987, *Language and social networks*. Oxford: Blackwell.

2001, The social categories of race and class: language ideology and sociolinguistics, in N. Coupland, S. Sarangi and C. Candlin (eds.), *Sociolinguistics and social theory* (pp. 235–60). London: Longman.

Milroy, J. and Milroy, L., 1998, *Authority in language: investigating standard English*. London: Routledge.

Milmoe, S., Rosenthal, R., Blane, H., Chaftez, M. and Wolf, I., 1967, The doctor's voice: postdictor of successful referral of alcohol patients. *Journal of abnormal psychology* 72, 78–84.

Mitchell, R., 1991, Multilingualism in British schools: future policy directions, in P. Meara and A. Ryan (eds.), *Language and nation* (pp. 107–116). London: BAAL and CILT.

Moore, S., 1991, *Looking for trouble: writings on film, consumption and the tyranny of gender*. London: Serpent's Tail Press.

Morley, D., 1980, *The nationwide audience*. London: British Film Institute.

Morrish, J., 1999, The accent that dare not speak its name. *The Independent on Sunday*, 21 March.

Mugglestone, L., 2003, *Talking proper: the rise of accent as social symbol*. Oxford: Oxford University Press.

Mutonya, M., 1997, Language attitudes of educated Africans towards varieties of African English. Unpublished MA thesis, Michigan State University.

Nabi, R., 2002, *Discrete emotions and persuasion*, in J. Dillard and M. Pfau (eds.), pp. 289–308.

Nesdale, D. and Rooney, R., 1996, Evaluations and stereotyping of accented speakers by pre-adolescent children. *Journal of language and social psychology* 15, 133–54.

Niedzielski, N. and Preston, D., 2000, *Folk linguistics*. New York: Mouton.

O'Barr, W., 1982, *Linguistic evidence: language, power and strategy in the courtroom*. New York: Academic Press.

O'Barr, W. and Atkins, B., 1980, 'Womens' language' or 'powerless language'?, in S. McConnell-Ginet, R. Borker and N. Furman (eds.), *Women and language in literature and society* (pp. 93–110). New York: Praeger.

O'Keefe, B., 1988, The logic of message design: individual differences in reasoning about communication. *Communication monographs* 55, 80–103.

O'Mara, E., 2007, Worker sacked because his accent 'wasn't English enough'. *Northampton Chronicle*, 24 November.

Oppenheim, A., 1992, *Questionnaire design, interviewing, and attitude measurement*. London: Pinter.

Oppenheim, B., 1982, An exercise in attitude measurement, in G. Breakwell, H. Foot and R. Gilmour (eds.), pp. 38–56.

Osgood, C., Suci, G. and Tannenbaum, P., 1957, *The measurement of meaning*. Urbana, IL: University of Illinois Press.

Oskamp, S., 1977, *Attitudes and opinions*. Englewood Cliffs, NJ: Prentice Hall.

Ostrom, T., 1969, The relationship between the affective, behavioural, and cognitive components of attitude. *Journal of experimental social psychology* 5, 12–30.

Ostrom, T., Bond, C., Krosnik, J. and Sedikides, C., 1994, *Attitude scales: how we measure the unmeasurable*, in S. Shavitt and T. Brock (eds.), pp. 15–42.

Paltridge, J. and Giles, H., 1984, Attitudes towards speakers of regional accents of French: effects of regionality, age and sex of listeners. *Linguistische berichte* 90, 71–85.

Parry, D., 1990, The conservative English dialects of north Carmarthenshire, in N. Coupland (ed.), *English in Wales: diversity, conflict and change* (pp. 151–61). Clevedon: Multilingual Matters.

Parton, S., Siltanen, S., Hosman, L. and Langenderfer, J., 2002, Employment interview outcomes and speech style effects. *Journal of language and social psychology* 21, 144–61.

Pegrum, M., 2004, Selling English: advertising and the discourses of ELT. *English today* 77, vol. 20 (1), 3–10.

Pennington, D., Gillen, K. and Hill, P., 1999, *Essential social psychology*. London: Hodder Arnold.

Perloff, R., 1993, *The dynamics of persuasion* (first edition). Hillsdale, NJ: Erlbaum.

2003, *The dynamics of persuasion: communication and attitudes in the 21st Century* (second edition). Mahwah, NJ: Erlbaum.

2008, *The dynamics of persuasion: communication and attitudes in the 21st Century* (third edition). New York: Erlbaum.

Petty, R. and Cacioppo, J., 1986, The elaboration likelihood model of persuasion, in L. Berkowitz (ed.), *Advances in experimental psychology* (vol. XIX, pp. 123–205). New York: Academic Press.

Pickles, W., 1949, *Between you and me*. London: Werner Laurie.

Pierson, H., Giles, H. and Young, L., 1987, Intergroup vitality perceptions during a period of political uncertainty: the case of Hong Kong. *Journal of multilingual and multicultural development* 8, 451–60.

Piller, I., 2001, Identity constructions in bilingual advertising. *Language in society* 30, 153–86.

2003, Advertising as a site of language contact. *Annual review of applied linguistics* 23, 170–83.

Plakans, B., 1997, Undergraduates' experiences with and attitudes toward international teaching assistants. *TESOL quarterly* 31, 95–119.

Platt, J. and Weber, H., 1984, Speech convergence miscarried: an investigation into inappropriate accommodation strategies. *International journal of the sociology of language* 46, 131–46.

Potter, J., 1998, Discursive social psychology: from attitudes to evaluative practices. *European review of social psychology* 9, 233–66.

Potter, J. and Wetherell, M., 1987, *Discourse and social psychology: beyond attitudes and behaviour*. London: Sage.

Powell, L., Callahan, K., Comans, C., McDonald, L., Mansell, J., Trotter, M. and Wiliams, V., 1984, Offensive language and impressions during an interview. *Psychological reports* 55, 617–18.

Powesland, P. and Giles, H., 1975, Persuasiveness and accent–message incompatibility. *Human relations* 28, 85–93.

Preston, D., 1989, *Perceptual dialectology: nonlinguists' views of areal linguistics*. Dordrecht: Foris.

1993, The uses of folklinguistics. *International journal of applied linguistics* 3, 181–259.

1996, Whaddayaknow?: The modes of folklinguistic awareness. *Language awareness* 5, 40–74.

Preston, D. (ed.), 1999, *Handbook of perceptual dialectology*, vol. 1. Amsterdam: Benjamins.

Preston, D., in press, Variation in language regard, in E. Ziegler, J. Scharloth and P. Gilles (eds.), *Empirische Evidenzen und theoretische Passungen sprachlicher Variation*. Frankfurt: Peter Lang.

Price, S., Fluck, M. and Giles, H., 1983, The effects of language of testing on bilingual pre-adolescents' attitudes towards Welsh and varieties of English. *Journal of multilingual and multicultural development* 4, 149–61.

Pumphrey, M., 1993, Masculinity, in E. Buscombe (ed.), *The BFI companion to the Western* (pp. 181–183). London: British Film Institute and Andre Deutsch.

Putman, W. and Street, R., 1984, The conception and perception of non-content speech performance: implications for speech accommodation theory. *International journal of the sociology of language* 46, 97–114.

Ralston, S. and Thameling, C., 1988, Effect of vividness on the information value of reference letters and job applicants' recommendations. *Psychological reports* 62, 867–70.

Ray, G., Ray, E. and Zahn, C., 1991, Speech behavior and social evaluation: an examination of medical messages. *Communication quarterly* 39, 119–29.

Reh, M., 2004, Multilingual writing: a reader-oriented typology – with examples from Lira Municipality Uganda. *International journal of the sociology of language* 170, 1–41.

Reinhard, J., 2002, Persuasion in the legal setting, in J. Dillard and M. Pfau (eds.), pp. 543–602.

Rey, A., 1977, Accent and employability: language attitudes. *Language sciences* 47, 7–12.

Rickford, J. and Traugott, E., 1985, Symbol of powerlessness and degeneracy, or symbol of solidarity and truth? Paradoxical attitudes towards pidgins and creoles, in S. Greenbaum (ed.), pp. 252–61.

Roberts, C., Davies, E. and Jupp, T., 1992, *Language and discrimination: a study of communication in multi-ethnic workplaces*. London: Longman.

Rodriguez, J., Cargile, A. and Rich, M., 2004, Reactions to African-American Vernacular English: do more phonological features matter? *The Western journal of Black Studies* 28, 407–14.

Rokeach, M., 1973, *The nature of human values*. New York: Free Press.

Ross, S. and Shortreed, I., 1990, Japanese foreigner talk: convergence or divergence? *Journal of Asian Pacific communication* 1, 135–46.

Roter, D., Hall, J. and Katz, N., 1987, Relations between physicians' behaviors and analogue patients' satisfaction, recall, and impressions. *Medical care* 25, 437–51.

Rubin, D., 1992, Nonlanguage factors affecting undergraduates' judgements of nonnative English-speaking teaching assistants. *Research in higher education* 33, 511–31.

Rubin, D. and Smith, K., 1990, Effects of accent, ethnicity, and lecturer topic on undergraduates' perceptions of nonnative English-speaking teaching assistants. *International journal of intercultural relations* 14, 337–53.

Rubin, D., DeHart, J. and Heintzman, M., 1991, Effects of accented speech and culture-typical compliance-gaining style on subordinates' impressions of managers. *International journal of intercultural relations* 15, 267–83.

Rubin, D., Healy, P., Gardiner, T., Zath, R. and Moore, C., 1997, Nonnative physicians as message sources: effects of accent and ethnicity on patients' responses to AIDS prevention counseling. *Health communication* 9, 351–68.

Ryan, E. B. and Capadano, H., 1978, Age perceptions and evaluative reactions toward adult speakers. *Journal of gerontology* 33, 98–102.

Ryan, E. B., Carranza, M. and Moffie, R., 1975, Reactions towards varying degrees of accentedness in the speech of Spanish-English. *Language and speech* 20, 267–73.

Ryan, E. B. and Giles, H. (eds.), 1982, *Attitudes towards language variation.* London: Arnold.

Ryan, E. B., Giles, H. and Hewstone, M., 1988, The measurement of language attitudes, in U. Ammon, N. Dittmar and K. Mattheier (eds.), *Sociolinguistics: an international handbook of the science of language and society* (pp. 1068–82). Berlin: Walter de Gruyter.

Ryan, E. B. and Sebastian, R., 1980, The effects of speech style and social class background on social judgements of speakers. *British journal of social and clinical psychology* 19, 229–33.

Salovey, P., Schneider, T. and Apanovitch, A. M., 2002, Message framing in the prevention and early detection of illness, in J. Dillard and M. Pfau (eds.), pp. 391–406.

Sarnoff, I., 1970, Social attitudes and the resolution of motivational conflict, in M. Jahoda and N. Warren (eds.), *Attitudes* (pp. 279–84). Harmondsworth: Penguin.

Sazer, L. and Kassinove, H., 1991, Effects of a counselor's profanity and subject's religiosity on content acquisition of a counseling lecture and behavioral compliance. *Psychological reports* 69, 1059–70.

Schmied, J., 1991, *English in Africa.* London: Longman.

Scollon, R. and Wong Scollon, S., 2003, *Discourses in place: language in the material world.* London: Routledge.

Sears, D., 1983, The persistence of early political predispositions: the role of attitude object and life stage, in L. Wheeler and P. Shaver (eds.),

Review of personality and social psychology (vol. 4, pp. 79–116). Beverly Hills, CA: Sage.

Sears, D. and Kosterman, R., 1994, Mass media and political persuasion, in S. Shavitt and T. Brock (eds.), pp. 251–78.

Seggie, I., 1983, Attributions of guilt as a function of accent and crime. *Journal of multilingual and multicultural development* 4, 197–206.

Seggie, I., Smith, N. and Hogkins, P., 1986, Evaluations of employment suitability based on accent alone: an Australian case study. *Language sciences* 8, 129–40.

Seiter, J., Larsen, J. and Skinner, J., 1998, 'Handcapped' or 'Handi-capable'?: the effects of language describing people with disabilities on perceptions of source credibility and persuasiveness. *Communication reports* 11, 1–11.

Seligman, C., Tucker, G. and Lambert, W., 1972, The effects of speech style and other attributes on teachers' attitudes towards pupils. *Language in society* 1, 131–42.

Sharp, D., Thomas, B., Price, E., Francis, G. and Davies, I., 1973, *Attitudes to Welsh and English in the schools of Wales*. Basingstoke: Macmillan.

Shavitt, S. and Brock, T. (eds.), 1994, *Persuasion: psychological insights and perspectives*. Boston, MA: Allyn and Bacon.

Sherif, M., 1967, Introduction, in C. Sherif and M. Sherif (eds.), *Attitude, ego-involvement, and change* (pp. 1–5). New York: Wiley.

Shohamy, E. and Gorter, D. (eds.), 2009, *Linguistic landscape: expanding the scenery*. London: Routledge.

Simard, L., Taylor, D. and Giles, H., 1976, Attribution processes and interpersonal accommodation in a bilingual setting. *Language and speech* 19, 374–87.

Smith, E. and Mackie, D., 2000, *Social psychology*. New York: Worth.

Smith, G., 1998, The political impact of name sounds. *Communication monographs* 65, 154–72.

Smith, M., 1982, Selection interviewing: a four step approach, in G. Breakwell, H. Foot and R. Gilmour (eds.), pp. 19–37.

Spolsky, B. and Cooper, R., 1991, *The languages of Jerusalem*. Oxford: Clarendon Press.

Stewart, M. and Ryan, E. B., 1982, Attitudes towards younger and older speakers: effects of varying speech rates. *Journal of language and social psychology* 1, 91–109.

Stewart, M., Ryan, E. B. and Giles, H., 1985, Accent and social class effects on status and solidarity evaluations. *Personality and social psychology bulletin* 11, 98–105.

Street, R., 1982, Evaluation of noncontent speech accommodation. *Language and communication* 2, 1–31.

  1991, Accommodation in medical consultations, in H. Giles, J. Coupland and N. Coupland (eds.), pp. 131–56.

Street, R., Brady, R. and Lee, 1984, Evaluative responses to communications: effects of speech rate, sex and interaction context. *Western journal of speech communication* 48, 14–27.

Street, R., Brady, R. and Putman, W., 1983, The influence of speech rate stereotypes and rate similarity on listeners' evaluations of speakers. *Journal of language and social psychology* 2, 37–56.

Strongman, K. and Woosley, J., 1967, Stereotypical reactions to regional accents. *British journal of social and clinical psychology* 6, 164–7.

Swift, M., 2007, Those who sound too different face social or career barriers. *San Jose Mercury News*, 15 April.

Tajfel, H., 1981, Social stereotypes and social groups, in J. Turner and H. Giles (eds.), *Intergroup behaviour* (pp. 144–65). Oxford: Blackwell.

Tajfel, H. and Turner, J., 1979, An integrative theory of intergroup conflict, in W. Austin and S. Worchel (eds.), *The social psychology of intergroup relations* (pp. 33–53). Monterey, CA: Brooks-Cole.

Tesser, A., 1993, The importance of heritability in psychological research: the case of attitudes. *Psychological review* 100, 129–42.

Thakerar, J. and Giles, H., 1981, They are – so to speak: noncontent speech stereotypes. *Language and communication* 1, 251–6.

Thurstone, L., 1931, The measurement of social attitudes. *Journal of abnormal and social psychology* 26, 249–69.

Trudgill, P., 1990, *The dialects of England*. Oxford: Blackwell.

1998, The meanings of words should not be allowed to vary or change, in L. Bauer and P. Trudgill (eds.), pp. 1–8.

Truss, L., 2003, *Eats, shoots & leaves*. London: Profile Books.

Tulp, S., 1978, Reklame en tweetaligheid: een onderzoek naar de geografische verspreiding van franstalige en nederlandstalige affiches in Brussel. *Taal en sociale integraties* 1, 261–88.

Urry, J., 2002, *The tourist gaze*. London: Sage.

van Bezooijen, R., 1994, Aesthetic evaluation of Dutch language varieties. *Language and communication* 14, 253–63.

Ward, D., 2000, Scousers put the accent on success. *The Guardian*, 22 September.

Webster, C., 1996, Hispanic and Anglo interviewer and respondent ethnicity and gender: the impact on survey response data. *Journal of marketing research* 33, 62–72.

Wegener, D., 1989, *White bears and other unwanted thoughts: suppression, obsession, and the psychology of mental control*. New York: Viking Press.

Wegener, D., Petty, R. and Smith, S., 1995, Positive mood can increase or decrease message scrutiny: the hedonic contingency view of mood and message processing. *Journal of personality and social psychology* 69, 5–15.

Wenzel, V., 1996, Reklame en tweetaligheid in Brussel: een empirisch onderzoek naar de spreiding van Nederlandstalige en Franstalige affiches, in Vrije Univeristeit Brussel (ed.), *Brusselse thema's 3* (pp. 45–74). Brussels: Vrije Universiteit.

White, S., 1989, Backchannels across cultures: a study of Americans and Japanese. *Language in society*, 18, 59–76.

Willemyns, M., Gallois, C., Callan, V. and Pittam, J., 1997, Accent accommodation in the job interview: impact of interviewer, accent and gender. *Journal of language and social psychology* 16, 3–22.

Williams, A. and Garrett, P., 2002, Communication evaluations across the lifespan: from adolescent storm and stress to elder aches and pains. *Journal of language and social psychology* 21, 101–26.

submitted, Teenagers' perceptions of communication and 'good communication' with peers, young adults and older adults.

Williams, A., Garrett, P. and Coupland, N., 1996, Perceptual dialectology, folklinguistics, and regional stereotypes: teachers' perceptions of variation in Welsh English. *Multilingua* 15, 171–99.

1999, Dialect recognition, in D. Preston (ed.), pp. 345–58.

Williams, A., Garrett, P. and Tennant, R., 2004, Young adults' perceptions of communication with peers and adolescents, in S. H. Ng, C. Candlin and C. Y. Chiu (eds.), *Language matters: communication, identity and culture* (pp. 111–36). Hong Kong: City University of Hong Kong Press.

Williams, A. and Giles, H., 1998, Communication of ageism, in M. Hecht (ed.), *Communication and prejudice* (pp. 136–60). Thousand Oaks, CA: Sage.

Williams, A. and Nussbaum, J., 2001, *Intergenerational communication across the lifespan*. Mahwah, NJ: Erlbaum.

Williams, A., Ylänne, V. and Wadleigh, P. M., 2007, Selling the 'Elixir of Life': images of the elderly in an Olivio advertising campaign. *Journal of aging studies* 21 (1), 1–21.

Williams, G., 1991, *The Welsh in Patagonia: the state and the ethnic community*. Cardiff: University of Wales Press.

Williams, M. and Burden, R., 1997, *Psychology for language teachers*. Cambridge: Cambridge University Press.

Wilson, S., 2002, *Seeking and resisting compliance*. Thousand Oaks, CA: Sage.

Winford, D., 1975, Teacher attitudes toward language varieties in a creole community. *International journal of the sociology of language* 8, 45–75.

Woolard, K., 1989, *Double talk: bilingualism and the politics of ethnicity in Catalonia*. Stanford, CA: Stanford University Press.

Woolard, K. and Gahng, T.-J., 1990, Changing language policies and attitudes in autonomous Catalonia. *Language in society* 19, 311–30.

Wright, J. and Hosman, L., 1983, Language style and sex bias in the courtroom: the effects of male and female use of hedges and intensifiers on impression formation. *The southern speech communication journal* 48, 137–52.

Yaeger-Dror, M. (ed.), 1992, Communicative accommodation: a new perspective on 'hypercorrect' speech. Special issue of *Language and communication* 12 (3&4).

Zahn, C. and Hopper, R., 1985, Measuring language attitudes: the speech evaluation instrument. *Journal of language and social psychology* 4, 113–23.

Zuengler, J., 1991, Accommodation in native–non-native interactions: going beyond the 'what' to the 'why' in second language research, in H. Giles, J. Coupland and N. Coupland (eds.), pp. 223–44.

Index

accent identical to your own 172–7
accent reduction 13, 16, 224
accommodation theory
    (see 'communication
    accommodation theory')
acquiescence bias 45, 56
advertisements, 23, 24, 25, 51, 73,
    142–58, 164, 170, 224
affected RP 54
Africa 46–8, 138 (see also 'Egypt',
    'Ghana', 'Kenya', 'South Africa',
    'Uganda')
African-American English 8, 75, 137
Afro-Caribbean English 173–7
age 73, 75, 94, 95–7, 114, 175, 196
Alabama 183
Andalucia 85
apostrophe 9
Arabic 39–40, 74, 154
Aragon 159
Argentina 86, 165, 225
Asturias 159
attitudes
    and behaviour 6, 19, 24, 103
    as input and output 21
    as learned phenomena 22
    components of 23
    definitions of 19–20
    development 22, 29
    dimensions of 55, 56, 73
    facets and manifestations 20
    hierarchies 74
    stability and durability 29–30, 229
attitudinal cognitorium 226
attitudinal differential 71, 198
audience design 111
Australia 22, 53, 60–2, 64, 65–9, 75, 94,
    110, 112, 123–4, 139, 187–99

Basque Country 159, 169
BBC 8, 13, 14, 49
BBC Voices study 160, 172–7
beliefs 19, 31, 179
Birmingham English 13, 99, 125, 172–7
boring 220
Bristolian English 13, 33, 97
Brussels 97

Canada 11, 45, 53, 64, 70–2, 88, 106,
    108–9, 129, 132, 138, 155
    (see also 'Montreal' and 'Quebec')
Cantonese 77, 86
Carolinas 180, 183
cartoons 14, 50
Catalan 84–6
causal attributions 110, 112, 120
ceremonial language use 148, 169
China 122, 155, 187 (see also 'Hong Kong')
Chinese (including Chinese-accented
    English) 131, 138
    codemixing 77
    Malaysian 123
    research participants 25, 131, 187
    written language 154, 155
cluster analysis 212–18, 222
Cockney 13, 64, 90, 91, 94, 173–7
codeswitching 2, 11–12, 75, 78,
    105, 228
'Comfort Factor' 4
communication accommodation
    theory 5, 12, 105–20, 228
    addressee foci 117
    basic notions 105
    constraints 108–10
    discourse attuning 117
    miscarried accommodation 112–15
    motivations 107–8

objective and subjective
    accommodation 111
optimal levels of accommodation 106
overaccommodation,
    hyperaccommodation and
    underaccommodation 106, 113
psychological accommodation 112–13
conceptual approach 42, 61, 172,
    196, 201
context 83–6, 97, 102, 179, 224–6
'controversy' 7
correctness 7, 183, 186
Costa Rica 77
'Cowbois' 156
Crocodile Dundee 190–1, 195
Cubans 111

Denmark 11, 43, 64, 79–82, 103
design logics 110
diaspora 86, 159, 160, 163–71, 227
direct approach 37–9, 42, 159–77,
    179, 228
discourse analysis 30, 159–63, 180, 227
domain priorities 169–70
double negatives in English 8
Dutch (including Dutch-accented
    English) 62, 153

educational contexts 128–31
    schools 4, 10, 13, 22, 33, 38, 39, 40,
        72, 75, 78, 80, 99, 128–30,
        203–18, 203–22
    universities 130–1
Egypt 74
eisteddfod 168, 170
elaboration likelihood model 100, 101,
    126, 140, 228
employment contexts 49, 89–90, 136–40
    job interviews 92, 110, 111, 136–9
English Only controversy 97, 100
ethnocentrism 98, 228
ethnolinguistic vitality 70, 83–6, 103,
    152, 160, 165, 227, 228
etiquette books 48–9
expertise 101
expletives 5, 132, 137, 219

fatigue effects 61, 63, 65
Finland 160–3
Finnish 160

Flemish 153
folklinguistics 179–99, 228
fonts 155
foreigner talk 112–13
France 72–4
French 1
    in Belgium 153
    in Canada 70–2, 88, 92, 108–9
    in France 72–4, 98, 155
    in Japan 143–5, 154
    in Switzerland 145–7
French-accented English 54, 60, 172–7

gender 3, 48–51, 196, 197 (*see also* 'sex')
German-accented English 60, 139, 172–7
Ghana 118
globalisation 66, 151, 152, 153, 160,
    164, 172, 227

habits 31
Hawaii 128, 183
health contexts 114–15, 132–6
    diagnostic interviews 134
    ethnicity 135
    medical jargon 132
    positivity and negativity 133–4
    question asking 132
    speech rates 133
Hebrew 39–40
Hong Kong 77, 86, 155
'hopefully' 6
hypothetical questions 43

ideology 2, 7, 8, 15, 19, 33, 34–5, 43,
    54, 65, 83, 103, 156, 158, 175,
    177, 195, 229
imposed norm hypothesis 5, 228
Indian-accented English 13, 14, 92,
    173–7
indirect approach 30, 37, 38, 42, 82, 228
inherent value hypothesis 5, 228
intergenerational research 117–19
interpretive repertoires 161
interviewer characteristics 45
Ireland 78, 108, 128, 155
Irish English 54, 78, 99, 172–7, 193

Japan 74, 136, 143–5, 154, 187
Japanese
    English 74, 106, 112

Japanese (*cont.*)
  language 112
  participants 46, 112, 136, 187

Kenya 103
keywords 187, 205–10, 218–22, 225
Korean 154

language expectancy theory 1, 228
language ideology (*see* 'ideology')
language myths 8–9
legal contexts
  attributions of guilt 122, 124
  audiofit 126–8
  courtrooms 122–3
  police 122
lexical diversity 89–90, 228
lexical provenance 88–9
linguistic landscape 151–7, 228
Lwo 153

Malaysian English 123, 131
Maori 11, 30, 62
matched guise technique 17, 37,
    39–41, 42, 45, 46, 53–87, 88, 92,
    95, 108–10, 114, 135, 138, 159,
    172, 179, 226, 228
  defined 41
  pros and cons 57–9
media 2, 7, 12–14, 15, 22, 46, 49,
    51, 66, 80, 84, 111, 143, 162,
    188–99, 211
message framing 134
Mexican Americans 76, 89, 93, 94, 99,
    102, 137, 138
Michigan 180–6
Montreal 42, 70, 151
mood 99–101
multidimensional scaling 212–18, 222
multidimensionality 83, 97, 103,
    132, 225–6
multiple questions 44

New York City 147, 183–6
New Zealand 11, 30, 53, 62–3, 65–9,
    112, 187–99
newsreaders 14, 111
North America 54, 86, 112, 118, 131, 135,
    147–51, 163–71, 172–7, 195, 225
    (*see also* 'Canada', 'USA')

opinions 19, 32
ordering effects 65

Pakeha 62
Papua New Guinea 12
Patagonia 163–71
perceptual dialectology 180–7,
    203–22, 229
perceptual maps 212–18
personal names 3–4
phonoaesthetics 4, 229
physical appearance 91–3
pidgins and creoles 11, 12
political correctness 5
powerful and powerless language 122,
    130, 137
psychological reactance 152

Quebec 70, 71, 92–3
Queen's English 173–7

Received Pronunciation (RP) 12, 13–15,
    41, 46, 54, 60, 62, 63, 64, 65, 74, 78,
    82, 89, 90, 91, 94, 96, 97, 99, 102,
    107, 123, 125, 131, 135, 138, 172–7,
    201–22
regional standard 64, 195
reinforcement expectancy theory 133
Russia 122

Scottish English 1, 13, 60, 64, 74, 102,
    172–7
Scottish Gaelic 37–8, 44
semantic differential scales 53, 55–6,
    61, 71, 73, 78, 187, 197, 203–5,
    210–18
sentence final prepositions in English 9
sex 5, 94, 95, 175, 196 (*see also* 'gender')
Singapore 112
slanted questions 43
social class 33, 34, 62, 66, 91, 92, 93–4,
    103, 175
social constructionism 30, 46, 159–63
social desirability bias 44, 56, 57,
    75, 226
social identity 12, 107, 113, 143, 147, 164
    (*see also* 'Welsh identity')
social identity theory 107, 108, 229
societal treatment approach 37, 46–51,
    142–58, 229

South Africa 118, 124

Spanish (including Spanish-accented English) 23, 122, 138, 144, 154, 166, 173–7

speech rate 90, 95, 102, 106, 107, 136, 229
  employment contexts 136
  health contexts 133

split infinitives in English 9

standard language ideology (*see* ideology)

stereotypes 4–5, 6, 10, 11, 14, 15, 19, 23, 32–3, 50, 60, 71, 76, 78, 95, 98, 124, 128, 132, 135, 140, 142, 143, 146, 174, 191, 197, 199, 207, 209, 216, 221, 224, 229

Sweden 130

Switzerland 145–7

teachers' attitudes 4, 132, 203–18

teenagers' attitudes 38, 39, 40, 80, 203–22

theory of reasoned action 26, 229

therapy sessions 117

Tokyo 154

travel agency 115–17

Trinidad 128

Tripartite model 23, 229

Uganda 153

UK 3, 7, 13, 14, 15, 33, 40–1, 53–4, 61, 74, 90, 97, 103, 112, 118, 125, 172, 187–99

university students' suitability as respondents 140

USA 3–4, 7, 13, 16, 22, 25, 33, 44, 46, 53, 63, 64, 65–9, 74, 75, 76, 90, 97, 99, 103, 122, 130, 137, 139, 159, 164, 169, 180–99 (*see also* 'North America')

values 31

verbal guise 41, 53–87, 88, 129, 159, 187, 201, 226, 229

vivid language 122, 228, 229

Wales 3, 11, 17, 21, 38, 46, 53–4, 58, 65, 86, 149, 156–7, 159, 163–71, 176, 201–22

Walpiri 11

Welsh English 12, 46, 58, 82, 86, 89, 99, 107, 116, 138, 172–7, 201–22

Welsh identity 12, 83, 108, 163, 213

Welsh language 12, 21, 38–9, 46, 82, 86, 147–51, 156, 159

Welsh Language Board 156

Y Drych 147–51, 164